NURTURING PROGRAM
For Parents and Children Birth to Five Years

Activities Manual for Parents
Home-Based Program

2nd Edition

Stephen J. Bavolek, Ph.D.
Juliana Dellinger-Bavolek, M.S.E.

NP2-AMP-H

Family Development Resources, Inc.
3160 Pinebrook Road
Park City, UT 84060

To reorder this book and other components of the Nurturing Program,
call (801) 649-5822, or FAX (801) 649-9599

About the Authors

Stephen J. Bavolek, Ph.D., is a nationally recognized leader in the fields of parent education and prevention and treatment of child abuse and neglect. He has a professional background working with emotionally disturbed children and adolescents in schools and residential settings, and abused children and abusive parents in treatment programs. He completed a postdoctoral internship at the Kempe Center for the Prevention and Treatment of Child Abuse in Denver, Colorado, and was selected by Phi Delta Kappa as one of 75 young educators in the country who represent the best in educational leadership, research, and services. Dr. Bavolek has conducted extensive research in the prevention and treatment of child abuse and neglect and parent education. He is the author of *A Handbook for Understanding Child Abuse and Neglect,* a comprehensive examination of maltreatment to children, and The *Adult—Adolescent Parenting Inventory*; a valid measure designed to assess high risk parenting attitudes. In addition, Dr. Bavolek is the principal author of the *Nurturing Program for Parents and Children 4 to 12 Years*; *Nurturing Program for Parents and Adolescents*; and *Nurturing Program for Teenage Parents and Their Families.*

Juliana Dellinger-Bavolek, M.S.E., is a parent-child training specialist. Ms. Dellinger-Bavolek's professional background includes extensive experience with preschool handicapped children and their families, both as a classroom teacher/home visitor and as a facilitator of support groups for parents of infants and toddlers with special needs. As a training specialist with the Portage Project Region V Head Start Training Center, Ms. Dellinger-Bavolek provided training and technical assistance to Head Start home visit staff in implementing services for culturally disadvantaged parents and their preschool children. Ms. Dellinger-Bavolek served as the Education/Handicap Services Coordinator for Head Start and Parent-Child Centers in a seven county area in Wisconsin. She continues to work as a consultant to special education programs in the public schools and to Head Start and Parent-Child Centers nationally.

Materials Needed

Materials listed below are required to complete some of the activities in this program. Many of the materials listed can be found in most households; others may need to be purchased. Check each session's agenda for materials needed for the session.

Writing paper
Pens/Pencils
Butcher block paper
Magic markers
Puppets
Crayons
VCR or filmstrip projector
Medium-sized ball
Coat hangers
String
Construction paper
Paste
Scissors
Magazines
Small object (ball, eraser)
Grocery bags
Tissue paper
Cardboard
Paper plates
Blanket
Pillow
Bell
Rug or mat
Paint brushes
Clay
Large bed sheet
Food coloring
Paper towels
Tape

Ivory Flakes
Measuring cup
Mixing bowl and spoon
Tempera paints
Straws
Scarf
Marbles
Shoe box
Shaving cream
Finger paint
Paint smocks (old shirts)
Safety pins
5 large pie plates
Newspapers
Old phone book
Cotton balls
Sand paper
Toothpicks
Washpan
Old towels or rags
Flashlight
White facial mask
Make-up
Mirrors
Washcloths
Crayon sharpener or vegetable grate
Clothes iron
Wax paper

Nurturing Program for Parents and Children Birth to Five Years

Family Record Form

PARENTS:

Father's Name: _____

Phone (Home): _____   (Work): _____

Mother's Name: _____

Phone (Home): _____   (Work): _____

Address: _____

City: _____   State _____   Zip _____

CHILDREN:

	Name	**Age**
1.	_____	_____
2.	_____	_____
3.	_____	_____
4.	_____	_____

Additional Information About the Family:

Family Schedule and Performance Chart

Complete the information at the end of each session by entering the date you introduced the concept. Place a check in **either** the *Needs More Work* column OR *Understands/Accepts* column. If more work is needed, review during the next session. When the concept is understood and accepted, place the date in the *Understands/Accepts* column. The concept should be understood and accepted before advancing to the next concept. Use the *Notes* column for any comments you wish to make.

Concept	Date Introduced	Needs More Work	Understands/ Accepts	Notes
1. Orientation				
2. Nurturing Philosophy of Raising Children				
3. Discipline and Punishment				
4. Family Rules				
5. Personal Needs and Payoffs to Behavior				
6. Spoiling Your Children				
7. Personal Power				
8. Praise for Being and Doing				
9. Red, White, and Bruises				
10. Hurting Touch				
11. Baby Proofing				
12. Verbal and Physical Redirection				
13. Touch and Talk				
14. Time-Out				
15. Ages and Stages				
16. Skill Strips				
17. Troublesome Feelings				
18. Handling Stress				
19. Nurturing Diapering and Dressing Routines				
20. Nurturing Feeding Routine				
21. Nutrition and Dinner Time				
22. Nurturing Bath Time Routine				
23. Nurturing Bedtime Routine				
24. Anger				
25. Managing Behavior				
26. Ignoring				
27. Personal Space				
28. Bodies, Conception, and Pregnancy				
29. Scary Touch, Love, and AIDS				
30. Body Map				
31. Criticism and Confrontation				
32. I Statements and You Messages				
33. Problem Solving and Decision Making				
34. Helping Children with Feelings				
35. Improving Specific Self-Esteem				
36. Stimulating and Communicating				
37. Toilet Training				
38. Verbal Management				
39. Self-Expression				
40. People and Possessions				
41. Situations and Solutions; Review of Behavior Management				
42. Positive Self-Talk				
43. Families and Chemical Use				
44. Emergency Parenting and Survival Kits				
45. Closing Program Activities				

Contents

NURTURING PROGRAM FOR PARENTS AND CHILDREN BIRTH TO FIVE YEARS
SESSION 1

BEHAVIOR CONSTRUCT: Behavior Management

SESSION CONCEPT: Orientation

BRIEF DESCRIPTION: Families will be introduced to the program, share their hopes and fears, and complete pretest assessments of parenting attitudes and knowledge. Children learn to be dynamic doers and draw pictures of themselves and family.

INTENDED USE: For parents of children birth to 5 years

PREREQUISITE KNOWLEDGE: None

AGENDA

Parent Activities

Parent Activities	Materials
1.1 Icebreaker: Hopes and Fears	Paper, pens
1.2 Orientation	*Parent Handbooks*
1.3 Assessing Parenting Strengths	Adult-Adolescent Parenting Inventory, Nurturing Quiz, Family Social History Questionnaire, pencils
1.4 Home Practice Exercise	*Parent Handbooks*

Family Activities*

Family Activities*	Materials
1.5 Family Nurturing Time	*Nurturing Book for Babies and Children*
1.6 Hello Time: Happy to See You	None
1.7 Red Light-Green Light	Large area free of obstacles
1.8 Circle Time: Dynamic Doers	Large sheet of white paper, magic markers, puppets
1.9 Picture Yourself/Picture Your Family and Family Hug	Paper, crayons, magic markers

*For parents with infants or toddlers, use activities presented in *Nurturing Book for Babies and Children*. For parents with preschoolers (ages 3-5), use the activities listed below Family Nurturing Time.

PARENT ACTIVITY: 1.1 Icebreaker: Hopes and Fears
CONSTRUCT: Self-Awareness
MATERIALS: Paper, pens

GOAL:

To begin the process of forming close and supportive relationships.

OBJECTIVES:

1. To identify feelings.

2. To express hopes and fears of participating in the program.

PROCEDURES:

1. Explain to the parents that at the beginning of each session, the activities will start with an icebreaker. There are no right or wrong answers in icebreakers, only opinions and feelings. While everyone is encouraged to respond to each statement, an individual may pass if he/she cannot or does not want to respond to a statement. If a person passes, return to the person who passed the first time (after other family members finish responding to the statements) and check if he/she now chooses to respond. Encourage a response.

2. Begin by encouraging parents to complete the following statements:

   - Right now, I am feeling _____.

   - My favorite fantasy is _____.

3. Due to the nature of the program and the fact it is the first meeting, there is probably an abundant amount of anxiety present. To begin to relieve the anxiety, ask the parents to respond to the following:

   - As a result of participating in the program and spending time together, one hope I have is _____.

   - One fear I have is _____.

4. Write the hopes and fears down, and explain that you will review their hopes and fears at the end of the program to see if they came true.

IF'S, AND'S, OR BUT'S:

Family members will probably be nervous about sharing information during the first icebreaker. You may want to respond first to model the depth of information you are seeking from them.

GOAL:

To clarify the structure of the program.

OBJECTIVES:

1. To explain structure of meetings.

2. To share expectations for participation in the program.

PROCEDURES:

1. Explain that the program activities will focus on their role as parents and on their personal strengths and weaknesses as people.

2. The **Nurturing Program for Parents and Children Birth to Five** consists of 45 home-based sessions. Each session lasts 1 1/2 hours.

3. The format of each home-based session is as follows:

   a. **Icebreaker and Home Practice Check In**. Explain that each session will begin with an icebreaker much like today's session began. This will be followed by a brief check-in time to see how they are doing and to see how successful they were in completing their home practice exercise. The Icebreaker and Home Practice Check In will last 15 minutes.

   b. **Discussion**. After the icebreaker and check in time, we will discuss issues related to their role as parents or issues about themselves. The focus is on developing a nurturing self and a nurturing parent. The discussion will last 45 minutes.

   c. **Family Nurturing Time**. The Family Nurturing Time follows the parent activities. Parents and their children will spend 30 minutes together to play, laugh, sing songs, and learn about positive touch.

   d. **Group/Family Hug**. Each session ends with a family hug. During the family hug, we can say positive things and discuss the home practice exercise. Children are included in the family hug. The family hug will last 3 minutes.

4. Instruct parents that each week, they will be responsible for trying their best to complete the home practice exercise. Sometimes it involves writing a few things, but most of the time they will be practicing new skills.

5. A constant part of their weekly home practice exercise is to spend 30 minutes each day with their children in play/fun time. That means no TV. Suggest that they read books and practice the new nurturing touch techniques.

6. The *Parent Handbook* is a resource book/workbook that contains weekly information and exercises. Each parent should have his/her own copy and bring it to each session.

Please note: The *Parent Handbook* includes Home Practice Exercises for both the Home-Based model and the Group-Based model. Since there are 45 home-based sessions, group-based participants are to complete two Home Practice Exercises per week.

7. The *Nurturing Book for Babies and Children* has seven sections. This book is to be used as a scrapbook, informational guide, and activities guide. The sections are as follows:

   a. Memories and Developmental Milestones

   b. Infant and Child Massage

   c. Activities for Infants

   d. Activities for Toddlers

   e. Activities for Preschoolers

   f. Special Day Celebrations

   g. Flu Bug Blues

   The Infant and Child Massage section will be used to help parents and their children learn gentle touch, stress relaxation, and positive parent-child interactions. Each weekly Home Practice Exercise will include activities from the following sections: Infant and Child Massage, Activities for Infants, Activities for Toddlers, and Activities for Preschoolers.

8. Parents are expected to keep a weekly Family Log of the changes occurring with themselves, their children, and their family. Changes can be either good or bad. Family Logs will be turned in weekly for review by the facilitator and returned to the parents. Parents are to keep their Family Logs in a notebook or folder.

9. There are three inventories to complete at the beginning and end of the program. The purpose of these inventories is to see how much the participants have gained in knowledge and awareness. The facilitator will review and discuss results of the inventories.

10. General expectations for the program sessions.

   a. To be honest—good or bad.

   b. To do home practice exercises.

   c. To ask questions if a concept is not understood.

   d. To make a commitment to growing.

   e. To laugh and have a good time.

IF'S, AND'S, OR BUT'S:

Be responsive to any questions the parents may have.

GOAL:

To increase parents' awareness of parenting and nurturing strengths and weaknesses.

OBJECTIVES:

1. To assess parents' attitudes and knowledge of age appropriate expectations.

2. To assess parents' attitudes of children's needs.

3. To assess parents' attitudes and knowledge of behavior management.

4. To assess parents' awareness of self needs.

PROCEDURES:

1. Explain the purpose of the pretesting/posttesting component of the program. An accurate understanding of the testing will ensure more honest test responses.

2. Distribute copies of the Adult-Adolescent Parenting Inventory (AAPI), Nurturing Quiz, and Family Social History Questionnaire (FSHQ) to the parents. Have the parents complete the AAPI first, then the Nurturing Quiz, then the FSHQ.

3. Explain how to respond to the inventories: circle only one response to each question; answer every question. Make sure parents put their names on all forms.

4. After parents have completed the tests, allow parents to discuss tests in general. A good statement to facilitate discussion is:

   - Something new I learned about myself is _____.

IF'S, AND'S, OR BUT'S:

You may get some parents who feel they have to respond with the socially desirable answer rather than their true feelings. Assure them that there is no advantage to doing this and that you expect their honest responses.

GOAL:

To increase parents' awareness of approaches they use to manage their children's behaviors.

OBJECTIVES:

1. To identify current behavior management strategies.

2. To increase personal awareness of appropriate and inappropriate behavior management strategies.

3. To initiate a plan for change.

4. To establish a warm and supportive environment.

PROCEDURES:

1. Share with the parents the philosophy of the Home Practice Exercise: practice the skill, try your best, share experiences and responses with the home visitor.

2. Instruct parents to locate the Home Practice Exercise on page 139 in their Handbooks. Review the exercise with them:

   a. List the ways you currently manage your children's behavior. What punishments and rewards do you use?

   b. Which of these techniques do you like; which don't you like?

   c. What do you think you would like to learn instead to manage your children's behavior?

   d. Complete family log.

3. Tell parents that in addition to the Home Practice Exercise, they are to spend 30 minutes each day with each of their children in nurturing playtime activities. Playtime is a time with the parent and child alone—no TV, no other distractions. Playing a game or reading books are good activities. From the *Nurturing Book for Babies and Children*, have the parents practice activities listed in the following sections: Activities for Infants, Activities for Toddlers, or Activities for Preschoolers. Tell parents to begin completing the Memories and Developmental Milestones section of the *Nurturing Book for Babies and Children*. Have the parents remember what they did and report the next week.

IF'S, AND'S, OR BUT'S:

1. Encourage the parents to try their hardest to complete the home practice exercise. Writing skills, spelling, and grammar are not important.

2. Remind parents to complete their weekly log prior to the start of the next visit.

FAMILY ACTIVITY:	**1.5 Family Nurturing Time**
CONSTRUCT:	**Empathy, Self-Awareness**
MATERIALS:	**Nurturing Book for Babies and Children**

ACTIVITIES FOR INFANTS (Birth to 15 months):

Utilizing the *Nurturing Book for Babies and Children*, select activities from the section entitled Activities for Infants. Engage parents in practicing songs, play, and stimulation activities with their infants.

ACTIVITIES FOR TODDLERS (15 months to 3 years):

Utilizing the *Nurturing Book for Babies and Children*, select activities from the section entitled Activities for Toddlers. Engage parents in practicing songs, play, language, and movement activities.

ACTIVITIES FOR PRESCHOOLERS (3-5 years):

Use the following activities when working with preschool children and their parents. Use the activities as the basis for involving infants and toddlers if you are conducting a home visit with children ages birth to five years.

FAMILY ACTIVITY:	**1.6 Hello Time: Happy to See You**
CONSTRUCT:	**Empathy**
MATERIALS:	**None**

GOAL:

To begin to build family cohesion.

OBJECTIVES:

1. To personally greet each child and parent.
2. To experience successful interactions in a family setting.
3. To get parents and children to have fun.

PROCEDURES:

1. Have everyone sit on the floor in a circle.
2. Explain that we will take turns singing a song to each person in the group.
3. Go around the circle and sing the following song to each person (to the tune of "This is the Way We Wash Our Clothes").

We're happy to see you here today, here today, here today,

We're happy to see you here today, happy to see you _____(name)_____.

4. After the name, ask the person, "How are you today?"

5. All children and adults should be sung to and asked how they are.

IF'S, AND'S, OR BUT'S:

1. After a person has been sung to, he or she may choose the next person for the group to sing to.

2. Touch each person in some way when they are being greeted (e.g., shake hands, touch their arm, pat their shoulder), but do not force this if a person is uncomfortable. Ask the person how they would like to be touched.

3. In a family setting, parents may be called by their first name or by their role (mom, dad, pop, mother, etc.). Check with the parent to see which they prefer prior to beginning the activity.

FAMILY ACTIVITY:	**1.7 Red Light-Green Light**
CONSTRUCT:	**Behavior Management**
MATERIALS:	**Large area free of obstacles**

GOAL:

To reinforce behavioral control.

OBJECTIVES:

1. To reinforce concept of natural consequences to behavior.

2. To reinforce family interactions.

PROCEDURES:

1. Have all family members seated on the floor in a semicircle prior to starting the activity.

2. Explain the rules of the game. One person stands in front of the group with his/her back toward the group. The remaining group members are standing behind. The goal is to sneak up on the person in front without being caught. The person in front says "Green Light," which gives the others permission to sneak up. At any time the person in front may yell "Red Light" and quickly turn around. If anyone is caught moving, he or she must return to the rear of the group and start over. The game ends when the person in front is touched by another. That person then gets to stand in front of the group. The game begins again.

3. Repeat the game for others to get a chance to be leader.

IF'S, AND'S, OR BUT'S:

1. Remind children to touch the one in front lightly.

2. Controversy may arise regarding whether a person was caught moving or not. You may have to act as the game official, whose job is to settle disputes.

3. A reminder: It is always wise to have people seated in a semicircle prior to the beginning of each activity. Such action serves to reduce inattentive behaviors and reinforces group cohesiveness.

FAMILY ACTIVITY:	**1.8 Circle Time: Dynamic Doers**
CONSTRUCT:	**Behavior Management**
MATERIALS:	**Large sheet of white paper, magic markers, puppets**

GOAL:

To reinforce the concept of following established home visit rules.

OBJECTIVES:

1. To build group unity and cohesion.

2. To establish an effective disciplinary system during home visits.

3. To build self-concept through reinforcement of following rules.

4. To explain Do's and Don'ts and Dynamic Doer Chart.

PROCEDURES:

1. Have all family members sit in a circle with the home visitor.

2. Explain to the children that this time is Circle Time; a time you will talk about special things. Introduce the puppets to the children by their names (or have kids give them names). Explain to the children that the puppets are good puppets but sometimes do things that aren't always the right things to do. The kids will have to help the puppets decide and choose the right things to do.

3. Explain to all family members that the group will need rules to operate by. Get input from the kids and parents as to what group rules they want to create. Keep the rules to a maximum of four.

4. Draw three columns. Label the first column FAMILY NAMES; the second column DO'S; and the third column DON'TS. Identify four things you want all group members to do—and things you don't want them to do. Whatever you choose to list as Do's and Don'ts, remember to be specific.

DYNAMIC DOERS

FAMILY NAMES	DO'S	DON'TS
	1. Do stay in room.	1. Don't run out of room.
Jimmy	2. Do handle things with care.	2. Don't throw things.
Mom	3. Do treat others with kindness.	3. Don't hit anyone.
Sally	4. Do work and play with others nicely.	4. Don't fight with others.

5. Write the words "Dynamic Doers" on top of the chart. Point to the chart and say, "Every time we see someone being a Dynamic Doer (following the rules), that person will get to place a (sticker, mark, star, dot, etc.) next to their name. At the end of the day, we will count the total number of (stickers, marks, dots, etc.) you have earned. Each week see if you can get more and more (stickers, dots, etc.)."

6. Utilizing the puppets, play act situations where the rules discussed will be challenged. For example, if one of the rules is "No throwing things; handle things with care", have two puppets playing together, and one puppet gets angry (or silly) and throws a toy (or other obstacle) across the room, on the floor, or at the wall. Ask how the puppet should handle things.

7. Repeat the scenario with each of the rules stressing what the puppets should be instead. Model the appropriate behaviors you want the children to learn with the puppets. That is, after the puppet throws a toy, ask what the puppet should have done instead. (Model the puppet handling things with care.)

IF'S, AND'S, OR BUT'S:

1. Substitutes may be made for stickers. Be creative. The only important aspect is that the children receive some tangible form of reward when they are adhering to the rules.

2. In a family setting, work out how you want parents praised for complying with the group rules. You may ask parents to make a mark next to their name when they are following the rules. It will model appropriate behaviors.

3. It is important to stress what you want instead. Model the appropriate behavior with the puppets.

4. The Dynamic Doer Rules will probably be different from the family rules that you will be establishing later in the program. These rules are specific to your home visit or class environment.

GOAL:

To increase family member's awareness of self and self within family.

OBJECTIVES:

1. To draw a picture of self.

2. To draw a picture of self with family.

3. To increase knowledge of child and family.

4. To serve as preprogram perceptions of self and family.

5. To reinforce comfort in using nurturing touch.

PROCEDURES:

1. Instruct family members to make two drawings: one drawing of self, and one of self with their family.

2. In both pictures the children may depict a portrait of self and/or family, or an action picture.

3. After pictures of self and family have been drawn, ask each family member to identify their pictures.

4. Write each family member role (father, mother, etc.) under each figure.

FAMILY HUG:

1. Today we will begin a new experience that will continue throughout the program. We will end each session we're together with a family hug.

2. Say that some problems can be solved by talking about them, others need new experiential learning.

3. Explain that touching is not always the easiest thing for a lot of parents and children to do.

4. Everyone get in a circle and put your arms around the people next to you. During the family hug time, anyone can say anything they like. It is a time for free expression.

5. At a natural time, close the activities for the day.

IF'S, AND'S, OR BUT'S:

1. Keep the pictures for comparison in the last week of the program. Pictures may show some significant interaction patterns and family characteristics.

2. Encourage the children to share with you who the family members are and what they are doing.

NURTURING PROGRAM FOR PARENTS AND CHILDREN BIRTH TO FIVE YEARS
SESSION #2

BEHAVIOR CONSTRUCT: Self-Awareness

SESSION CONCEPT: Nurturing Philosophy of Raising Children

BRIEF DESCRIPTION: Parents will learn the philosophy of the Nurturing Program and review tests taken during the previous meeting. Children will share information about themselves and make a me mobile.

INTENDED USE: For parents of children birth to 5 years

PREREQUISITE KNOWLEDGE: None

AGENDA

Parent Activities

		Materials
2.1	Icebreaker and Home Practice Check In	*Parent Handbooks*
2.2	Nurturing Parenting	*Parent Handbooks*, **Nurturing and Parenting** AV presentation, AV equipment
2.3	Assessment Review	Results of AAPI, Nurturing Quiz, and FSHQ

Family Activities*

		Materials
2.4	Family Nurturing Time	*Nurturing Book for Babies and Children*
2.5	Hello Time: Watch the Ball	One ball
2.6	Duck, Duck, Goose	None
2.7	Circle Time: Getting to Know You	None
2.8	Me Mobile and Family Hug	Coat hangers, string, construction paper, paste, crayons, scissors, magazines

*For parents with infants or toddlers, use activities presented in *Nurturing Book for Babies and Children*. For parents with preschoolers (ages 3-5), use the activities listed below Family Nurturing Time.

PARENT ACTIVITY: 2.1 Icebreaker and Home Practice Check In
CONSTRUCT: Self-Awareness, Empathy
MATERIALS: Parent Handbooks

GOAL:

To increase awareness of self-strengths.

OBJECTIVES:

1. To share characteristics of self with others.

2. To reinforce empathic awareness of the needs of others.

3. To reinforce sharing between staff and parents.

PROCEDURES:

1. Begin today's parent activities by having each adult respond to the following:

   ● In order to know who I really am, three things you need to know about me are:
   _____ , _____ , and _____.

2. After each parent has had an opportunity to respond to the statements above, review the Home Practice Exercise from the previous meeting. Also discuss perceived changes in family members and their interactions as reported in the family log.

IF'S, AND'S, OR BUT'S:

Parents can share any three things about themselves. However, to avoid surface facts, you may want to begin by sharing feelings, experiences, meaningful moments.

PARENT ACTIVITY: 2.2 Nurturing Parenting
CONSTRUCT: Self-Awareness, Behavior Management, Empathy, Child Development
MATERIALS: Parent Handbooks, Nurturing and Parenting AV presentation, AV equipment

GOAL:

To increase parents' awareness of parent-child interaction difficulties.

OBJECTIVES:

1. To enable parents to understand their parenting and nurturing strengths and weaknesses.

2. To increase parents' awareness of four parenting program constructs.

3. To increase parents' awareness of rationale of the program.

PROCEDURES:

1. If you are using the audio-visual programs, present the AV entitled **Nurturing and Parenting**.

2. Instruct parents to locate the information entitled **The Nurturing Program for Parents and Children** on pages 1-4 in their Handbooks. Utilize the information presented in the handbook to discuss the following major concepts with the parents:

   a. Some argue that parenting is instinctual: people are born to be natural parents.

   b. The philosophy of the Nurturing Program is that parenting is learned.

   c. Parenting is learned through modeling. Our parents model a style of parenting that we use later in our lives as parents. In turn our children model our style and so on.

   d. The Nurturing Program has four main goals:

      • Increase positive self-concept and self-esteem.

      • Increase empathy — the ability to be aware of the needs of others.

      • Teach alternatives to corporal punishment.

      • Help parents learn age appropriate developmental tasks of childhood.

3. Ask parents to focus on the constructs and to select one they feel is their strongest — and one they feel is their weakest.

IF'S, AND'S, OR BUT'S:

Spend time focusing on the constructs of the program. A clear rationale of the program goals may ease some parent anxiety.

PARENT ACTIVITY: 2.3 Assessment Review
CONSTRUCT: Self-Awareness
MATERIALS: Results of AAPI, Nurturing Quiz, and FSHQ

GOAL:

To increase awareness of parenting strengths and weaknesses.

OBJECTIVES:

1. To review responses to the AAPI.

2. To review responses to the Nurturing Quiz.

3. To review responses to the Family Social History Questionnaire.

4. To develop a specific parent education program.

PROCEDURES:

1. Review with the parents the results of their responses to the AAPI and the Nurturing Quiz.

2. Review only the general findings by indicating assessed strengths and weaknesses. For example:

   > Ms. Smith, in reviewing your responses to the items on the AAPI, Nurturing Quiz, and the Family Social History Questionnaire, I have found several strengths and areas for improvement. Your strengths are in _____. Areas that need some improvement are _____.

3. Avoid using any label. Parents will be a bit defensive and anxious; don't feed these fears.

IF'S, AND'S, OR BUT'S:

Your skill as a caring educator needs to come through here. Assessment is always best used for remediation — not judgment.

FAMILY ACTIVITY:	**2.4 Family Nurturing Time**
CONSTRUCT:	**Empathy, Self-Awareness**
MATERIALS:	**Nurturing Book for Babies and Children**

ACTIVITIES FOR INFANTS (Birth to 15 months):

Utilizing the *Nurturing Book for Babies and Children*, select activities from the section entitled Activities for Infants. Engage parents in practicing songs, play, and stimulation activities with their infants. Have parents begin completing the Memories and Developmental Milestones section of the book.

ACTIVITIES FOR TODDLERS (15 months to 3 years):

Utilizing the *Nurturing Book for Babies and Children*, select activities from the section entitled Activities for Toddlers. Engage parents in practicing songs, play, language, and movement activities. Vary the activities weekly to promote interest. Have parents begin completing the Memories and Developmental Milestones section of the book.

ACTIVITIES FOR PRESCHOOLERS (3-5 years):

Use the following activities when working with preschool children and their parents. Use the activities as the basis for involving infants and toddlers if you are conducting a home visit with children ages birth to five years.

FAMILY ACTIVITY: 2.5 Hello Time: Watch the Ball
CONSTRUCT: Empathy
MATERIALS: One ball

GOAL:

To increase positive family interactions

OBJECTIVES:

1. To have children greet others by their name.

2. To increase children's awareness of the feelings of others in group.

3. To reinforce positive peer and family interactions.

PROCEDURES:

1. Assemble children and adults in a circle sitting on the floor.

2. Explain the rules: I will call a person by name and roll the ball to him/her. After s/he catches the ball, I will ask, "Hello _____, how are you today?"

3. The person who responded gets to roll the ball to another person. S/he may ask the other child or adult any question or may offer a statement of praise.

4. Keep the game going by having each child receive and roll the ball. You can do it several times, asking different questions.

IF'S, AND'S, OR BUT'S:

The only hazard to the game could be a child who rolls the ball with increased speed. Management will prevent inappropriate throwing of the ball.

FAMILY ACTIVITY: 2.6 Duck, Duck, Goose
CONSTRUCT: Developmental
MATERIALS: None

GOAL:

To increase positive social interactions among children and parents.

OBJECTIVES:

1. To increase children's ability to follow simple rules.

2. To use big and small muscle movements.

3. To play cooperatively in structured activity.

4. To have fun.

PROCEDURES:

1. Have children and adults sit in a circle. Remove obstacles in immediate area for room to run around circle.

2. Select one child who will be "It." "It" walks around the circle tapping each child and adult on the shoulder saying, "Duck."

3. After tapping several people, "It" must tap someone saying, "Goose!" and then "Goose" chases "It" back to the empty spot in the circle.

4. If "It" is tagged by "Goose" before sitting down, the person remains "It." If not, "Goose" becomes "It" and Steps 2 and 3 are repeated.

IF'S, AND'S, OR BUT'S:

This is a very popular game among children. Although it serves as a nice gross motor exercise, caution the overuse of the game.

FAMILY ACTIVITY:	**2.7 Circle Time: Getting To Know You**
CONSTRUCT:	**Self-Awareness**
MATERIALS:	**None**

GOAL:

To encourage children and adults to share some aspect of themselves.

OBJECTIVES:

1. To increase children's knowledge of self and others.

2. To increase the child's ability to share within a group.

3. To increase the child's ability to trust other adults and children.

PROCEDURES:

1. The topic for discussion is "Getting to Know You." Use the following questions to facilitate discussion. Allow each person a chance to answer the questions.

    *   How old are you, and when is your birthday?

    *   Who is your favorite friend?

    *   What is your favorite TV show?

    *   Do you have any pets?

    *   Who is your favorite adult/child?

    *   If you could be anyone, who would you be?

    *   If you could do anything, what would you do?

1. Keep the conversation moving

2. If someone doesn't want to answer, they can pass.

FAMILY ACTIVITY:	2.8 Me Mobile and Family Hug
CONSTRUCT:	Self-Awareness
MATERIALS:	Coat hangers, string, construction paper, paste, crayons, scissors, magazines

GOAL:

To increase children's awareness of various aspects of self.

OBJECTIVES:

1. To express self through art.

2. To recognize aspects of self.

3. To display different aspects of self.

4. To increase comfort in touching.

5. To break down barriers.

6. To develop closeness.

7. To provide closure of activities.

PROCEDURES:

1. Cut five various shapes out of construction paper of different colors. Label one shape "Things I Like"; another, "This Is My House"; another, "I Am ____ Years Old"; the other shapes could be of related content: my favorite color, my favorite food, etc.

2. Have the children cut and paste pictures from magazines, or draw pictures on the different shapes. The items can be both positive and negative aspects of self. Paste pictures and/or drawings to paper for hanging.

3. Attach each drawing, picture, etc., to a string of different sizes and hang from the coat hanger.

4. Place the name of the child in the center of the hanger (below the hook) by taping or stapling the paper.

FAMILY HUG:

1. Remind family members that touching is not always the easiest thing for a lot of parents and children to do.

2. Say that some problems can be solved by talking about them, others need new experiential learning.

3. Today we will continue to end each session we're together with a family hug.

4. Everyone get in a circle and put your arms around the people next to you. During the family hug time, anyone can say anything they like. It is a time for free expression.

5. At a natural time, close the activities for the day.

IF'S, AND'S, OR BUT'S:

1. Other ideas of things to put on the mobiles are: family, hand or thumb prints, things that "make me happy, sad, angry, etc.," self-portrait, things "I do well."

2. Another option would be to make a "Me Poster" rather than a mobile.

NURTURING PROGRAM FOR PARENTS AND CHILDREN BIRTH TO FIVE YEARS

SESSION 3

BEHAVIOR CONSTRUCT:	Behavior Management
SESSION CONCEPT:	Discipline and Punishment
BRIEF DESCRIPTION:	Parents learn the difference between discipline and punishment, and begin formulating family rules. Children will play the Nurturing Game and enhance their self-awareness, empathy, ability to touch, and knowledge of behavior management.
INTENDED USE:	For parents of children birth to 5 years
PREREQUISITE KNOWLEDGE:	Nurturing Program Philosophy

AGENDA

Parent Activities
Materials

3.1	Icebreaker	None
3.2	Behavior Management: Discipline and Punishment	*Parent Handbooks*, **Behavior Management** AV presentation, AV equipment
3.3	Home Practice Exercise	*Parent Handbooks*

Family Activities*
Materials

3.4	Family Nurturing Time	*Nurturing Book for Babies and Children*
3.5	Hello Time: The Farmer in the Dell	None
3.6	Tall and Small	None
3.7	Circle Time: Nurturing Game	Nurturing Game
3.8	Nurturing Coloring Book and Family Hug	Coloring books, crayons

*For parents with infants or toddlers, use activities presented in *Nurturing Book for Babies and Children*. For parents with preschoolers (ages 3-5), use the activities listed below Family Nurturing Time.

PARENT ACTIVITY:	3.1 Icebreaker
CONSTRUCT:	Behavior Management, Self-Awareness
MATERIALS:	None

GOAL:

To increase parent's awareness of the ways they were punished and disciplined as children.

OBJECTIVES:

1. To increase parent's willingness to share.

2. To lay the groundwork for discussion on punishment and discipline.

3. To gain an understanding of the parent's childhood background.

4. To gain an awareness of the type of relationship the parent had with his/her parents.

5. To discuss changes in family interactions.

PROCEDURES:

1. Begin today's parent activities by having each adult respond to the following:

   - When I was growing up, my parents used to punish and discipline me by _____ .

   - If I could tell my parents anything about the way I was punished and disciplined, I would say _____ .

2. Discuss changes parents notice in family members and their interactions.

IF'S, AND'S, OR BUT'S:

As with all Icebreaker activities, getting parents to begin to share their thoughts and feelings is a primary purpose. Discuss with each parent their responses, but do not let conversation drag on.

PARENT ACTIVITY:	3.2 Behavior Management: Discipline and Punishment
CONSTRUCT:	Behavior Management
MATERIALS:	Parent Handbooks, Behavior Management AV presentation, AV equipment

GOAL:

To increase parent's knowledge of the concepts of behavior management.

OBJECTIVES:

1. To enable parents to understand that behavior is purposeful and goal directed.

2. To help parents identify goals of behavior of children and selves.

3. To increase parent's awareness of the concepts: behavior management, discipline, and punishment.

4. To introduce the concept of family rules.

PROCEDURES:

1. If you are using audio-visual programs, present the AV entitled **Behavior Management**.

2. Instruct parents to locate the information entitled **Behavior Management** on pages 5-8 in their Handbooks. Utilize the information presented to discuss the following major concepts with the parents:

   a. Children need to learn right from wrong. Learning right from wrong is important because children want to please Mom and Dad. Doing the right things please Mom and Dad.

   b. There are appropriate and inappropriate ways to help children learn how to behave appropriately.

   c. Consistent use of nurturing behavior management helps children learn appropriate ways to behave.

   d. Discipline is a form of behavior management. Discipline is rules, standards, guidelines, and expectations for appropriate behavior.

   e. Punishment is a form of behavior management. Punishment is a penalty administered by the parents when a child has chosen to act inappropriately.

   f. For punishment to be effective, it must immediately follow the misbehavior; it must be administered every time the misbehavior occurs; it must not be abusive.

3. Issues in the handbook that you can mention but will be discussed in more detail later:

   a. Effective punishments are time-out, loss of privilege, and restitution (paying back). Spanking and hitting children are not effective punishment. They punish children not the behavior.

   b. For punishment to be just, family rules have to be established.

      • Rules must be clear.

      • Rules must be consistent.

      • Rules must be fair.

IF'S, AND'S, OR BUT'S:

Some parents may begin to feel awkward about using spanking to punish and discipline their children. Don't press the issue or come across as condemning. You want to establish a sharing communication with the parents.

GOAL:

To increase parents' knowledge of appropriate ways to help children manage their behavior.

OBJECTIVES:

1. To reinforce the difference between the concepts of punishment and discipline.

2. To continue to build the groundwork for change in family interactions.

3. To identify behavior management strategies currently used at home.

4. To establish a warm supportive environment.

PROCEDURES:

1. Instruct parents to locate the Home Practice Exercise on page 139 in their Handbooks. Review the exercise with them:

    a. List ways you currently manage your children's behavior. What punishments and rewards do you use?

    b. Which of these techniques do you like; which don't you like?

    c. Complete family log.

2. Tell parents that in addition to the Home Practice Exercise, they are to spend 30 minutes each day with each of their children in nurturing playtime activities. Playtime is a time with the parent and child alone — no TV, no other distractions. Playing a game or reading books are good activities. From the *Nurturing Book for Babies and Children*, have the parents practice activities listed in the following sections: Activities for Infants, Activities for Toddlers, or Activities for Preschoolers. Tell parents to complete information in the Memories and Developmental Milestones section of the *Nurturing Book for Babies and Children*. Have the parents remember what they did and report the next week.

IF'S, AND'S, OR BUT'S:

Encourage the parents to try to complete the home practice exercise.

FAMILY ACTIVITY:	3.4 Family Nurturing Time
CONSTRUCT:	Empathy, Self-Awareness
MATERIALS:	Nurturing Book for Babies and Children

ACTIVITIES FOR INFANTS (Birth to 15 months):

Utilizing the *Nurturing Book for Babies and Children*, select activities from the section entitled Activities for Infants. Engage parents in practicing songs, play, and stimulation activities with their infants. Vary the activities weekly to promote interest.

ACTIVITIES FOR TODDLERS (15 months to 3 years):

Utilizing the *Nurturing Book for Babies and Children.* select activities from the section entitled Activities for Toddlers. Engage parents in practicing songs, play, language, and movement activities. Vary the activities weekly to promote interest.

ACTIVITIES FOR PRESCHOOLERS (3-5 years):

Use the following activities when working with preschool children and their parents. Use the activities as the basis for involving infants and toddlers if you are conducting a home visit with children ages birth to five years.

FAMILY ACTIVITY:	3.5 Hello Time: The Farmer in the Dell
CONSTRUCT:	Empathy
MATERIALS:	None

GOAL:

To build positive parent-child interactions.

OBJECTIVES:

1. To help parents and children relate in a positive, nurturing way.

2. To help parents learn to enjoy their children.

PROCEDURES:

1. This is the traditional version of the Farmer in the Dell game.

2. Assemble children and adults holding hands in a circle.

3. Choose one child to stand in the center of the circle and be the "farmer."

4. The group moves in a circle around the "farmer" while singing. As the song calls for the farmer to "take a wife," have the child in the center of the circle choose another child or adult to join him inside the circle.

5. Continue in the same way until the verse "the cheese stands alone." Have the "cheese" stand in the center of the circle while the children sing that verse.

6. If the game is repeated, the person who was the "cheese" becomes the "farmer" for the new game.

The Farmer in the Dell

The farmer in the dell, the farmer in the dell,
Hi ho the dairy-o, the farmer in the dell.

The farmer takes a wife, the farmer takes a wife,
Hi ho the dairy-o, the farmer takes a wife.

The wife takes a child, the wife takes a child,
Hi ho the dairy-o, the wife takes a child.

The child takes a nurse, the child takes a nurse,
Hi ho the dairy-o, the child takes a nurse.

The nurse takes a dog, the nurse takes a dog,
Hi ho the dairy-o, the nurse takes a dog.

The dog takes a cat, the dog takes a cat,
Hi ho the dairy-o, the dog takes a cat.

The cat takes a rat, the cat takes a rat,
Hi ho the dairy-o, the cat takes a rat.

The rat takes the cheese, the rat takes the cheese,
Hi ho the dairy-o, the rat takes the cheese.

The cheese stands alone, the cheese stands alone,
Hi ho the dairy-o, the cheese stands alone.

IF'S, AND'S, OR BUT'S:

In small families you may want to use objects such as dolls or pets to participate in the game.

GOAL:

To increase family cohesion through movement activities.

OBJECTIVES:

1. To practice gross motor movement.

2. To increase language and cognition.

3. To experience success through participation and repetition.

4. To reinforce patience (appropriate need delay).

PROCEDURES:

1. Children and adults are seated in a circle on the floor.

2. Introduce activity by demonstrating the exercise. Children should watch during this time.

   Words: Now I'm small.
   Movement: Squat or crouch position on floor.

   Words: But now I'm tall.
   Movement: Jump up and reach up with arms.

   Words: Now I'm so little you can't see me at all.
   Movement: Crouch on floor and hide face with hands.

   Words: See me grow, grow, grow.
   Movement: Slowly stand up and reach arms up.

   Words: Now I'm a giant with a ho-ho-ho.
   Movement: Stand on tip-toes and pat stomach while saying "ho-ho-ho."

3. Repeat activity and encourage children to participate. Proceed slowly so that all children in the group can keep up with the pace.

4. Repeat the activity 2 or 3 times until children are able to perform the actions with the accompanying words.

IF'S, AND'S, OR BUT'S:

With a very young child, or a child who is reluctant to participate, an adult may attempt to assist the child by gently, physically prompting the child through the movements.

FAMILY ACTIVITY:	3.7 Circle Time: Nurturing Game
CONSTRUCT:	Behavior Management
MATERIALS:	Nurturing Game

GOAL:

To reinforce appropriate social interactions through cooperative play.

OBJECTIVES:

1. To reinforce concepts of behavior management.

2. To increase self-awareness.

3. To foster positive touch interactions.

PROCEDURES:

1. Assemble children and adults in a circle sitting on the floor.

2. The goal of the game is to all begin at start and end up at "home." To get home, each player has to roll one die and move his/her game piece the appropriate number of squares.

3. Players land on colored squares that correspond to:

   Orange squares represent **self-awareness**.

   Green squares represent **behavior management**.

   Pink squares represent **touch**.

   Yellow squares represent **praise**.

   Blue squares represent **feelings**.

4. When a player lands on a square s/he picks up a card and completes the activity. There are no cards for pink and yellow squares. Each time a player (adult or child) lands on a pink square, s/he hugs or touches someone in a nice way. Each time a player lands on a yellow square, s/he praises someone else.

5. The behavior management cards indicate a particular behavior occurred appropriately or inappropriately. The player may be rewarded by moving ahead one to three squares or penalized one to three squares for inappropriate behavior. Chance dictates behavior management.

6. Blue feeling cards and orange self-awareness cards are action cards the players have to respond to. When the behavior is completed, the next person rolls the die.

IF'S, AND'S, OR BUT'S:

1. The goal is to encourage interactions between children and adults. The game is based on the programs' constructs and reinforces concepts presented throughout the program.

2. Younger children will need help and encouragement to play.

FAMILY ACTIVITY: 3.8 Nurturing Coloring Book and Family Hug
CONSTRUCT: Self-Awareness
MATERIALS: Coloring books, crayons

GOAL:

To reinforce program concepts of self-awareness, empathy, behavior management, and developmental expectations.

OBJECTIVES:

1. To have children work on individual coloring books.

2. To increase children's pride in accomplishments.

3. To reinforce comfort in using nurturing touch.

PROCEDURES:

1. Hand out one coloring book per child. Immediately have children put their names on their book.

2. Have crayons available for children to use. Instruct the children that they can color in their book.

FAMILY HUG:

1. End each home visit with a family hug. Everyone get in a circle and put your arms around the people next to you. During the family hug time, anyone can say anything they like. It is a time for free expression.

2. At a natural time, close the activities for the day.

IF'S, AND'S, OR BUT'S:

1. Have the children share the colored pictures before the end of the session.

2. Make sure each child puts his/her name on their book.

3. Family members should be getting a bit more comfortable with the closing hug activity. If there is discomfort, don't give in to pressure. Keep the hug as part of the closing activity.

NURTURING PROGRAM FOR PARENTS AND CHILDREN BIRTH TO FIVE YEARS

SESSION 4

BEHAVIOR CONSTRUCT: Behavior Management

SESSION CONCEPT: Family Rules

BRIEF DESCRIPTION: Parents work on developing family rules. Children learn more about themselves and others and increase their social skills through the Ask It, Tell It game.

INTENDED USE: For parents of children birth to 5 years

PREREQUISITE KNOWLEDGE: Behavior Management discussion

AGENDA

Parent Activities	Materials
4.1 Icebreaker and Home Practice Check In	*Parent Handbooks*
4.2 Family Rules	*Parent Handbooks*
4.3 Home Practice Exercise	*Parent Handbooks*

Family Activities*	Materials
4.4 Family Nurturing Time	*Nurturing Book for Babies and Children*
4.5 Hello Time: Hokey Pokey	None
4.6 Over and Under	Small objects to pass
4.7 Circle Time: Ask It, Tell It	Ask It, Tell It Game
4.8 Nurturing Coloring Book and Family Hug	Coloring books, crayons

*For parents with infants or toddlers, use activities presented in *Nurturing Book for Babies and Children*. For parents with preschoolers (ages 3-5), use the activities listed below Family Nurturing Time.

PARENT ACTIVITY: 4.1 Icebreaker and Home Practice Check In
CONSTRUCT: Behavior Management, Self-Awareness
MATERIALS: Parent Handbooks

GOAL:

To increase parents' awareness of rules and their impact on family interactions.

OBJECTIVES:

1. To increase parent willingness to share.

2. To identify written and unwritten family rules.

3. To increase awareness of feelings regarding family rules.

4. To identify impact of rules on growing up.

5. To reinforce parents' attempts at completing the home practice exercise.

6. To discuss changes in family interactions.

PROCEDURES:

1. Begin today's parent activities by having each adult respond to the following:

   - Two rules that my family had when I was growing up were:_____ .

   - One message I received from my parents regarding rules was _____ .

2. After each parent has had an opportunity to respond to the statements above, review the Home Practice Exercise from the previous meeting. Also discuss perceived changes in family members and their interactions as reported in the family log.

IF'S, AND'S, OR BUT'S:

Process the above statements with the parents. Discuss the impact written and unwritten family rules had on them when they (the parents) were children. Remember to also respond to your own family rules and messages you received when you were growing up.

PARENT ACTIVITY: 4.2 Family Rules
CONSTRUCT: Behavior Management
MATERIALS: Parent Handbooks

GOAL:

To initiate the development of family rules.

OBJECTIVES:

1. To review the differences between discipline and punishment.

2. To discuss the purpose of family rules.

3. To identify rewards and consequences.

4. To initiate the process of communication among family members.

5. To develop a positive view of children's behavior.

PROCEDURES:

1. Review the concepts discipline and punishment. Discipline is the standards; the rules. Punishment is something administered after a family member has chosen to break a family rule.

2. Instruct parents to review the information entitled **Behavior Management** on pages 5-8 in their Handbooks and read the section on Family Rules. Family rules must be clear, consistently enforced, and fair.

3. Instruct parents to locate the information entitled **Tentative List of Family Rules** on page 10 in their Handbooks. With the parents and children (if possible), brainstorm a list of four or five rules that will serve as rules for that family. Write the rules on the **Tentative List of Family Rules** worksheet in the Handbook. Allow children to have input into the type of rules that all members of the family will follow. Ask parents to openly share their rules.

4. Identify rewards and consequences that will be associated with each rule. Some examples of rewards might be tangibles such as stars, stickers, money, allowance, or special privileges such as extra time watching TV, reading a story with mom, or playing a game, etc. Some examples of consequences could be loss of privilege such as playing time, being grounded, time-out, or paying back in chores for something purposefully broken, or a loss of tangibles such as not playing with an object for awhile, or loss of dessert, etc. The consequences for children do not have to be the same as consequences for adults.

IF'S, AND'S, OR BUT'S:

1. Be very careful in helping families decide on rules, rewards and punishments. Make sure the rules are very specific and not vague. Specific rule: Put toys in the toy box. Vague rule: No running in the house. In the latter rule, it could be that there is a time running in the house would be appropriate; e.g., to answer the phone, get a rag to wipe up a spilled drink, etc.

2. Hitting is not an acceptable consequence for a broken rule. Hitting as an unacceptable consequence is discussed in **Behavior Management** on pages 5-8 in the *Parent Handbook*.

3. Remember these are family rules. All members obey them. However, not all consequences have to be the same. Time-out would be appropriate for young children, not appropriate for teens or adults. Being grounded is appropriate for teens, paying a fine or doing an extra chore is appropriate for teens and adults.

PARENT ACTIVITY: 4.3 Home Practice Exercise
CONSTRUCT: Behavior Management
MATERIALS: Parent Handbooks

GOAL:

To work on establishing a set of rules agreeable to all family members.

OBJECTIVES:

1. Share proposed rules with other family members.

2. Get input from other family members and make appropriate additions and deletions.

3. Identify a proposed list of rewards and consequences.

4. To establish a warm supportive environment.

5. To increase comfort in nurturing touch.

PROCEDURES:

1. Instruct parents to locate the Home Practice Exercise on page 139 in their Handbooks. Review the exercise with them:

   a. Review the proposed list of rules with other family members to get their input.

   b. Make appropriate changes in rules, rewards, and consequences.

   c. Be prepared to implement the rules by the next session.

   d. Complete family log.

2. Tell parents that in addition to the Home Practice Exercise, they are to spend 30 minutes each day with each of their children in nurturing playtime activities. Playtime is a time with the parent and child alone—no TV, no other distractions. Playing a game or reading books are good activities. From the *Nurturing Book for Babies and Children*, have the parents practice activities listed in the following sections: Activities for Infants, Activities for Toddlers, Activities for Preschoolers, or Infant and Child Massage. Have the parents remember what they did and report the next week.

IF'S, AND'S, OR BUT'S:

Some parents may balk at having to set rules, rewards, and consequences. Encourage them by reminding them that if you want desirable behavior, children must know what is expected. The rewards and punishment will help establish the worth of the rules.

ACTIVITIES FOR INFANTS (Birth to 15 months):

Utilizing the *Nurturing Book for Babies and Children*, review with parents the information on Infant and Child Massage on pages 26-31. Have parents begin massaging their infant's legs and feet. Encourage parents to begin using massage as a part of their nurturing playtime activities.

ACTIVITIES FOR TODDLERS (15 months to 3 years):

Utilizing the *Nurturing Book for Babies and Children*, review with the parents the information on Infant and Child Massage on pages 26-31. Have parents begin massaging their toddler's legs and feet. Encourage parents to begin using massage as a part of their nurturing playtime activities.

ACTIVITIES FOR PRESCHOOLERS (3-5 years):

Use the following activities when working with preschool children and their parents. Use the activities as the basis for involving infants and toddlers if you are conducting a home visit with children ages birth to five years.

FAMILY ACTIVITY:	4.5 Hello Time: Hokey Pokey
CONSTRUCT:	Empathy
MATERIALS:	None

GOAL:

To increase positive parent-child interactions through music and dance.

OBJECTIVES:

1. To help parents and children learn to relate in a positive way.

2. To help parents learn to enjoy their children.

3. To provide an opportunity for the children to be with the parents in a safe atmosphere.

PROCEDURES:

1. Have parents and children stand in a circle. Ask if everyone knows how to do the Hokey Pokey. If not, model a few verses and movements.

Hokey Pokey

Put your right hand in, take your right hand out, Put your right hand in and shake it all about.

Do the hokey pokey and turn yourself around (hands in air, body swaying as you turn around in place), That's what it's all about.

(Repeat words only substituting: left hand, right and left arms, right and left foot, right and left leg, use all parts, let children suggest.)

IF'S, AND'S, OR BUT'S:

Some parents may feel a little silly at first doing the Hokey Pokey. Have patience, they will get more comfortable if you are.

FAMILY ACTIVITY: 4.6 Over and Under
CONSTRUCT: Developmental
MATERIALS: Small objects to pass

GOAL:

To facilitate group interactions through play.

OBJECTIVES:

1. To help children play cooperatively with others.

2. To increase children's appropriate social interactions.

3. To increase children's fine and gross motor coordination.

PROCEDURES:

Listed below is a game that requires adults and children to cooperate.

Over and Under

Have children and adults line up with their legs apart.

The first person passes an object (ball, eraser, etc.) over his/her head to the second person, who passes it through his/her legs to the third person, who passes it over his/her head and so on.

The last person runs to the beginning of the line and starts the object over his/her head again.

When the first person returns to the head of the line, the relay is finished.

IF'S, AND'S, OR BUT'S:

1. If you have enough people for two teams, you can have a friendly race.

2. Add some excitement to the game by requiring speed — the faster you pass the object, the better.

FAMILY ACTIVITY: 4.7 Circle Time: Ask It, Tell It
CONSTRUCT: Empathy
MATERIALS: Ask It, Tell It Game

GOAL:

To increase positive family interactions through awareness.

OBJECTIVES:

1. To increase children's self-awareness.

2. To increase children's awareness of others.

3. To increase children's communication skills.

PROCEDURES:

1. Direct children and adults to sit around a small table or in a circle on the floor.

2. Place the Ask It, Tell It game board and cards in the center.

3. Each person will have a turn to spin. If the spinner stops in a **yellow area**, the person chooses a **yellow Ask It Card**. If the spinner stops in an **orange area**, the person chooses an **orange Tell It Card**. The person should respond to the statement on the chosen card accordingly.

4. When everyone has had a turn, repeat. The game ends when either the cards or time expires.

IF'S, AND'S, OR BUT'S:

1. Children will like playing this game. If you have a very large group, the game will be more fun if you break into smaller groups with each group having its own game board and cards.

2. Some young children will need help reading the card statements. See if other children can help out.

GOAL:

To reinforce program concepts of self-awareness, empathy, behavior management, and developmental expectations.

OBJECTIVES:

1. To have children work on individual coloring books.

2. To increase children's pride in accomplishments.

3. To reinforce comfort in using nurturing touch.

PROCEDURES:

1. Instruct the children that they can color in their coloring books. Have crayons available for children to use.

2. Have children share their colored pictures with their family before the end of the session.

FAMILY HUG:

1. End each home visit with a family hug. Everyone get in a circle and put your arms around the people next to you. During the family hug time, anyone can say anything they like. It is a time for free expression.

2. At a natural time, close the activities for the day.

IF'S, AND'S, OR BUT'S:

Thank family members for sharing their attitudes and feelings.

NURTURING PROGRAM FOR PARENTS AND CHILDREN BIRTH TO FIVE YEARS

SESSION 5

BEHAVIOR CONSTRUCT: Self-Awareness

SESSION CONCEPT: Personal Needs and Payoffs to Behavior

BRIEF DESCRIPTION: Parents will discuss what needs are and ways people choose to get their needs met. Payoffs to behavior will also be discussed. Children and adults will exercise to music and complete a giant drawing of themselves.

INTENDED USE: For parents of children birth to 5 years

PREREQUISITE KNOWLEDGE: None

AGENDA

Parent Activities	Materials
5.1　Icebreaker and Home Practice Check In	*Parent Handbooks*
5.2　Parents' Needs and Payoffs	*Parent Handbooks*
5.3　Home Practice Exercise	*Parent Handbooks*

Family Activities*	Materials
5.4　Family Nurturing Time	*Nurturing Book for Babies and Children*
5.5　Hello Time: Where is _____?	None
5.6　Circle Time: Dancercise	Cassette player and cassettes or record player and records
5.7　Giant Self-Drawing and Family Hug	Large butcher block paper, magic markers, crayons, old magazines, paste, scissors

*For parents with infants or toddlers, use activities presented in *Nurturing Book for Babies and Children*. For parents with preschoolers (ages 3-5), use the activities listed below Family Nurturing Time.

PARENT ACTIVITY: 5.1 Icebreaker and Home Practice Check In
CONSTRUCT: Empathy, Self-Awareness
MATERIALS: Parent Handbooks

GOAL:

To increase parents' awareness of self needs.

OBJECTIVES:

1. To identify current feelings.

2. To identify unmet needs.

3. To maintain sharing

4. To continue to develop a positive relationship.

PROCEDURES:

1. Begin today's parent activities by having each adult respond to the following:

   • Right now I am feeling _____ .

   • One need I presently have which is not being met is _____ .

2. After each parent has had an opportunity to respond to the statements above, review the Home Practice Exercise from the previous meeting. Also discuss perceived changes in family members and their interactions as reported in the family log.

IF'S, AND'S, OR BUT'S:

1. Allowing the parents to state a need and listening closely develops the ability to share self with others. Not "solving" the need instantly develops patience and also respect for the person. By keeping the attention focused on their needs, parents begin to develop an ability to be empathic to the needs of others.

2. Remember to share your feelings and unmet needs.

3. Finalize Family Rules using the Rules for the _____ Family worksheet located in the Parent Handbook. Post the rules in a place where all family members can see them.

PARENT ACTIVITY: 5.2 Parents' Needs and Payoffs
CONSTRUCT: Appropriate Developmental Expectations, Empathy, Self-Awareness
MATERIALS: Parent Handbooks

GOAL:

To increase parents' ability to identify and meet their own needs.

38

OBJECTIVES:

1. To increase parents' awareness of a need which is not being met.

2. To increase parents' confidence in their own ability to get their needs met.

3. To encourage parents to accept responsibility for blocking the process by which some of their needs could be met.

4. To increase parents' understanding of their own needs and the needs of others.

5. To teach parents a planning process by which they can plan to accomplish a goal.

6. To break down parents' sense of isolation or of self-pity by helping them to see that others also have unmet needs.

PROCEDURES:

1. Instruct parents to locate the information entitled **Needs and Payoffs for Adults and Children** on pages 12-14 in their Handbooks.

2. Write the following words on a piece of paper:
   - SELF-ESTEEM
   - SELF-CONCEPT
   - NEEDS

3. Discuss each word with the family to obtain a practical level of understanding.
   - SELF-ESTEEM: The way people feel about themselves. Elicit words from the group used to describe feelings toward self.
   - SELF-CONCEPT: Different from self-esteem, but related. Self-concept is the way people think about themselves. Elicit words from the group used to describe thoughts about self. *NOTE:* Making a distinction between feelings and thoughts is critical to making the distinction between a person's self-esteem and self-concept. Use as many examples as necessary to convey this difference.
   - NEEDS: The forces that drive people to behave the way they do.

4. Needs can be thought of in six general categories:
   - *Social Needs.* The need for friendship and companionship.
   - *Emotional Needs.* The need for friendship, love, praise, or sex.
   - *Physical Needs.* The need for food, sleep, or exercise.
   - *Intellectual Needs.* The need for stimulation from new ideas or thoughts.
   - *Creative Needs.* The need to make something, dance, or write a poem.
   - *Spiritual Needs.* The need to understand that we are part of something bigger than ourselves and that we can increase our sensitivity to it.

5. Explain that all behavior has one purpose — to meet a need. We constantly strive to get our needs met. Get examples from the family (tired, go to sleep; hungry, eat food; lonely, make friends, etc.). Behavior is related to how a person feels and thinks about him/herself. When people like themselves, they behave in positive ways; when they don't like themselves, they behave in negative ways.

6. Write the word BEHAVIOR on a piece of paper. Underneath, write the word SELF with a double arrow.

BEHAVIOR

↕

SELF

7. Mention that self and behavior are inseparable. You can't have one without the other. The word BEHAVIOR is meant to include everything from sleeping, to crying, to thinking, to eating supper. Feelings are behavior because the body expresses them: anger, sadness, jealousy, etc.

8. The way people think and feel about themselves usually dictates their behavior. People's behavior is related to their self-esteem and self-concept.

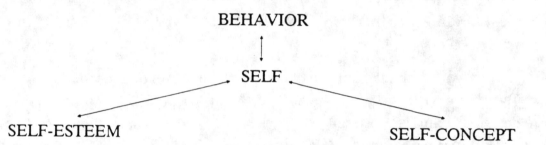

9. Positive (+) SE (self-esteem) and positive (+) SC (self-concept) is reflected in people's behavior. When you think good thoughts about yourself and have good feelings about yourself, you usually treat others the same way. Your positive behavior is a reflection of your positive thoughts and feelings. People behave solely upon how they feel towards themselves and others.

10. Get some examples of the relationship between positive SE and SC and positive, healthy behaviors. Example: A person who is kind to others behaves that way because he/she likes him/herself.

11. Repeat steps #9 and #10 using negative (-) SE (self-esteem) and negative (-) SC (self-concept). Focus on child abuse, spouse abuse, drug abuse, etc.

12. Emphasize that adults and children behave the way they do for a reason, or a purpose. All behavior is purposeful — that is, to get payoffs. A payoff is something we get when we try to get our needs met. Payoffs can be either good or bad. Some payoffs are attention, food, fat, sex, a hangover, good appearance, loneliness, companionship, etc.

13. The way we feel about ourselves influences the way we get our needs met and our payoffs. People who feel lousy about themselves generally do things to keep them feeling lousy. Feeling lousy is their payoff. The same is true with people who feel good about themselves. They do things to help them feel good about themselves.

14. Complete the exercise presented in the resource material on positive and negative payoffs. Generate a list of Good Payoffs (payoffs people want) and Bad Payoffs (payoffs people don't want). Do the exercise for both adults and children.

15. Have each parent identify one need that they would like to have met. Then instruct each parent to identify ways he or she blocks getting the need met. It is a fact that we often block getting our own needs met.

16. When we block getting our needs met, what are our payoffs—both positive and negative. Finally, brainstorm ways parents can get their needs met in an appropriate way.

IF'S, AND'S, OR BUT'S:

1. A lot of information is presented in this activity that is critical for the continuing change in family interactions. Make sure parents have an understanding of the concept of needs prior to discussing additional program concepts.

2. It may take two sessions to help parents fully comprehend all this information.

PARENT ACTIVITY:	5.3 Home Practice Exercise
CONSTRUCT:	Self-Awareness, Empathy
MATERIALS:	Parent Handbooks

GOAL:

To increase parents' awareness of needs and their relationship to behavior.

OBJECTIVES:

1. To help parents practice meeting their needs.

2. To help parents meet the needs of their children.

3. To reinforce nurturing parent-child relationships.

4. To establish a warm and supportive atmosphere.

PROCEDURES:

1. Instruct parents to locate the Home Practice Exercise on page 139 in their Handbooks. Review the exercise with them:

   a. Do at least one thing to meet a need of your own. How did you feel?

   b. Do at least one thing to meet a need of your children. How do you think your children felt?

   c. Complete family log.

2. Tell parents that in addition to the Home Practice Exercise, they are to spend 30 minutes each day with each of their children in nurturing playtime activities. Playtime is a time with the parent and child alone—no TV, no other distractions. Playing a game or reading books are good activities. From the *Nurturing Book for Babies and Children*, have the parents practice activities listed in the following sections: Activities for Infants, Activities for Toddlers, Activities for Preschoolers, or Infant and Child Massage.

IF'S, AND'S, OR BUT'S:

Highlight the concept that parents have needs and their behavior is designed to meet those needs.

FAMILY ACTIVITY:	**5.4 Family Nurturing Time**
CONSTRUCT:	**Empathy, Self-Awareness**
MATERIALS:	**Nurturing Book for Babies and Children**

ACTIVITIES FOR INFANTS (Birth to 15 months):

Utilizing the *Nurturing Book for Babies and Children*, review the information on stomach massage on pages 32-34. Have parents practice massaging their infant's stomach. Encourage parents to massage the legs, feet, and stomach as a part of their nurturing playtime activities.

ACTIVITIES FOR TODDLERS (15 months to 3 years):

Utilizing the *Nurturing Book for Babies and Children*, review the information on stomach massage on pages 32-34. Have parents practice massaging their toddler's stomach. Encourage parents to massage the legs, feet, and stomach as part of their nurturing playtime activities.

ACTIVITIES FOR PRESCHOOLERS (3-5 years):

Use the following activities when working with preschool children and their parents. Use the activities as the basis for involving infants and toddlers if you are conducting a home visit with children ages birth to five years.

FAMILY ACTIVITY: 5.5 Hello Time: Where is _____?
CONSTRUCT: Empathy
MATERIALS: None

GOAL:

To have children gain an awareness of others in the group.

OBJECTIVES:

1. To greet each child and adult by their first name.

2. To increase recognition of the needs of others.

3. To have fun in family interactions.

PROCEDURES:

1. Children and adults should be seated in a circle on the floor.

2. Ask everyone if they know the tune "Frere Jacques." Hum the tune and see if they recognize the melody. It is a good idea to have the children hum or sing the tune with you without any words a couple of times to ensure they know the song.

3. Using the tune of "Frere Jacques," sing the following words, first alone, and then once with the group. Use your first name (or the name of a parent) and identify an activity (suggest running or hopping).

Where is _____ ?

Where is __(name)__? Where is __(name)__?

Please stand up, please stand up.

(Dance, hop, run, tip toe, etc.) around the group_____.
(Dance, hop, run, tip toe, etc.) around the group_____.

Then sit down, then sit down.

4. Explain that everyone will have a chance to get up and move when it is their turn.

5. Choose a child to begin. Sing the song, inserting the movement. Allow the child to choose the next person, or the adult may choose who is next.

IF'S, AND'S, OR BUT'S:

1. For variation, ask for movement suggestions from the group. Children especially like to choose movements for adults and view this as a good joke. The response of the adult to this teasing provides a good model for behavior.

2. Noncompliant children may be encouraged if they are allowed to take a turn with a friend. Vary the song to include two people. Example: "Where are Jesse and Chad?"

FAMILY ACTIVITY: 5.6 Circle Time: Dancercise
CONSTRUCT: Developmental
MATERIALS: Cassette player and cassettes or record player and records

GOAL:

To increase family interactions through music.

OBJECTIVES:

1. To involve children and parents in group cooperative musical activities.
2. To practice gross motor movement.
3. To foster creative expression through dance.
4. To enhance self-awareness through dance.
5. To have fun.

PROCEDURES:

1. This activity will serve as a mini-dancercise movement. Have children and adults assemble in a circle.
2. Play music on a cassette player or a record player.
3. Demonstrate easy dance activities that generally use gross motor movements. The movements should change every 30 seconds to one minute to keep the interest going. Some gross motor movements may include the following:

   30 seconds, jumping jacks

   30 seconds, standing leg lifts (bending leg at hip and knee to form right angle)

   30 seconds, body twisting (turning at waist with hands on hips)

IF'S, AND'S, OR BUT'S:

1. Some parents may feel silly dancing around. Have patience and encourage the parents to participate. Soon they will see it's fun.
2. Select music that will encourage movement. You may want to ask one of the children to pick out their favorite song to dance to.

FAMILY ACTIVITY:	5.7 Giant Self-Drawing and Family Hug
CONSTRUCT:	Self-Awareness
MATERIALS:	Large butcher block paper, magic markers, crayons, old magazines, paste, scissors

GOAL:

To increase children's awareness of self and others.

OBJECTIVES:

1. To reinforce appropriate child-adult interactions.

2. To increase the child's knowledge of self.

3. To reinforce positive aspects of adult touch.

4. To reinforce comfort in using nurturing touch.

PROCEDURES:

1. Have one child at a time lay down on a piece of paper the entire length of his/her body.

2. Have the child lay on his/her back while the adult traces the outline of the body on the paper.

3. Allow each child the opportunity to fill in his/her own body drawing by cutting out words and pictures from the magazines and pasting them to their figure, and/or by coloring in body parts with crayons or markers.

4. Have each child cut out his/her figure and tape or tack each figure on the bulletin board.

5. When finished, hang in the family "Hall of Fame."

FAMILY HUG:

1. End each home visit with a family hug. Everyone get in a circle and put your arms around the people next to you. During the family hug time, anyone can say anything they like. It is a time for free expression.

2. At a natural time, close the activities for the day.

IF'S, AND'S, OR BUT'S:

1. Some children may feel awkward having their body drawn on paper. Encourage them by allowing them to watch or by helping trace the bodies on paper.

2. Monitor the use of the scissors.

3. Try to get parents to draw their giant selves. They can hang their pictures with their children's.

4. By sharing information about themselves, parents are always risking their self-esteem and self-concept. Appreciate that fact and thank them for taking risks.

NURTURING PROGRAM FOR PARENTS AND CHILDREN BIRTH TO FIVE YEARS

SESSION 6

BEHAVIOR CONSTRUCT: Empathy

SESSION CONCEPT: Spoiling Your Children

BRIEF DESCRIPTION: Parents will discuss the concept of spanking as it related to raising children. Children will practice recognizing feelings by role playing messages drawn from a hat.

INTENDED USE: For parents of children birth to 5 years

PREREQUISITE KNOWLEDGE: None

AGENDA

Parent Activities

		Materials
6.1	Icebreaker and Home Practice Check In	*Parent Handbooks*
6.2	Spoiling Your Children	*Parent Handbooks*, **Spoiling Your Child** AV presentation, AV equipment
6.3	Home Practice Exercise	*Parent Handbooks*

Family Activities*

		Materials
6.4	Family Nurturing Time	*Nurturing Book for Babies and Children*
6.5	Hello Time: This is the Way	None
6.6	Feeling Song	None
6.7	Circle Time: Charades	Small pieces of paper, pencil, bag
6.8	Tissue Art and Family Hug	White paper, pieces of different colored tissue, glue

*For parents with infants or toddlers, use activities presented in *Nurturing Book for Babies and Children*. For parents with preschoolers (ages 3-5), use the activities listed below Family Nurturing Time.

PARENT ACTIVITY: 6.1 Icebreaker and Home Practice Check In
CONSTRUCT: Self-Awareness
MATERIALS: Parent Handbooks

GOAL:

To initiate discussion regarding the concept of spoiling children.

OBJECTIVES:

1. To increase parent awareness of how they were spoiled.

2. To increase parent awareness of how their children are spoiled.

3. To allow parents to verbalize feelings related to spoiled children.

PROCEDURES:

1. Begin today's parent activities by having each adult respond to the following:

    ● As a child, my mother and/or father spoiled me by _____ .

    ● I think spoiled children deserve _____ .

2. After each parent has had an opportunity to respond to the statements above, review the Home Practice Exercise from the previous meeting. Also discuss perceived changes in family members and their interactions as reported in the family log.

IF'S, AND'S, OR BUT'S:

1. Some parents may want you to "define" what a spoiled child is. Decline the request and tell them to respond to the statements with their current perceptions of what a spoiled child is.

2. A more detailed discussion of spoiling children appears in the following activity.

PARENT ACTIVITY: 6.2 Spoiling Your Children
CONSTRUCT: Empathy
MATERIALS: Parent Handbooks, Spoiling Your Child AV presentation, AV equipment

GOAL:

To increase parents' knowledge of the myths and facts surrounding spoiling children.

OBJECTIVES:

1. To dispel myths of spoiling children.

2. To increase parents' ability to provide nurturing touch.

3. To promote an empathic awareness of childrens' needs.

PROCEDURES:

1. If you are using audio-visual programs, present the AV entitled **Spoiling Your Child**.

2. Instruct parents to locate the information entitled **Spoiling Your Children** on pages 15-18 in their Handbooks. Utilize the information to discuss the following major concepts with the parents.

   a. A spoiled child is one whose normal developmental needs for comfort, sameness, and attention are excessive and demanding.

   b. Children become spoiled by:
   - Doing everything for them.
   - Anticipating their requests.
   - Spending all of your time with them.
   - Not being separated for brief times from their parents.
   - Being held only when crying.
   - Inconsistent limit setting.
   - Blaming the child for being demanding.

   c. Myths and facts of spoiling.

   d. Reducing spoiled behaviors.

   e. Encouraging healthy behaviors.

3. Ask each parent to respond to the following: "If my child(ren) is(are) spoiled in any one area, it probably is _____." Encourage each parent to recognize how their child is spoiled.

4. Then ask each parent the following: "The way I contributed in spoiling my child(ren) was by _____." Let each parent take his/her share of the ownership of teaching the child undesirable behavior.

5. After each parent has identified a "spoiled behavior" in their child, brainstorm ways to remedy the situation.

IF'S, AND'S, OR BUT'S:

Parents may feel some guilt for spoiling their children or be overwhelmed by the magnitude of the behaviors. Be supportive and encouraging. Use the problem solving techniques to generate alternative behaviors.

GOAL:

To reduce the incidence of "spoiled child behaviors."

OBJECTIVES:

1. To begin to remediate unacceptable, "spoiled" behaviors.

2. To promote positive nurturing parent-child interactions.

3. To promote independence in parent and child.

4. To establish a warm and supportive atmosphere.

PROCEDURES:

1. Instruct parents to locate the Home Practice Exercise on page 139 in their Handbooks. Review the exercise with them:

   a. Attempt reducing the spoiled, unacceptable behavior of the child by practicing the suggestions presented in the earlier activity. Follow the recommendations offered.

   b. Complete family log.

2. Tell parents that in addition to the Home Practice Exercise, they are to spend 30 minutes each day with each of their children in nurturing playtime activities. Playtime is a time with the parent and child alone — no TV, no other distractions. Playing a game or reading books are good activities. From the *Nurturing Book for Babies and Children*, have the parents practice activities listed in the following sections: Activities for Infants, Activities for Toddlers, Activities for Preschoolers, or Infant and Child Massage. Have the parents remember what they did and report the next week.

IF'S, AND'S, OR BUT'S:

1. If the parents are not convinced that they had any hand in reinforcing the current undesirable "spoiled" behavior, they will be less likely to take an active role in remediating the situation.

2. Some dysfunctional families need one or more members of their family to display inappropriate behavior to keep from focusing on the real issues: husband/wife conflicts, alcoholism, depression, etc. The need to keep some children the scapegoat is not all uncommon.

FAMILY ACTIVITY:	6.4 Family Nurturing Time
CONSTRUCT:	Empathy, Self-Awareness
MATERIALS:	Nurturing Book for Babies and Children

ACTIVITIES FOR INFANTS *(Birth to 15 months):*

Utilizing the *Nurturing Book for Babies and Children*, review with parents chest and head massage on pages 35-37. Have parents practice chest and head massage. Encourage parents to practice chest and head massage as part of their nurturing playtime activities.

ACTIVITIES FOR TODDLERS *(15 months to 3 years):*

Utilizing the *Nurturing Book for Babies and Children*, review with parents chest and head massage on pages 35-37. Have parents practice chest and head massage. Encourage parents to practice chest and head massage as part of their nurturing playtime activities.

ACTIVITIES FOR PRESCHOOLERS *(3-5 years):*

Use the following activities when working with preschool children and their parents. Use the activities as the basis for involving infants and toddlers if you are conducting a home visit with children ages birth to five years.

FAMILY ACTIVITY:	6.5 Hello Time: This is the Way
CONSTRUCT:	Behavior Management
MATERIALS:	None

GOAL:

To build positive social interactions among family members.

OBJECTIVES:

1. To increase children's ability to communicate.

2. To reinforce positive peer interactions.

PROCEDURES:

1. Have children and adults stand in a circle.

2. Explain to them that today we are going to sing hello. Sing the following song to the tune of "This is the Way We Wash Our Clothes," and demonstrate the actions to the children.

This is the Way

This is the way we say hello (wave open hand-fingers pointing up),
Say hello (continue waving), say hello (continue waving),
This is the way we say hello, early in the morning.

This is the way we greet our friends (bow to one another)
Greet our friends, greet our friends,
This is the way we greet our friends, happy to see you here today.

3. Continue with "This is the way we . . . . (smile and laugh, shake other's hands, dance and sing).

IF'S, AND'S, OR BUT'S:

Have a good time with the song. Be creative and add your own lyrics.

FAMILY ACTIVITY:	**6.6 Feeling Song**
CONSTRUCT:	**Empathy**
MATERIALS:	**None**

GOAL:

To reinforce appropriate adult/child interactions.

OBJECTIVES:

1. To help parents and children learn to enjoy each other.

2. To provide an opportunity for the children to be with the parents in a safe atmosphere.

3. To physically and emotionally nourish children and parents.

4. To increase awareness of feelings.

PROCEDURES:

1. Have adults and children stand in a circle.

2. Explain the activity. We are going to sing a song that has lots of feelings. The song goes like this:

Feeling Song

When you're happy and you know it, clap your hands,
When you're happy and you know it, clap your hands,
When you're happy and you know it, then your face will surely show it,
When you're happy and you know it, clap your hands.

3. Repeat singing the song with the children clapping their hands.

4. Repeat the song with the following stanzas:

> When you're mad . . . stamp your feet.
> When you're sad . . .wipe your eyes.
> When you're scared . . . scream out loud (Ahh!).
> When you're cold . . . shake and shiver (shake body).
> When you're hot . . . sweat and faint (bend to knees).

IF'S, AND'S, OR BUT'S:

1. Encourage everyone to participate even though some may feel somewhat hesitant.

2. Ask children for suggestions for additional activities.

FAMILY ACTIVITY: **6.7 Circle Time: Charades**
CONSTRUCT: **Empathy**
MATERIALS: **Small pieces of paper, pencil, bag**

GOAL:

To give children practice in combining facial expressions, gestures, and postures to communicate feelings.

OBJECTIVES:

1. To increase children's awareness of facial expressions of others.

2. To help children learn to communicate through gesture.

3. To reinforce positive adult-child interactions.

PROCEDURES:

1. Write the following messages on small pieces of paper and put in a bag:

I like you.	We won!	I am sad.	Will you help me?
I am angry.	I love you.	I am scared.	I am happy.
I am hurt.	Be quiet!	Go away.	I won't do it!

2. Tell children and adults they will be playing a game called charades. The game is played by having others guess what one person is saying or feeling.

3. Begin by having one person (adult or child) pick a message from the bag. That person has to act out the message while the others try to guess what it is. The person with the message is not allowed to talk.

4. When the message is correctly identified, another person picks a message from the bag and acts it out.

IF'S, AND'S, OR BUT'S:

Some young children may need help reading or understanding. Help when appropriate.

FAMILY ACTIVITY: 6.8 Tissue Art and Family Hug
CONSTRUCT: Developmental
MATERIALS: White paper, pieces of different colored tissue, glue

GOAL:

To increase children's self-concept and self-esteem through accomplishment of age appropriate tasks.

OBJECTIVES:

1. To foster creative expression through art.

2. To increase fine motor skills.

3. To reinforce comfort in using nurturing touch.

PROCEDURES:

1. Assemble children around a table.

2. Fill a large container with various shapes and sizes of different colored tissue.

3. Provide each child with his/her own sheet of white paper.

4. Instruct the children that they are to glue the different sizes and colors of tissue onto the sheet of white paper, making a mosaic. The tissue should overlap each other creating different colors and patterns.

FAMILY HUG:

1. End each home visit with a family hug. Everyone get in a circle and put your arms around the people next to you. During the family hug time, anyone can say anything they like. It is a time for free expression.

2. At a natural time, close the activities for the day.

IF'S, AND'S, OR BUT'S:

1. You will need to cut the tissue in various shapes and sizes before beginning the activity.

2. Have children display their works of art by hanging them on a wall.

NURTURING PROGRAM FOR PARENTS AND CHILDREN BIRTH TO FIVE YEARS

SESSION 7

BEHAVIOR CONSTRUCT: Self-Awareness

SESSION CONCEPT: Personal Power

BRIEF DESCRIPTION: Parents and children will learn what personal power is and how to use their personal power to build their self-esteem and self-concept.

INTENDED USE: For parents of children birth to 5 years

PREREQUISITE KNOWLEDGE: Parent Needs and Behavior Payoffs

AGENDA

Parent Activities		Materials
7.1	Icebreaker and Home Practice Check In	*Parent Handbooks*
7.2	Personal Power	*Parent Handbooks*, **Personal Power** AV presentation, AV equipment
7.3	Home Practice Exercise	*Parent Handbooks*

Family Activities*		Materials
7.4	Family Nurturing Time	*Nurturing Book for Babies and Children*
7.5	Hello Time: Super Power	None
7.6	Simon Says	None
7.7	Circle Time: Personal Power	Puppets
7.8	Personal Power Vests and Family Hug	Scissors, large paper grocery bags, magic markers, crayons

*For parents with infants or toddlers, use activities presented in *Nurturing Book for Babies and Children*. For parents with preschoolers (ages 3-5), use the activities listed below Family Nurturing Time.

PARENT ACTIVITY: 7.1 Icebreaker and Home Practice Check In
CONSTRUCT: Self-Awareness
MATERIALS: Parent Handbooks

GOAL:

To increase parents' awareness of their ability to effect change in their lives.

OBJECTIVES:

1. To introduce the concept of power.

2. To increase parents' awareness of positive and negative aspects in their lives.

PROCEDURES:

1. Begin today's parent activities by having each adult respond to the following:

   ● If I had the power to go back in time and change anything I wanted, two things I would definitely change would be _____ and _____ .

   ● Two things I would definitely keep the same are _____ and _____ .

2. After each parent has had an opportunity to respond to the statements above, review the Home Practice Exercise from the previous meeting. Also discuss perceived changes in family members and their interactions as reported in the family log.

IF'S, AND'S, OR BUT'S:

The focus this session is on power — personal power. Being aware that one has power is a necessary prerequisite to changing one's lifestyle and environment.

PARENT ACTIVITY: 7.2 Personal Power
CONSTRUCT: Self-Awareness
MATERIALS: Parent Handbooks, Personal Power AV presentation, AV equipment

GOAL:

To increase parents' ability to use their personal power to help meet their own needs.

OBJECTIVES:

1. To define personal power.

2. To understand the difference between personal power and control.

3. To help parents foster feelings of personal power in their children.

4. To differentiate between positive and negative personal power.

PROCEDURES:

1. Instruct parents to locate the information entitled **Personal Power** on pages 19-21 in their Handbooks. Begin by asking them to define the word "power." Use the brainstorming technique to facilitate the discussion.

2. Next, define the term "personal power" presented in the Handbook. Personal power is not how physically strong we are, but the use of our knowledge and our feelings to act in a manner to get our needs met. In this way, self-esteem and self-concept and personal power are all related to each other. We use our personal power to act on what we know and how we feel about ourselves.

3. If you are using the audio-visual programs, present the AV entitled **Personal Power**. During the AV presentation, the family will be asked to discuss ways the characters in the presentation are using their personal power. At the end of each brief story, stop the program and ask the family to discuss the questions presented in the AV presentation. Allow around five minutes per discussion for each situation presented.

4. Now focus on the children. Brainstorm with the family situations when the children use their personal power. Do young infants know the difference between good and bad behavior? Do babies purposefully use their personal power in a negative way? When is it necessary to control the behavior of children? When can they foster the positive use of their personal power?

5. Ask parents to complete the following statements:

   • Within my family, one area I use my personal power in a positive way is _____. When this happens, I feel _____.

   • Within my family, one area I use my personal power in a negative way is _____. When this happens, I feel _____; but what I can do instead is _____.

IF'S, AND'S, OR BUT'S:

1. The theme of personal power will be used continually throughout the program. Know the concept well because you will be asking parents how they can use their personal power in a positive way to get their needs met.

2. Focus on how infants use their personal power to get their needs met.

3. If you are not using the audio-visual programs, use the information in the Handbook to foster discussion.

PARENT ACTIVITY: 7.3 Home Practice Exercise
CONSTRUCT: Behavior Management, Self-Awareness, Empathy
MATERIALS: Parent Handbooks

GOAL:

To foster the concepts of personal power in parents and children.

OBJECTIVES:

1. To provide parents with practice in using positive control to manage children's behavior.

2. To allow parents to practice their personal power.

3. To build personal power in children.

4. To establish a warm and supportive atmosphere.

PROCEDURES:

1. Instruct parents to locate the Home Practice Exercise on page 139 in their Handbooks. Review the exercise with them:

   a. Practice using positive control to manage behavior.

   b. Practice using your personal power to enhance self-esteem.

   c. Provide children an opportunity to use their personal power to take responsibility for their behavior.

   d. Praise yourself and your children for being and doing at least twice.

   e. Complete family log.

2. Tell parents that in addition to the Home Practice Exercise, they are to spend 30 minutes each day with each of their children in nurturing playtime activities. Playtime is a time with the parent and child alone — no TV, no other distractions. Playing a game or reading books are good activities. From the *Nurturing Book for Babies and Children*, have the parents practice activities listed in the following sections: Activities for Infants, Activities for Toddlers, Activities for Preschoolers, or Infant and Child Massage. Have the parents remember what they did and report the next week.

IF'S, AND'S, OR BUT'S:

Praise parents' attempts at meeting their homework responsibility. Suggest to them it is one way of using their personal power.

FAMILY ACTIVITY: **7.4 Family Nurturing Time**
CONSTRUCT: **Empathy, Self-Awareness**
MATERIALS: **Nurturing Book for Babies and Children**

ACTIVITIES FOR INFANTS (Birth to 15 months):

Utilizing the *Nurturing Book for Babies and Children*, review with parents the information on arms and hand massage on pages 38-39. Have parents practice massaging their infant's arms and hands. Encourage parents to practice massaging their infant's arms and hands as part of their nurturing playtime activities.

ACTIVITIES FOR TODDLERS (15 months to 3 years):

Utilizing the *Nurturing Book for Babies and Children*, review with parents the information on arms and hand massage on pages 38-39. Have parents practice massaging their toddler's arms and hands. Encourage parents to practice massaging their toddler's arms and hands as part of their nurturing playtime activities.

ACTIVITIES FOR PRESCHOOLERS (3-5 years):

Use the following activities when working with preschool children and their parents. Use the activities as the basis for involving infants and toddlers if you are conducting a home visit with children ages birth to five years.

FAMILY ACTIVITY: 7.5 Hello Time: Super Power
CONSTRUCT: Self-Awareness
MATERIALS: None

GOAL:

To increase children's personal feelings of power.

OBJECTIVES:

1. To enhance children's sense of control.

2. To increase awareness of self-power.

3. To reinforce appropriate social interactions among family members.

4. To identify a personal super power.

PROCEDURES:

1. Children and adults should be seated in a circle on the floor.

2. Begin with the following statements and ask everyone to complete them:

   • Today I am feeling _____ .

   • If you could choose to do anything you wanted, what would you choose?

   • How would you feel being able to _____ ?

IF'S, AND'S, OR BUT'S:

1. Encourage the children to offer why they chose that super power. Responses can provide insight into children's needs.

2. If a child cannot think of a super power they would like to have, let them pass and take their turn later.

FAMILY ACTIVITY: 7.6 Simon Says
CONSTRUCT: Behavior Management
MATERIALS: None

GOAL:

To increase child's ability to respond to behavior management.

OBJECTIVES:

1. To increase children's ability to follow directions.

2. To increase children's ability to identify body parts.

3. To increase children's auditory memory.

4. To give children an opportunity to give commands.

PROCEDURES:

1. Explain the rules of "Simon Says." When Simon says to do something, the players must follow the command.

2. Two versions of the game can occur:

   a. Adult is Simon giving children commands. Commands can be gross motor movements (hopping, jumping, etc.), fine motor movements (writing, cutting, etc.), or identification of body parts (touch ears, eyes, etc.).

   b. Children can be Simon taking turns giving the adult and other children commands.

IF'S, AND'S, OR BUT'S:

1. You may want to change the name "Simon Says" to the name of the person giving the commands; e.g., "Billy says."

2. Make sure everyone gets a turn.

3. Kids will love giving adults commands.

FAMILY ACTIVITY: 7.7 Circle Time: Personal Power
CONSTRUCT: Behavior Management
MATERIALS: Puppets

GOAL:

To increase the awareness of children to exercise personal power to manage their own lives.

OBJECTIVES:

1. To increase children's awareness of their own personal power.

2. To help children learn how to avoid physical and emotional abuse by using their personal power.

3. To increase the child's ability to effectively manage their own safety when being punished by a parent.

PROCEDURES:

1. Assemble children and parents in a circle on the floor.

2. Today we will talk about power. Can anyone tell me what power is? (Wait for response and reinforce.) We all have power that is called "personal power." Personal power means we decide to do or not to do certain things. Can anyone tell me how they use their personal power to do or not to do certain things? (Personal power can be used to decide what to wear, who to be friends with, who to play with, etc.).

3. Personal power can be used in a bad way. Some people use personal power to hurt others. Acting like a bully, fighting, and yelling are ways some people misuse personal power.

4. We can use our personal power when we are being punished by our parents. Does anyone know what punishment is? (Something that happens to you when you do something wrong.) What kinds of punishment do parents use? (Spanking, yelling, being sent to room, time-out, etc.) How do you feel when your parents hit you or yell at you? We are going to discuss ways in which we can use our personal power to avoid being hit and yelled at. I'll read you some situations, and you tell me what should be done.

5. Use the puppets to act out the skits. Let one of the parents act out one of the puppet roles.

   a. Mom is really angry at you because you have been making too much noise in the house and she has told you twice to stop. She says to you, "I have asked you to quit making noise in the house. If you continue to make noise, you will take a three-minute time-out." You continue to make noise and she tells you to take a three-minute time-out. What should you do? How can you use your personal power? Has anybody here had to take a time-out at home?

   b. Your dad tells you to take a two-minute time-out because you have done something wrong. You go to your time-out area and begin to make a lot of noise. What's going to happen if you continue making noise? How could you use your power?

   c. Mom is angry at you because you were naughty. She says you deserve to be spanked. What could you do to not get hit? Could you take a time-out instead?

   d. Use a situation appropriate to the family.

IF'S, AND'S, OR BUT'S:

Discuss with the children the alternatives to being hit, like time-out. Encourage children to take their time-outs appropriately or to initiate a self time-out to avoid spankings.

GOAL:

To increase the child's ability to become assertive in letting others know his/her needs and abilities.

OBJECTIVES:

1. To increase children's ability to express their needs.

2. To increase children's feelings of power.

3. To increase children's ability to receive positive comments.

4. To reinforce comfort in using nurturing touch.

PROCEDURES:

1. Prior to initiating the activity, spend a few moments with the family explaining how feelings can sometimes be frightening. Explain how some children are more vulnerable than others in receiving praise or criticism, or being able to talk about how they feel and what they need. To help the children increase their ability to communicate their feelings and needs, each of them will make a "Personal Power Vest." This vest helps children give and receive positive comments, ask for things, and talk about how they feel.

2. Have children use paper grocery bags. Cut holes in the front of the bags for arms and in the top for the head. Do this by placing the bag on the back of the child and measuring for shoulder and arms.

3. Allow children to decorate vest in any manner they choose.

4. Children can wear their vests any time they choose. The purpose is to help children understand and gain feelings of assertiveness through power in decision making.

FAMILY HUG:

1. End each home visit with a family hug. Everyone get in a circle and put your arms around the people next to you. During the family hug time, anyone can say anything they like. It is a time for free expression.

2. At a natural time, close the activities for the day.

IF'S, AND'S, OR BUT'S:

1. Younger children may need help assembling and cutting their vest. Have parents help out.

2. Allow children to wear their vest anytime.

3. Remind children power vests help them to make decisions that make them feel good.

NURTURING PROGRAM FOR PARENTS AND CHILDREN BIRTH TO FIVE YEARS

SESSION 8

BEHAVIOR CONSTRUCT: Behavior Management

SESSION CONCEPT: Praise for Being and Doing

BRIEF DESCRIPTION: Parents and children learn what praise is and how to praise self and others.

INTENDED USE: For parents of children birth to 5 years

PREREQUISITE KNOWLEDGE: None

AGENDA

Parent Activities	Materials
8.1 Icebreaker and Home Practice Check In	*Parent Handbooks*
8.2 Praise for Being and Doing	*Parent Handbooks*, **Praise** AV presentation, AV equipment
8.3 Home Practice Exercise	*Parent Handbooks*

Family Activities*	Materials
8.4 Family Nurturing Time	*Nurturing Book for Babies and Children*
8.5 Hello Time: Something Good About Me	None
8.6 Hopping Song	None
8.7 Circle Time: Praise	Feeling Faces, Puppets
8.8 Tear and Paste and Family Hug	Old magazines, phone book pages or tissue paper, glue, cardboard, paper plates, construction paper

*For parents with infants or toddlers, use activities presented in *Nurturing Book for Babies and Children*. For parents with preschoolers (ages 3-5), use the activities listed below Family Nurturing Time.

PARENT ACTIVITY: 8.1 Icebreaker and Home Practice Check In
CONSTRUCT: Self-Awareness
MATERIALS: Parent Handbooks

GOAL:

To increase parents' awareness of the need to be recognized.

OBJECTIVES:

1. To increase parent willingness to share.

2. To identify areas for recognition.

3. To learn the value of praise.

PROCEDURES:

1. Begin today's parent activities by having each adult respond to the following:

   ● Right now I am feeling _____ .

   ● One day I would like someone to praise me for _____ .

2. After each parent has had an opportunity to respond to the statements above, review the Home Practice Exercise from the previous meeting. Also discuss perceived changes in family members and their interactions as reported in the family log.

IF'S, AND'S, OR BUT'S:

1. Parents will begin to recognize that there are a number of things they do for others that they receive no thanks or recognition for. Some might want to be praised for who they are and not for what they do. Listen closely for their praise needs. Maybe sometime during the meetings you have with the parents you might get the chance to praise them in their identified area.

2. Praise will be discussed in more detail in the next activity.

PARENT ACTIVITY: 8.2 Praise for Being and Doing
CONSTRUCT: Behavior Management
MATERIALS: Parent Handbooks, Praise AV presentation, AV equipment

GOAL:

To increase parents' knowledge of the theory and techniques of using praise.

OBJECTIVES:

1. To understand the steps involved in praise.

2. To understand the importance of praise.

3. To experience giving and receiving praise.

4. To give parents information on praise for being and praise for doing.

5. To increase individual self-esteem.

PROCEDURES:

1. If you are using the audio-visual programs, present the AV entitled **Praise**. Utilize the discussion frames at the end of the presentation to review the major concepts of the program.

2. Instruct parents to locate the information entitled **Praising a Child's Behavior** on pages 22-24 in their Handbooks. Utilize the information presented to discuss the following major concepts with the parents:

   a. Praise for being recognizes children for who they are. It tells them they are special for who they are — not because they have done something.

   b. Praise for doing acknowledges children and others for the things they do, attempt, try, or complete — not for who they are. When you offer praise, praise for either being or doing — but not together.

3. Have parents practice praise for being and praise for doing.

4. In praising children:
   - Focus attention on the child.
   - Make eye contact.
   - Look pleasant.
   - Describe exactly what behavior you are praising.
   - Share your pleasure.
   - Touch the child if possible.
   - Focus on the behavior, not the child.

5. Practice the steps involved in praising. Role play that you're the child and have the parent praise you, incorporating all the steps of praising.

6. Point out that there are many ways to give praise, such as giving money, kissing, smiling, or even remaining silent instead of criticizing. See if the parents think of other ways to praise.

7. Pair off the family members. Ask each pair to make physical contact with each other in a way that's comfortable for both of them. Have them maintain that contact. (Holding hands, touching knees, etc.).

8. Person A begins by praising Person B for being or doing. Person B can only say "thank you", smile, or nod approvingly, but cannot refute the praise. Person A has to praise Person B for being and doing for about 1 minute.

9. Reverse roles. Person B praises Person A for being and doing. The same ground rules apply: Person A cannot refute the praise. Proceed for about 1 minute.

10. Afterwards, discuss the activity. Was it easier to praise or be praised? What were they feeling when they were getting praised? Why do we feel that way?

11. Discuss the following: How important is giving praise to children? What are three praise statements you could say to your child? Have each parent practice saying three praise statements to that can be said to a young child.

12. Promote the idea of self-praise. Explain that it's not bragging or being conceited, but giving yourself a pat on the back when you deserve it.

IF'S, AND'S, OR BUT'S:

1. Some parents will have difficulty giving and/or receiving praise. Process feelings with the parents.

2. Have parents think about praising their children. Share any concerns they might have.

PARENT ACTIVITY:	**8.3 Home Practice Exercise**
CONSTRUCT:	**Behavior Management, Empathy**
MATERIALS:	**Parent Handbooks**

GOAL:

To reinforce the use of praise as an effective means of helping children increase their self-concept and self-esteem.

OBJECTIVES:

1. To practice giving praise for being and doing.

2. To reinforce positive aspects of self.

3. To focus on desirable behaviors of children.

4. To help children begin to manage their behavior.

5. To establish a warm and supportive atmosphere.

PROCEDURES:

1. Instruct parents to locate the Home Practice Exercise on page 140 in their Handbooks. Review the exercise with them:

   a. Praise each child twice: once for being, once for doing.

   b. Praise yourself twice for either being or doing.

   c. Complete family log.

2. Tell parents that in addition to the Home Practice Exercise, they are to spend 30 minutes each day with each of their children in nurturing playtime activities. Playtime is a time with the parent and child alone—no TV, no other distractions. Playing a game or reading books are good activities. From the *Nurturing Book for Babies and Children*, have the parents practice activities listed in the following sections: Activities for Infants, Activities for Toddlers, Activities for Preschoolers, or Infant and Child Massage. Have the parents remember what they did and report the next week.

IF'S, AND'S, OR BUT'S:

Praise is a very powerful incentive to change behavior. Encourage parents to use praise as their number one way to help children learn desirable behavior.

FAMILY ACTIVITY:	**8.4 Family Nurturing Time**
CONSTRUCT:	**Empathy, Self-Awareness**
MATERIALS:	**Nurturing Book for Babies and Children**

ACTIVITIES FOR INFANTS (Birth to 15 months):

Utilizing the *Nurturing Book for Babies and Children*, review with parents the information on back massage on pages 40-41. Have parents practice massaging their infant's back. Encourage parents to practice massaging their infant's back as part of their nurturing playtime activities.

ACTIVITIES FOR TODDLERS (15 months to 3 years):

Utilizing the *Nurturing Book for Babies and Children*, review with parents the information on back massage on pages 40-41. Have parents practice massaging their toddler's back. Encourage parents to practice massaging their toddler's back as part of their nurturing playtime activities.

ACTIVITIES FOR PRESCHOOLERS (3-5 years):

Use the following activities when working with preschool children and their parents. Use the activities as the basis for involving infants and toddlers if you are conducting a home visit with children ages birth to five years.

FAMILY ACTIVITY: 8.5 Hello Time: Something Good About Me
CONSTRUCT: Self-Awareness
MATERIALS: None

GOAL:

To increase positive self-concept and self-esteem.

OBJECTIVES:

1. To reinforce positive verbal self-expression.

2. To increase positive perceptions of self.

PROCEDURES:

1. Children and adults should be seated in a circle on the floor.

2. Have each child and adult respond to the following statements:

   • Right now I am feeling _____ .

   • Something good about me is _____ .

IF'S, AND'S, OR BUT'S:

1. Have the parents help their children come up with something good about themselves. Those who say nothing is good about them need extra praise for being and doing.

2. Encourage parents to be supportive and encouraging.

FAMILY ACTIVITY: 8.6 Hopping Song
CONSTRUCT: Empathy
MATERIALS: None

GOAL:

To increase positive family interactions through music.

OBJECTIVES:

1. To involve children in active and cooperative musical activities.

2. To foster creative expression through music.

PROCEDURES:

1. Assemble children and adults in a circle to participate in the song activity.

2. Sing words to the tune of "99 Bottles of Beer."

There is one person hopping, hopping all around,
Hopping, hopping, hopping,
Hopping all around.

Movement: Kids hop and increase to 2 kids, 3 kids, etc. or have everyone participate at the same time. Ask the children what activity should be performed.

Example: There is one family hopping, hopping all around.

IF'S, AND'S, OR BUT'S:

Use gross motor movements such as hopping, skipping, jumping, running backwards, etc. The idea is movement.

FAMILY ACTIVITY:	8.7 Circle Time: Praise
CONSTRUCT:	Empathy, Self-Awareness
MATERIALS:	Feeling Faces, Puppets

GOAL:

To increase children's knowledge of the concept of praise.

OBJECTIVES:

1. To identify the concept of praise.

2. To identify feelings associated with praise.

PROCEDURES:

1. Assemble everyone in a circle sitting on the floor. Explain that today we are going to learn about an important way to talk to people. It is called praise. Praise is saying something nice to others.

2. Explain that there are two kinds of praise: the kind we get from others and the kind we give to others. In this way, praise is like a gift. Some gifts we get from people, other gifts we give to people.

   • Has anyone here ever received a present from someone? How do you feel when you get present?

   • Has anyone here ever given a present to someone else? How do you feel when you give presents?

   Giving and getting praise is much like giving and getting presents. It feels good.

3. Let's practice giving praise. Who can say something nice? Encourage children to give examples of praise. Some examples are:

   Praise for being: I like you.
   You are a nice friend.
   I like to be with you.

68

Praise for doing: I like the way you play.

You cleaned your room well.

I like the way you talk with indoor voices.

4. Help the children to recognize how they feel when someone praises them. Praise feels good, warm, happy, etc. Using a happy face, hold up the picture and let the children see a smiling boy/girl who has just been praised. The focus is on feelings associated with being praised or giving praise.

5. Ask the following questions to get children in touch with praise:

   - When are you praised?

   - When was the last time someone praised you?

   - When was the last time you praised someone?

6. When someone gives us praise, we should say "thank you."

7. Have the two puppets appear. "Well, hello _____ and _____. How are you today?"

   Puppet #1: I feel real good today.

   Puppet #2: Oh . . . I guess I feel okay.

   Puppet #1: (to Puppet #2) Boy-o-boy, don't you look nice! Is that a new haircut you have?

   Puppet #2: (shyly) Yes, but this ol' raggy mop never looks good.

   Puppet #1: Well, you do have on new jeans and you really look good in them.

   Puppet #2: (shyly) They're new alright, but my legs are too (thin, fat, short, long). I don't like my body.

   Puppet #1: I bet your new gym shoes can make you run fast as the wind.

   Puppet #2: (shyly) I'm no good at running. And furthermore, I don't like it when you praise me.

   Leader (ask the group):

   - What is the matter with Puppet #2?

   - How is Puppet #2 feeling?

   - Why do you think Puppet #2 doesn't like to be praised?

   Leader: Let's see what we can do to help Puppet #2 accept praise. What should we tell him/her to do when someone is praising him/her? (To say thank you; to accept praise; to feel good about praise.)

   Puppet #1: (to Puppet #2) No matter what I praise, you don't like my praise.

   Puppet #2: Sorry, but it just feels kind of funny.

   Puppet #1: Maybe the kids and adults can all give you some praise so you can practice saying "thank you" and accepting the praise.

   Leader: Encourage kids and adults to give Puppet #2 lots of praise. Have Puppet #2 say thank you to each child and adult who offers praise.

Puppet #2: (to Puppet #1) Boy-o-boy, I am feeling better since the kids and adults gave me some praise. From now on, every time I receive praise, I'm gonna say "thank you." And I'm also gonna praise other kids and adults, too. I know how good it feels. Thanks for the lesson. Bye!

Puppet #1: Bye!

IF'S, AND'S, OR BUT'S:

1. Praise is not always easy for children to give and receive. Encourage the children to practice praise with each other in the group. Don't forget to model praise whenever you can throughout the program.

2. If there is time, let some children use the puppets to act out their own script on praise.

3. In a family situation, let one of the parents take on the role of one of the puppets.

FAMILY ACTIVITY:	**8.8 Tear and Paste and Family Hug**
CONSTRUCT:	**Developmental**
MATERIALS:	**Old magazines, phone book pages or tissue paper, glue, cardboard, paper plates, construction paper**

GOAL:

To encourage creative expression through the use of developmental capabilities.

OBJECTIVES:

1. To create in art.

2. To enhance fine motor movement.

3. To increase the ability to control finger muscles.

4. To increase the child's awareness of shapes, sizes, and proportions.

5. To reinforce comfort in using nurturing touch.

PROCEDURES:

1. Assemble everyone around a table or on the floor with some protective covering.

2. Provide old magazines, phone book pages, or tissue paper and let the children tear out pieces of paper to their heart's content.

3. Practice tearing together. Talk about the "pinching" fingers. Keep both pinchers together to get the paper to do what you want it to do. Children can learn to control the torn edge by moving their fingers inch by inch as they tear.

4. Practice tearing the paper into shapes. Let's tear a small piece from our big piece. Let's tear our paper right in half. Tear, together, long skinny strips, tiny bits, and so on.

5. Have the children paste their shapes on cardboard, paper plates, or construction paper.

6. Let the children participate in cleanup.

FAMILY HUG:

1. End each home visit with a family hug. Everyone get in a circle and put your arms around the people next to you. During the family hug time, anyone can say anything they like. It is a time for free expression.

2. At a natural time, close the activities for the day.

IF'S, AND'S, OR BUT'S:

Have parents assist their child in their art activity.

NURTURING PROGRAM FOR PARENTS AND CHILDREN BIRTH TO FIVE YEARS

SESSION 9

BEHAVIOR CONSTRUCT: Behavior Management

SESSION CONCEPT: Red, White, and Bruises

BRIEF DESCRIPTION: Parents discuss the nonvalue hitting has as a way of punishing behavior. Reasons why hitting is used by parents is also discussed. Children review personal power.

INTENDED USE: For parents of children birth to 5 years

PREREQUISITE KNOWLEDGE: Behavior Management and Family Rules

AGENDA

Parent Activities		Materials
9.1	Icebreaker and Home Practice Check In	*Parent Handbooks*
9.2	Red, White, and Bruises	*Parent Handbooks*, **Red, White, and Bruises** AV presentation, AV equipment, paper, pens
9.3	Home Practice Exercise	*Parent Handbooks*

Family Activities*		Materials
9.4	Family Nurturing Time	*Nurturing Book for Babies and Children*
9.5	Hello Time: Something I Do Good	None
9.6	Are You Sleeping?	Blanket, pillow, bell, rug or mat
9.7	Circle Time: Personal Power Review	Puppets
9.8	Power Painting and Family Hug	Paint brushes, paints, butcher block paper

*For parents with infants or toddlers, use activities presented in *Nurturing Book for Babies and Children*. For parents with preschoolers (ages 3-5), use the activities listed below Family Nurturing Time.

PARENT ACTIVITY: 9.1 Icebreaker and Home Practice Check In
CONSTRUCT: Self-Awareness
MATERIALS: Parent Handbooks

GOAL:

To share feelings resulting from being spanked as a child.

OBJECTIVES:

1. To increase awareness of commonality of feelings.

2. To become aware of the negative impact of hitting.

3. To begin to consider alternatives to hitting.

PROCEDURES:

1. Begin today's parent activities by having each adult respond to the following:

   • When I was spanked (hit) as a child, I usually felt _____ and I learned _____ .

2. After each parent has had an opportunity to respond to the statements above, review the Home Practice Exercise from the previous meeting. Also discuss perceived changes in family members and their interactions as reported in the family log.

IF'S, AND'S, OR BUT'S:

Encourage parents to get in touch with how they felt after they were hit and to verbalize what they learned as a result.

PARENT ACTIVITY: 9.2 Red, White, and Bruises
CONSTRUCT: Behavior Management
MATERIALS: Parent Handbooks, Red, White, and Bruises AV presentation, AV equipment, paper, pens

GOAL:

To increase parents' awareness of the limitations of hitting as a form of punishment.

OBJECTIVES:

1. To present information about the effects of spanking.

2. To help parents evaluate the effects of being spanked as children.

3. To encourage parents to think about the undesirability of spanking.

4. To begin to free parents from their perceived roles as bad and incompetent caregivers.

PROCEDURES:

1. Assemble family members in a circle. Inform them that today's home visit will focus on the limitations of hitting.

2. Mention the word HITTING. Brainstorm other words and phrases that are used to describe the word.

    - SPANKING

    - LOVE TAP

    - KICK IN THE BUTT

    - BEATING

    - THE HELL KICKED OUT OF SOMEONE

3. Next, brainstorm reasons why parents hit children:

    - To teach them right from wrong.

    - To protect them from getting hurt.

4. Explain the philosophy of the Nurturing Program:

    - Hitting for any reason in a parent-child relationship is not acceptable. As a way for human beings to treat each other, it clearly shows a lack of respect. It is also a poor way to teach what to do. It only teaches what not to do.

5. If you are using the audio-visual programs, present the AV entitled **Red, White, and Bruises**.

6. Instruct parents to locate the information entitled **Red, White, and Bruises** on pages 25-29 in their Handbooks. Utilize the information to discuss the following major concepts with the parents:

    a. Hitting people has been around for a long time.

    b. Spanking is the most common form of hitting used by parents.

    c. Parents use spanking for two main reasons: to educate and to punish.

    d. The disadvantages to spanking are:

        - It teaches children fear.

        - It develops a poor self-concept in the child.

        - It teaches the child to want to seek revenge.

        - It teaches children it's OK to hit those you love.

        - The behavior for which the child was hit usually appears again.

    e. Several myths and facts are presented in the Handbook. Review each myth and fact with the parents.

IF'S, AND'S, OR BUT'S:

1. Some parents will have a difficult time remembering when they were spanked. Others will deny the experiences, while still others will remember the hurt very easily. Allow time for the parents to process all their feelings.

2. It may take two sessions to share this information.

PARENT ACTIVITY: 9.3 Home Practice Exercise
CONSTRUCT: Self-Awareness, Behavior Management
MATERIALS: Parent Handbooks

GOAL:

To reinforce nurturing parent-child interactions.

OBJECTIVES:

1. To encourage parents to use alternatives to hitting.

2. To reinforce positive regard for children.

3. To build positive regard for self in the role of a parent.

4. To implement family rules.

5. To establish a warm and supportive atmosphere.

PROCEDURES:

1. Instruct parents to locate the Home Practice Exercise on page 140 in their Handbooks. Review the exercise with them:

   a. Identify two times during the week when you felt like hitting your children but didn't.

   b. Identify what you did instead of hitting.

   c. Identify instances when the family rules seemed to be working or not working.

   d. Complete family log prior to the start of the next session.

2. Tell parents that in addition to the Home Practice Exercise, they are to spend 30 minutes each day with each of their children in nurturing playtime activities. Playtime is a time with the parent and child alone — no TV, no other distractions. Playing a game or reading books are good activities. From the *Nurturing Book for Babies and Children*, have the parents practice activities listed in the following sections: Activities for Infants, Activities for Toddlers, Activities for Preschoolers, or Infant and Child Massage. Have the parents remember what they did and report the next week.

IF'S, AND'S, OR BUT'S:

If parents are not using stickers, stars, etc. as a type of reward for following rules, encourage them to start using the system immediately.

FAMILY ACTIVITY:	**9.4 Family Nurturing Time**
CONSTRUCT:	**Empathy, Self-Awareness**
MATERIALS:	**Nurturing Book for Babies and Children**

ACTIVITIES FOR INFANTS (Birth to 15 months):

Utilizing the *Nurturing Book for Babies and Children*, review with parents the information on massage exercises on pages 42-43. Have parents practice the massage exercises on their infants. Encourage parents to use massage as a part of their nurturing playtime activities.

ACTIVITIES FOR TODDLERS (15 months to 3 years):

Utilizing the *Nurturing Book for Babies and Children*, review with parents the information on massage exercises on pages 42-43. Have parents practice the massage exercises on their toddlers. Encourage parents to use massage as a part of their nurturing playtime activities.

ACTIVITIES FOR PRESCHOOLERS (3-5 years):

Use the following activities when working with preschool children and their parents. Use the activities as the basis for involving infants and toddlers if you are conducting a home visit with children ages birth to five years.

FAMILY ACTIVITY:	**9.5 Hello Time: Something I Do Good**
CONSTRUCT:	**Self-Awareness, Empathy**
MATERIALS:	**None**

GOAL:

To increase positive self-concept and self-esteem.

OBJECTIVES:

1. To increase children's ability to recognize positive aspects of self.
2. To reinforce children's ability to praise self.
3. To increase children's ability to share positive aspects of self.
4. To increase recognition of feelings.

PROCEDURES:

1. Have everyone sit in a circle on the floor.

2. Have each child and adult respond to the following statements:
   - Right now I am feeling _____ .
   - Something I do good is _____ .

IF'S, AND'S, OR BUT'S:

Being "good" and doing something good may be confusing to the children. Help them understand the differences.

FAMILY ACTIVITY:	**9.6 Are You Sleeping?**
CONSTRUCT:	**Empathy**
MATERIALS:	**Blanket, pillow, bell, rug or mat**

GOAL:

To express and accept nurturing gestures appropriately among children and their parents.

OBJECTIVES:

1. To increase positive parent-child nurturing interactions.

2. To engage in cooperative activity between children and parents.

PROCEDURES:

1. Have children and parents sit in a circle on the floor.

2. Begin to discuss the concept of nurturing. Start by using examples:

   a. When they are frightened, the feeling of comfort when someone holds them.

   b. The feelings of comfort after someone helped them do a difficult task.

   In this instance, nurturing is being equated to the feeling of being comforted.

3. Describe the game for parents and children. One child lies down on the rug and pillow and is covered with the blanket by the parent. Appropriate nurturing-type interactions may be demonstrated such as tucking the blanket around the child, touching him/her and saying "good night" softly. The small bell should be placed near the pillow. The child on the rug pretends to sleep while the group sings softly:

   ### Are You Sleeping?

   Are you sleeping, Are you sleeping,
   Brother (Sister) _____ , Brother (Sister) _____ .

---

4. The group sings loudly and claps:

> Morning bells are ringing, Morning bells are ringing,
> Ding, ding, dong; Ding, ding, dong.
> (The sleeping person jumps up and rings the bell.)

5. Activity continues until all children have been tucked in by their parents.

IF'S, AND'S, OR BUT'S:

1. This is a good activity to use to provide appropriate physical contact in a nurturing way to children and their parents who may not ordinarily be receptive to it.

2. The activity allows children to experience appropriate nurturing behaviors.

3. Build up the suspense of being quiet while a child is "sleeping" and clapping and singing loudly when he/she "wakes up." This helps children wait for their turn.

4. Encourage parents who may be feeling awkward that night time nurturing behaviors have a positive impact upon the sleeping styles of young children.

FAMILY ACTIVITY:	9.7 Circle Time: Personal Power Review
CONSTRUCT:	Behavior Management
MATERIALS:	Puppets

GOAL:

To reinforce the ability of children to exercise personal power.

OBJECTIVES:

1. To teach children to use personal power to avoid being hit.

2. To increase children's awareness of how they may precipitate their own maltreatment.

3. To teach children how to effectively use personal power to manage their own lives.

PROCEDURES:

1. Have children and adults sit in a circle on the floor.

2. Remember when we talked about personal power and the different ways we could use our personal power? Who can tell me what personal power is?

3. Calling puppets by their first names, act out the following situations:

Puppet #1: Look at that kid over there. He is on his bicycle. Let's push him down and take his bicycle.

Puppet #2: Oh, I don't know if we should.

Puppet #1: Come on, it will be fun!

Leader: What should Puppet #2 do? How can he/she use his/her personal power? Finish skit in manner suggested by the children.

Puppet #1: Hey, look! There's some candy in the candy store. Let's take it!

Puppet #2: It's not our candy. We have to buy it before we can eat it. I don't think we should take it.

Puppet #1: Oh, it's okay. Nobody will miss the candy.

Puppet #2: I'm not sure.

Leader: What should Puppet #2 do? How can he/she use his/her personal power? Finish skit in manner suggested by the children.

Act out a situation relevant to your group where personal power can be used to reinforce a rule, lesson, etc.

IF'S, AND'S, OR BUT'S:

Continue to use the concept of personal power throughout the program. How could you use your personal power to _____ ?

FAMILY ACTIVITY:	**9.8 Power Painting and Family Hug**
CONSTRUCT:	**Developmental**
MATERIALS:	**Paint brushes, paints, butcher block paper**

GOAL:

To reinforce the concept of personal power through personal expression in art.

OBJECTIVES:

1. To enhance ability to gain personal power.

2. To increase child's self-concept through task completion.

3. To increase fine motor skills.

4. To enhance social sharing interactions.

5. To reinforce comfort in using nurturing touch.

PROCEDURES:

1. The theme of the painting is power. Have the children and adults draw the most powerful thing they know. Or, have them draw themselves in a very powerful position.

2. Let the paintings dry by hanging them.

3. Encourage everyone to discuss their paintings. What is the power in the painting? How are you powerful in the painting?

FAMILY HUG:

1. End each home visit with a family hug. Everyone get in a circle and put your arms around the people next to you. During the family hug time, anyone can say anything they like. It is a time for free expression.

2. At a natural time, close the activities for the day.

IF'S, AND'S, OR BUT'S:

Younger children may have some difficulty understanding the theme of the painting. Nevertheless, encourage them to paint "power."

NURTURING PROGRAM FOR PARENTS AND CHILDREN BIRTH TO FIVE YEARS

SESSION 10

BEHAVIOR CONSTRUCT: Empathy

SESSION CONCEPT: Hurting Touch

BRIEF DESCRIPTION: Parents and children will discuss hurting touch and how they feel after they experience hurting touch.

INTENDED USE: For parents of children birth to 5 years

PREREQUISITE KNOWLEDGE: Red, White, and Bruises, Behavior Management

AGENDA

Parent Activities	Materials
10.1 Icebreaker and Home Practice Check In	*Parent Handbooks*
10.2 Hurting Touch	Paper, pen
10.3 Home Practice Exercise	*Parent Handbooks*

Family Activities*	Materials
10.4 Family Nurturing Time	*Nurturing Book for Babies and Children*
10.5 Hello Time: Loud and Soft	None
10.6 Boat Song	None
10.7 Circle Time: Hurting Touch	None
10.8 Paper Mountain and Family Hug	Construction paper, scissors, glue or tape

*For parents with infants or toddlers, use activities presented in *Nurturing Book for Babies and Children*. For parents with preschoolers (ages 3-5), use the activities listed below Family Nurturing Time.

PARENT ACTIVITY: 10.1 Icebreaker and Home Practice Check In
CONSTRUCT: Empathy, Self-Awareness
MATERIALS: Parent Handbooks

GOAL:

To increase parents' awareness of touch.

OBJECTIVES:

1. To increase parents' awareness of how touch has impacted their lives.

2. To increase parents' sensitivity to providing positive touch to their children.

PROCEDURES:

1. Begin today's parent activities by having each adult respond to the following:

   • I'd like to be able to touch more easily, but _____ .

   • To me, touching means _____ .

2. After each parent has had an opportunity to respond to the statements above, review the Home Practice Exercise from the previous meeting. Also discuss perceived changes in family members and their interactions as reported in the family log.

IF'S, AND'S, OR BUT'S:

Touch is a very powerful topic for many parents to discuss. Some parents may relate ease in touching other adults but not their children. Encourage parents to think about all aspects of touch.

PARENT ACTIVITY: 10.2 Hurting Touch
CONSTRUCT: Empathy
MATERIALS: Paper, pen

GOAL:

To increase parents' awareness of inappropriate "hurting" parent-child relationships.

OBJECTIVES:

1. To increase parents' awareness of hurting touch experiences.

2. To increase parents' desire to use alternatives to hitting and spanking.

PROCEDURES:

1. To discuss with the parents that this week the focus is on hurting touch.

2. Write the words HURTING TOUCH on a large sheet of paper. Ask parents to brainstorm the types of hurting touch they experienced as children. Write all the types down on paper.

3. Ask the parents to identify how they felt about themselves and about the person doing the hurting touch after it was over. Write the feelings on the paper.

4. In a series, without giving time to answer each question orally, conduct an Internal Interview. Pause after each statement.

> Why were you spanked? What did your parents think they were teaching you? What were your feelings about your parents while they were spanking you? After they spanked you? What were your feelings about yourself? About your world? What did you actually learn?

5. Allow parents to share anything they wish to share.

6. Explain "rules" of brainstorming:

   a. Any idea goes — wild, funny, reasonable, anything goes.

   b. No evaluations, comments, or judgments while brainstorming.

   c. Keep ideas short.

   d. Repeats are fine; building on other's suggestions is OK.

7. On the top of a sheet of paper, write the words: WHAT TO DO INSTEAD. The goal of the exercise is to identify what to do instead of hitting or yelling at your child. You don't have to write out the whole statement. What to do instead will focus the thinking more on the alternatives than on the hitting or yelling.

8. Brainstorm with the parents alternatives to hitting and yelling at children. Write the ideas down. Afterwards, congratulate the parents on a large and creative list and encourage the parents to feel pride.

9. Ask each parent to identify two things s/he can do instead of hitting or yelling. Have them state why s/he can do these things. Ask parents to pick out two alternatives they feel they can't do. Have them state why not.

10. Do a very short guided fantasy for two minutes. Have parents assume a comfortable position and close their eyes. Then say:

> Now imagine the person who spanked you the most is standing right in front of you. Now imagine yourself speaking to them and saying: "Well, mom, dad (or whomever), I didn't like it much when you spanked me. It was not a pleasant experience, but I want you to know I am no longer the child you spanked. The child you spanked no longer exists. I am a loving and capable adult human being." Have them open their eyes and share anything they wish to share.

IF'S, AND'S, OR BUT'S:

Some parents might confuse hurting touch (spanking) with scary touch (sexual touch). Although there are times hurting touch can be scary and vice versa, try to help parents understand the distinction.

GOAL:

To increase parents' ability to talk about hurting touch.

OBJECTIVES:

1. To recognize hurting touch interactions.

2. To reinforce alternatives to hitting.

3. To establish a warm and supportive atmosphere.

PROCEDURES:

1. Instruct parents to locate the Home Practice Exercise on page 140 in their Handbooks. Review the exercise with them:

   a. Find a chance to talk to other family members about hurting touch. See what they remember of the experiences. Other family members can include children, husbands/wives, grandparents, siblings, parents, etc.

   b. Complete family log.

2. Tell parents that in addition to the Home Practice Exercise, they are to spend 30 minutes each day with each of their children in nurturing playtime activities. Playtime is a time with the parent and child alone — no TV, no other distractions. Playing a game or reading books are good activities. From the *Nurturing Book for Babies and Children*, have the parents practice activities listed in the following sections: Activities for Infants, Activities for Toddlers, Activities for Preschoolers, or Infant and Child Massage. Have the parents remember what they did and report the next week.

IF'S, AND'S, OR BUT'S:

There are often a number of resentful feelings left after hurting touch is administered. These feelings have a way of building up over time. Talking about hurting touch experiences with other family members can be very therapeutic.

FAMILY ACTIVITY:	10.4 Family Nurturing Time
CONSTRUCT:	Empathy, Self-Awareness
MATERIALS:	Nurturing Book for Babies and Children

ACTIVITIES FOR INFANTS (Birth to 15 months):

Utilizing the *Nurturing Book for Babies and Children*, select activities from the sections entitled Activities for Infants or Infant and Child Massage. Engage parents in practicing songs, play and stimulation activities, or massage. Vary the activities weekly to promote interest.

ACTIVITIES FOR TODDLERS (15 months to 3 years):

Utilizing the *Nurturing Book for Babies and Children*, select activities from the sections entitled Activities for Toddlers or Infant and Child Massage. Engage parents in practicing songs, play, language, and movement activities, or massage. Vary the activities weekly to promote interest.

ACTIVITIES FOR PRESCHOOLERS (3-5 years):

Use the following activities when working with preschool children and their parents. Use the activities as the basis for involving infants and toddlers if you are conducting a home visit with children ages birth to five years.

FAMILY ACTIVITY:	10.5 Hello Time: Loud and Soft
CONSTRUCT:	Self-Awareness
MATERIALS:	None

GOAL:

To have family members become aware of their self and others through selected verbal expression of feelings.

OBJECTIVES:

1. To greet each child and adult by first name.

2. To gain sensitivity to the feelings of others.

3. To encourage self-expression and ownership of feelings.

PROCEDURES:

1. Children and adults should be seated in a circle on the floor. A parent or home visitor should act as the leader of the activity.

2. The adult leading the activity explains the rules of the game. Rules: The group will take turns saying hello to everyone individually in either a loud or soft voice. The adult may say, "When it is your turn, you can tell us if you want us to say hello in a loud voice or a soft voice. When we ask, 'how are you?' you can answer in a loud or soft voice. After your turn, you can choose the next person for us to say hello to."

3. The adult chooses a child and asks whether they'd like a loud or soft voice. After the child indicates his choice, the group responds in a loud or soft voice by saying, "Hello _(name)_ ."

4. The adult asks, "How are you?" and the child is encouraged to respond. The adult may remark that the child appears happy, sad, etc., in response to the child's feeling.

5. The child chooses the next person to be greeted, and Steps 3 and 4 are repeated.

IF'S, AND'S, OR BUT'S:

1. Remind children that loud voices are for outside use but that it is okay to yell during this special activity.

2. When a child doesn't respond to "How are you?" or "Do you want loud or soft?" the group may be enlisted to interpret how the child is feeling and how they should talk to them.

   Example:

   Are you feeling sad, happy, etc.?
   How does Chad look? How do you think he feels?
   How do you think he'd like us to say hello?

FAMILY ACTIVITY:	10.6 Boat Song
CONSTRUCT:	Empathy
MATERIALS:	None

GOAL:

To increase positive parent-child interactions through music and touch.

OBJECTIVES:

1. To increase parents' ability to enjoy fun times with their children.

2. To have children practice gross motor coordination.

PROCEDURES:

1. This activity takes place on the floor. Adults and children pretend to be "boats" by sitting with their legs extended in front of them and spread apart. One or two children sit in each "boat" by sitting between an adult's legs, with their backs to the adult. The children hold onto the adult's hands and pretend that they are oars.

2. Sing the song "Michael, Row Your Boat Ashore" substituting each child's name for "Michael." As you sing, move your arms in a forward/backward movement simulating rowing a boat while holding hands with the children in each boat. Repeat the song until each person's name has been used once.

1. Repeat the activity with children in pairs. They can take turns being the "boat" or the "rower."

2. Emphasize taking turns by having the person whose name has been sung choose the next person to be sung about.

3. This is a good activity to provide appropriate physical contact between adults and children in a nonthreatening way. The activity also emphasizes cooperation in taking turns and waiting.

FAMILY ACTIVITY:	**10.7 Circle Time: Hurting Touch**
CONSTRUCT:	**Self-Awareness, Behavior Management**
MATERIALS:	**None**

GOAL:

To reinforce children's awareness of hurting touch.

OBJECTIVES:

1. To reinforce children's awareness of threatening situations.

2. To increase recognition of hurting touch.

3. To become aware of feelings associated with hurting touch.

PROCEDURES:

1. Have children and parents sit in a circle on the floor.

2. Today we are going to discuss a special kind of touch. The kind of touch we will talk about is hurting touch.

   - Can you tell me if you ever got hurt?

   - How did you get hurt?

3. Hurting touch is when we hit, push, spank, punch, slap, or grab someone else, or when that happens to us.

   - Has anyone ever had a hurting touch?

   - How do you feel after a hurting touch?

   - Has anyone ever given someone else a hurting touch?

   - How do you think the other person feels?

4. Sometimes our parents give us hurting touch. What kind of hurting touch do your parents give you?

5. What could you do instead of giving someone hurting touch? What could your mother/father do instead of giving you hurting touch?

1. The focus is on helping children become aware of hurting touch. Reinforce efforts to recognize hurting touch.

2. Parents should be supportive. Elicit parents' support for their children to learn alternatives to hurting touch.

FAMILY ACTIVITY:	**10.8 Paper Mountain and Family Hug**
CONSTRUCT:	**Developmental**
MATERIALS:	**Construction paper, scissors, glue or tape**

GOAL:

To increase children's self-concept and self-esteem through accomplishment of age appropriate tasks.

OBJECTIVES:

1. To foster creative expression through art.

2. To increase fine motor skills.

3. To reinforce comfort in using nurturing touch.

PROCEDURES:

1. Assemble children around a table.

2. Have each child choose a color of construction paper they like.

3. Model cutting the paper lengthwise into ½" strips. Have each child make a pile of colored strips of different lengths.

4. Tape or glue both ends of the different length strips on a sheet of construction paper to form arches.

5. Use random over and under patterns to form different patterns.

FAMILY HUG:

1. End each home visit with a family hug. Everyone get in a circle and put your arms around the people next to you. During the family hug time, anyone can say anything they like. It is a time for free expression.

2. At a natural time, close the activities for the day.

IF'S, AND'S, OR BUT'S:

Monitor the use of the scissors with young children.

NURTURING PROGRAM FOR PARENTS AND CHILDREN BIRTH TO FIVE YEARS

SESSION 11

BEHAVIOR CONSTRUCT: Child Development

SESSION CONCEPT: Baby Proofing

BRIEF DESCRIPTION: Parents will learn ways to change the living environment to increase the safety for small children. Utilizing the checklist, the home visitor and parent will baby proof the house. Children will review hurting touch and nice touch.

INTENDED USE: For parents of children birth to 5 years

PREREQUISITE KNOWLEDGE: None

AGENDA

Parent Activities	Materials
11.1 Icebreaker and Home Practice Check In	*Parent Handbooks*
11.2 Baby Proofing	*Parent Handbooks*, **Baby Proofing** AV presentation, AV equipment
11.3 Home Practice Exercise	*Parent Handbooks*

Family Activities*	Materials
11.4 Family Nurturing Time	*Nurturing Book for Babies and Children*
11.5 Hello Time: Happy and Sad	None
11.6 In and Out the Window	None
11.7 Circle Time: Ellie & Benny	Ellie & Benny pictures
11.8 Clay and Family Hug	Clay, newspaper, water

*For parents with infants or toddlers, use activities presented in *Nurturing Book for Babies and Children*. For parents with preschoolers (ages 3-5), use the activities listed below Family Nurturing Time.

PARENT ACTIVITY: 11.1 Icebreaker and Home Practice Check In
CONSTRUCT: Child Development
MATERIALS: Parent Handbooks

GOAL:

To increase parents' awareness of the impact their personal power has on their personal destiny.

OBJECTIVES:

1. To increase parents' awareness of their personal power.

2. To increase parents' awareness of how use of their personal power can change their destiny.

PROCEDURES:

1. Begin today's parent activities by having each adult respond to the following:

   - One thing that holds me back from doing what I really want to do is _____ .

   - One way I can get to do what I really want to do is by _____ .

2. After each parent has had an opportunity to respond to the statements above, review the Home Practice Exercise from the previous meeting. Also discuss perceived changes in family members and their interactions as reported in the family log.

IF'S, AND'S, OR BUT'S:

Many parents' wishes, dreams, and hopes are delayed or unmet because of what they believe to be restrictions. Getting them to focus on what these dreams are and how they can be achieved is a step toward self-sufficiency.

PARENT ACTIVITY: 11.2 Baby Proofing
CONSTRUCT: Child Development
MATERIALS: Parent Handbooks, Baby Proofing AV presentation, AV equipment

GOAL:

To increase parents' ability to create a safe environment for their children.

OBJECTIVES:

1. To increase parents' knowledge of the concept of baby proofing.

2. To increase parents' ability to baby proof their house.

3. To review general safety rules for household safety.

PROCEDURES:

1. If you are using the audio-visual programs, present the AV entitled **Baby Proofing**.

2. Instruct parents to locate the information entitled **Baby Proofing Your House** on pages 30-36 in their Handbooks. Utilize the information to discuss the major concepts of baby proofing a home.

3. If you're conducting a home visit, utilize the checklist and go through the house with the parents. If you are outside the parents' home, go through the checklist with the parents identifying areas of potential danger.

4. Review with the parents the **General Safety Rules** and the **Safety Reminders by Age**. Discuss each of the reminders ensuring the parents are aware of the point.

IF'S, AND'S, OR BUT'S:

Baby proofing a house not only helps prevent accidental injuries, but actually increases the nurturing interactions between parents and children. In a baby proofed house, the focus on the child's behavior doesn't always have to be a "restriction." That is, the "no-no's" are actually reduced and permit the child and parent to interact more positively.

PARENT ACTIVITY:	**11.3 Home Practice Exercise**
CONSTRUCT:	**Child Development**
MATERIALS:	**Parent Handbooks**

GOAL:

To increase the safety standards for children.

OBJECTIVES:

1. To encourage parents to baby proof their house.

2. To reinforce positive parent-child interactions.

3. To establish a warm and supportive atmosphere.

PROCEDURES:

1. Instruct parents to locate the Home Practice Exercise on page 140 in their Handbooks. Review the exercise with them:

   a. Use the baby proof checklist to modify your house environment, making the house safe for your child.

   b. Complete family log.

2. Tell parents that in addition to the Home Practice Exercise, they are to spend 30 minutes each day with each of their children in nurturing playtime activities. Playtime is a time with the parent and child alone – no TV, no other distractions. Playing a game or reading books are good activities. From the *Nurturing Book for Babies and Children*, have the parents practice activities listed in the following sections: Activities for Infants, Activities for Toddlers, Activities for Preschoolers, or Infant and Child Massage. Have the parents remember what they did and report the next week.

IF'S, AND'S, OR BUT'S:

Although many parents are apt to feel positive about making their house safe for children, some parents may resent having to change the house around because their child "won't listen." Pay close attention to the parents' responses to baby proofing the house. Their responses will give you an indication of their commitment to empathizing with their children's needs.

FAMILY ACTIVITY:	**11.4 Family Nurturing Time**
CONSTRUCT:	**Empathy, Self-Awareness**
MATERIALS:	**Nurturing Book for Babies and Children**

ACTIVITIES FOR INFANTS (Birth to 15 months):

Utilizing the *Nurturing Book for Babies and Children*, select activities from the sections entitled Activities for Infants or Infant and Child Massage. Engage parents in practicing songs, play and stimulation activities, or massage. Vary the activities weekly to promote interest.

ACTIVITIES FOR TODDLERS (15 months to 3 years):

Utilizing the *Nurturing Book for Babies and Children*, select activities from the sections entitled Activities for Toddlers or Infant and Child Massage. Engage parents in practicing songs, play, language, and movement activities, or massage. Vary the activities weekly to promote interest.

ACTIVITIES FOR PRESCHOOLERS (3-5 years):

Use the following activities when working with preschool children and their parents. Use the activities as the basis for involving infants and toddlers if you are conducting a home visit with children ages birth to five years.

FAMILY ACTIVITY:	**11.5 Hello Time: Happy and Sad**
CONSTRUCT:	**Self-Awareness**
MATERIALS:	**None**

GOAL:

To increase family members' sensitivity to the feelings of others.

OBJECTIVES:

1. To increase children's awareness of things that make them happy.

2. To increase children's awareness of things that make them sad.

PROCEDURES:

1. Have children and adults sit in a circle on the floor.

2. Have each child and adult respond to the following statements:

   - Something that makes me happy is _____ .
   - Something that makes me sad is _____ .

IF'S, AND'S, OR BUT'S:

Recognition of happy and sad feelings are very basic feelings for most children. They are also the only feelings many adults are aware of. With people who are not very good at expressing their feelings, happy/sad is a good place to begin.

FAMILY ACTIVITY:	**11.6 In and Out the Window**
CONSTRUCT:	**Empathy**
MATERIALS:	**None**

GOAL:

To build positive parent-child interactions.

OBJECTIVES:

1. To help parents and children relate in a positive, nurturing way.

2. To help parents learn to enjoy their children.

PROCEDURES:

1. Have all children and parents stand in a large circle without holding hands.

2. Choose one person to start the game by walking around the circle weaving behind and in front of each person as the group sings:

In and Out the Window

Go in and out the window, go in and out the window,
Go in and out the window, as we have done before.

3. The person stops and stands in front of someone in the circle as the group sings:

Now stand and face your partner, now stand and face your partner,
Now stand and face your partner, as we have done before.

4. The person takes the hands of his partner and they weave in and out of the circle as the group sings:

Now take her off to London, now take her off to London,
Now take her off to London, as we have done before.

5. This game continues until everyone has a turn.

IF'S, AND'S, OR BUT'S:

Have parents act as partners with each of their children.

FAMILY ACTIVITY: **11.7 Circle Time: Ellie & Benny**
CONSTRUCT: **Empathy**
MATERIALS: **Ellie & Benny pictures**

GOAL:

To increase the child's understanding of inappropriate adult-child interactions.

OBJECTIVES:

1. To increase children's awareness of threatening and overpowering interactions.

2. To enable children to recognize potentially abusive interactions.

3. To increase children's use of their personal power to reinforce positive feelings of self and others.

PROCEDURES:

1. Have the children and adults sit in a circle on the floor.

2. Introduce Ellie the elephant and Benny the bird. (Picture 1 of Ellie and Picture 2 of Benny).

3. Elicit responses from the children to the following questions:

   • How are Ellie and Benny different? (bigger, smaller, strong, weak, fly, walk).

   • Are you Benny the bird or Ellie the elephant? If you could be a bird or an elephant, which would you be?

   • Do you think Benny is afraid of Ellie? Is Ellie afraid of Benny? (Picture 3, bird sitting on top of elephant).

- Ellie likes to play outside and so does Benny. But when Ellie plays with Benny she forgets that she is so much bigger. Benny gets scared sometimes. Does anyone here ever get scared? (Picture 4, bird afraid of being stepped on.)

- Why do you suppose Benny is afraid to play with Ellie? (Benny may get hurt playing; continue to show Picture 4.)

- Do you think the elephant would want to hurt the bird on purpose? (Yes, if he was mad; or no, if he didn't know how strong he was.)

- What happened in this picture? (Show Picture 5.) The elephant squeezed the bird too hard. Touch was hurting.

- How do you suppose Benny feels when he is hurt? (sad, dejected, frightened).

- How could Ellie and Benny have used their personal power not to hurt others or be hurt?

- How can you use your personal power to avoid getting hurt?

IF'S, AND'S, OR BUT'S:

Elicit responses from the children regarding hurting touch. Some children may feel most uncomfortable. Be extra sensitive.

FAMILY ACTIVITY:	**11.8 Clay and Family Hug**
CONSTRUCT:	**Self-Awareness**
MATERIALS:	**Clay, newspaper, water**

GOAL:

To provide children and parents an opportunity to experience their own creativity and sensitivity.

OBJECTIVES:

1. To allow children the opportunity to express themselves in clay.

2. To enable children to express their feelings in a nonverbal form.

3. To help children learn about themselves in new ways.

4. To reinforce comfort in using nurturing touch.

PROCEDURES:

1. Cover floor with newspapers — thick layers so water won't soak through.

2. Hand out clay to each person — allow children and adults to take more if they want more or to put some back until they have an amount which feels good in their hands. Encourage them to pay attention to how the clay feels in their own hands.

3. Tell everyone that they are to make anything they want. It can be a lump, a ball, anything they choose.

4. When finished, ask parents and children to share their creations.

FAMILY HUG:

1. End each home visit with a family hug. Everyone get in a circle and put your arms around the people next to you. During the family hug time, anyone can say anything they like. It is a time for free expression.

2. At a natural time, close the activities for the day.

IF'S, AND'S, OR BUT'S:

A good way to begin to break down defensiveness toward touch is to encourage tactile stimulation. Over time, the word "touch" won't have such a scary sound.

NURTURING PROGRAM FOR PARENTS AND CHILDREN BIRTH TO FIVE YEARS

SESSION 12

BEHAVIOR CONSTRUCT: Behavior Management

SESSION CONCEPT: Verbal and Physical Redirection

BRIEF DESCRIPTION: Parents learn an appropriate strategy to discipline and guide the behavior of children. Children playact in the Blanket Game and review the differences between hurting touch and nice touch.

INTENDED USE: For parents of children birth to 5 years

PREREQUISITE KNOWLEDGE: Behavior Management, Praise

AGENDA

Parent Activities	Materials
12.1 Icebreaker and Home Practice Check In	*Parent Handbooks*
12.2 Verbal and Physical Redirection	*Parent Handbooks*, **Redirection** AV presentation, AV equipment
12.3 Home Practice Exercise	*Parent Handbooks*

Family Activities*	Materials
12.4 Family Nurturing Time	*Nurturing Book for Babies and Children*
12.5 Hello Time: London Bridge	None
12.6 Blanket Game	Large blanket or large bed sheet
12.7 Circle Time: Hurting/Nice Touch Review	Puppets
12.8 Food Coloring Painting and Family Hug	Paint brushes, food coloring, paper towels, containers with water, tape

*For parents with infants or toddlers, use activities presented in *Nurturing Book for Babies and Children*. For parents with preschoolers (ages 3-5), use the activities listed below Family Nurturing Time.

PARENT ACTIVITY: 12.1 Icebreaker and Home Practice Check In
CONSTRUCT: Self-Awareness, Empathy
MATERIALS: Parent Handbooks

GOAL:

To increase parents' desire to improve the quality of their relationships with their children.

OBJECTIVES:

1. To encourage parents to recall positive times during childhood.

2. To encourage parents to identify positive characteristics of their parents.

3. To reinforce the healthy elements of parent-child interactions.

PROCEDURES:

1. Begin today's parent activities by having each adult respond to the following:

   • When I think about my childhood, my fondest memories are when _____ .

   • The positive qualities I remember most about my parent(s) are _____ .

2. After each parent has had an opportunity to respond to the statements above, review the home practice exercise from the previous meeting. Also discuss perceived changes in family members and their interactions as reported in the family log.

IF'S, AND'S, OR BUT'S:

Encouraging parents to get in touch with fond memories of childhood helps parents recall positive parent-child interactions. The goal is to replicate those feelings associated with the memories more often in their role as parents with their children.

PARENT ACTIVITY: 12.2 Verbal and Physical Redirection
CONSTRUCT: Behavior Management
MATERIALS: Parent Handbooks, Redirection AV presentation, AV equipment

GOAL:

To increase parents' ability to manage the behavior of their young children.

OBJECTIVES:

1. To increase parents' knowledge of physical and verbal redirection.

2. To reinforce nonabusive punishment of children.

3. To teach parents to promote desirable behaviors in children.

PROCEDURES:

1. Mention to the family that for the next hour they will be discussing and role playing techniques of discipline.

2. Review with the family the goal of discipline — to encourage good behavior through setting guidelines. The parents will learn four techniques of discipline: family rules, redirection, choices and consequences, and ignoring. Mention that some of the techniques are only useful with certain ages of children.

3. The first technique they will learn is redirection. Instruct the parents to locate the information entitled **Verbal and Physical Redirection** on pages 37-41 in their Handbooks. Review the major points:

   - Redirection is a technique to help kids learn to do good things.

   - There are two types of redirection: verbal and physical.

   - Verbal redirection tells children what is not acceptable and what is.

   - Physical redirection removes children from dangerous activities and substitutes more appropriate activities.

   - Verbal and physical redirection work best when used together.

4. If you are using the audio-visual programs, present the AV entitled **Redirection**.

5. After the presentation, role play the redirection technique (you may choose to write the steps on a piece of paper.) Ask one parent to be the "child," the other to be the "parent."

   Situation: A young child is getting ready to put an object into an electric socket. The "parent" will use the following steps to redirect the "child."

   a. Walk towards the "child," stoop down, make eye contact, and while shaking your head tell the child, "No-o-o! Oweee! That can cause an oweee!"

   b. Make gentle, physical contact with the child's arm and back and physically lead him/her away from the socket. While you're leading the child away, use a more pleasant tone of voice and facial expression and say, "Come on over here. Oh look at the _____. Wouldn't that be fun to play with?"

   c. Once the child is engaged in the new activity praise the child: "Oh, what a good listener you are. Look how nicely you're playing with _____. I sure like it when you cooperate."

   d. If the child goes back to the socket, repeat a-d. It may be necessary to lead the child to another room.

6. Switch the role players. Have the "child" become the "parent" and the "parent" the "child." Role play a child going toward a hot stove, or near a stairwell, or heading toward the street.

7. Ask the parents to cite an example of their child's behavior that they feel needs to be redirected. What have they tried in their attempts to modify the behavior?

Parents of young children may be asking for specific ways to punish the behavior of their children. Impress upon them that the behavior of infants and toddlers is not punishable, simply because children aren't capable of remembering what is bad from what is curious to what is safe. Punishment only tends to confuse children, at best, and teaches them they are no good. Redirection helps children maintain their sense of exploration and learning in addition to reducing punishing parent-child interactions.

PARENT ACTIVITY: 12.3 Home Practice Exercise
CONSTRUCT: Behavior Management, Empathy
MATERIALS: Parent Handbooks

GOAL:

To increase parents' use of nurturing behavior management strategies.

OBJECTIVES:

1. To reinforce parents' ability to use verbal and physical redirection.

2. To increase positive parent-child relationships.

3. To establish a warm and supportive atmosphere.

PROCEDURES:

1. Instruct parents to locate the home practice exercise on page 140 in their Handbooks. Review the exercise with them:

   a. Practice verbal and physical redirection at least five times.

   b. Praise your child for cooperating.

   c. Complete family log.

2. Tell parents that in addition to the Home Practice Exercise, they are to spend 30 minutes each day with each of their children in nurturing playtime activities. Playtime is a time with the parent and child alone — no TV, no other distractions. Playing a game or reading books are good activities. From the *Nurturing Book for Babies and Children*, have the parents practice activities listed in the following sections: Activities for Infants, Activities for Toddlers, Activities for Preschoolers, or Infant and Child Massage. Have the parents remember what they did and report the next week.

IF'S, AND'S, OR BUT'S:

Five times may seem like a lot of redirecting, but with a toddler, that may occur in one day. Reinforce the parents.

FAMILY ACTIVITY:	**12.4 Family Nurturing Time**
CONSTRUCT:	**Empathy, Self-Awareness**
MATERIALS:	**Nurturing Book for Babies and Children**

ACTIVITIES FOR INFANTS (Birth to 15 months):

Utilizing the *Nurturing Book for Babies and Children*, select activities from the sections entitled Activities for Infants or Infant and Child Massage. Engage parents in practicing songs, play and stimulation activities, or massage. Vary the activities weekly to promote interest.

ACTIVITIES FOR TODDLERS (15 months to 3 years):

Utilizing the *Nurturing Book for Babies and Children*, select activities from the sections entitled Activities for Toddlers or Infant and Child Massage. Engage parents in practicing songs, play, language, and movement activities, or massage. Vary the activities weekly to promote interest.

ACTIVITIES FOR PRESCHOOLERS (3-5 years):

Use the following activities when working with preschool children and their parents. Use the activities as the basis for involving infants and toddlers if you are conducting a home visit with children ages birth to five years.

FAMILY ACTIVITY:	**12.5 Hello Time: London Bridge**
CONSTRUCT:	**Empathy**
MATERIALS:	**None**

GOAL:

To reinforce appropriate adult-child interactions.

OBJECTIVES:

1. To help parents and children enjoy each other.

2. To increase positive touch.

PROCEDURES:

1. Choose two persons to be the "bridge" by facing each other and holding hands with their arms lifted high enough for others to pass under.

2. Have the rest of the people form a line and pass under the bridge as everyone sings:

London Bridge

London Bridge is falling down, falling down, falling down,

London Bridge is falling down, my fair __(name)__ .

3. As the group sings "my fair ," the two people who are the bridge should lower their arms and "catch" someone. Have the group sing that person's name in the line "my fair _____ ."

4. The person who gets "caught" in the bridge takes the place of one of the people making up the bridge and that person joins the group moving under the bridge.

IF'S, AND'S, OR BUT'S:

Allow all children a chance to be a part of the bridge.

FAMILY ACTIVITY: 12.6 Blanket Game
CONSTRUCT: Age Appropriate Developmental Expectations
MATERIALS: Large Blanket or large bed sheet

GOAL:

To reinforce positive family interactions.

OBJECTIVES:

1. To reinforce positive trusting interactions with adults.

2. To use large muscles.

3. To reinforce creative imagination.

PROCEDURES:

1. Have all children and adults sit close together on the floor.

2. An adult covers the entire group with a large blanket. Make sure everyone is under the blanket.

3. The adult tells the group (under the blanket) to listen carefully, then says:

   When I take the blanket off, you will be (animal name) .
   (i.e., monkeys, birds, lions, cows, etc.)

4. Pull the blanket off the group (be dramatic about it) and encourage them to act like the animal named. Adults in the group should model expected behaviors. Let this go on for about 1/2 minute, then call the group back to sit on the floor again.

5. When the group is sitting on the floor, repeat the activity for a different animal.

IF'S, AND'S, OR BUT'S:

1. Be sure to reassure children who may be frightened of being under the blanket.

2. Call children back to group using the animal name; i.e., "Come on back to your pen, little pigs," or, "All the cows need to return to the barn," etc.

GOAL:

To reinforce the difference between the concepts of hurting touch and nice touch.

OBJECTIVES:

1. To provide children with alternatives to hurting touch.

2. To reinforce the concept of telling others if they are getting hurting touch.

3. To promote nice touch.

PROCEDURES:

1. Have children and adults sit in a circle on the floor.

2. Do you remember last time we talked about a special kind of touch? Who can remember the name of that touch? (Hurting touch) Who remembers what kind of touch is hurting touch? (hitting, slapping, spanking, etc.)

3. The following skits reinforce the difference between hurting touch and nice touch.

4. I bet Puppet #1 and Puppet #2 can fool you guys. They are sure you guys don't know the difference between nice touch and hurting touch. Let's see if they can fool us.

5. Act out the following situations:

   Puppet #1: (talking to children) Puppet #2 and I will now give each other nice touch.

   a. Two puppets hitting each other.

   b. One puppet spanking the other.

   c. One puppet pushing the other.

   After each, ask "Is that nice touch?"

   Puppet #1: (talking to children) Puppet #2 and I will now give each other hurting touch.

   a. Hugging each other.

   b. Holding hands.

   c. Playing nice together.

   After each ask, "Is that hurting touch?"

IF'S, AND'S, OR BUT'S:

Get dramatic with the fooler approach. The kids will love coming up with the right response.

FAMILY ACTIVITY: 12.8 Food Coloring Painting and Family Hug
CONSTRUCT: Developmental
MATERIALS: Paint brushes, food coloring, paper towels, containers with water, tape

GOAL:

To increase children's self-concept and self-esteem through accomplishment of age appropriate tasks.

OBJECTIVES:

1. To foster creative expression through art.

2. To increase fine motor skills.

3. To reinforce comfort in using nurturing touch.

PROCEDURES:

1. Assemble children around a table.

2. Pour water into small containers and add food coloring.

3. Give each child a plain white paper towel and tape it to the table.

4. Have each child dip their brush into the colored water and paint designs on their paper towels.

FAMILY HUG:

1. End each home visit with a family hug. Everyone get in a circle and put your arms around the people next to you. During the family hug time, anyone can say anything they like. It is a time for free expression.

2. At a natural time, close the activities for the day.

IF'S, AND'S, OR BUT'S:

Hang the finished products to dry and display.

NURTURING PROGRAM FOR PARENTS AND CHILDREN BIRTH TO FIVE YEARS

SESSION 13

BEHAVIOR CONSTRUCT:	Empathy
SESSION CONCEPT:	Touch and Talk
BRIEF DESCRIPTION:	Parents practice the use of praise and touch with a partner. Children also practice to give and receive praise in Strength Bombardment and learn to make soap clay.
INTENDED USE:	For parents of children birth to 5 years
PREREQUISITE KNOWLEDGE:	Praise

AGENDA

Parent Activities · Materials

13.1   Icebreaker and Home Practice Check In · *Parent Handbooks*

13.2   Touch and Talk; Discipline, Rewards, and Punishment · *Parent Handbooks*

13.3   Home Practice Exercise · *Parent Handbooks*

Family Activities* · Materials

13.4   Family Nurturing Time · *Nurturing Book for Babies and Children*

13.5   Hello Time: My Favorite Animal · None

13.6   I'm a Dynamic Doer · None

13.7   Circle Time: Strength Bombardment · Puppets

13.8   Soap Clay and Family Hug · Ivory Flakes, water, measuring cup, bowl, food coloring, spoon

*For parents with infants or toddlers, use activities presented in *Nurturing Book for Babies and Children*. For parents with preschoolers (ages 3-5), use the activities listed below Family Nurturing Time.

GOAL:

To encourage parents to recognize positive family changes and growth.

OBJECTIVES:

1. To increase awareness of positive changes in family.

2. To recognize positive changes in children.

3. To reinforce positive changes in self.

PROCEDURES:

1. Begin today's parent activities by having each adult respond to the following:

   • One area I have definitely noticed a change for the better in me is _____ .

   • One area I have definitely noticed a change for the better in my child(ren) is _____ .

   • One area I have definitely noticed a change for the better in my family is _____ .

2. After each parent has had an opportunity to respond to the statements above, review the Home Practice Exercise from the previous meeting. Also discuss perceived changes in family members and their interactions as reported in the family log.

IF'S, AND'S, OR BUT'S:

Focusing on the positive will encourage parents to view themselves, children, and family in more positive ways.

GOAL:

To increase parents' awareness of touch as a means of healthy communication.

OBJECTIVES:

1. To help parents experience nurturing touch with other group members.

2. To increase parents' awareness that touching can enhance communication.

3. To enhance parents' skill in behavior management.

PROCEDURES:

1. Have parents form pairs by sitting facing each other. Instruct parents to locate the information entitled **Touch and Talk** on pages 42-43 in their Handbooks.

2. Instruct each pair to breathe from their stomachs in rhythm with the other person. For a few minutes just be silent and breathe in the same rhythm. This is called "getting in synch," and people of any age do it unconsciously, including newborn babies and their mothers.

3. One person will speak while the other person listens. Have the speaker touch the listener and leave his/her hand on the listener as long as it is comfortable. Remove it whenever you want, replace it whenever you want.

4. Have the pairs check out with each other if the chosen place (leg, shoulder, arm, hand, etc.)) is comfortable for both.

5. Have the first parent repeat the first nine statements in the Handbook while touching his/her partner.

> You are a nice person.
> I like you.
> It's nice to touch you.
> I enjoy touching you.
> I like being in this group with you.
> I don't always feel this good about you.
> Sometimes I get upset with you.
> Sometimes I get angry at you.
> Sometimes I don't like you.

6. Change roles and repeat, starting with Procedure 2. Have the second parent repeat the second nine statements while touching his/her partner.

> I don't like what you are doing.
> You hurt my feelings when you said that.
> I felt sad when you did that.
> I feel good when you are nice to me.
> You usually are nice to me.
> I like you a lot.
> I feel love for you.
> This exercise hasn't been easy, but I've enjoyed doing it with you.
> I'm glad this turn is over.

7. Process the exercise. Was it easier saying the statements or receiving the statements? Why?

8. Mention that touch and praise are the two most important techniques to use in helping children learn appropriate behavior. The remaining time will be spent discussing the differences between discipline, rewards, and punishment.

9. Present the following ideas:

   a. Children need to learn right from wrong. Learning right from wrong is important to the children because they want to please mom and dad. Doing the right things pleases mom and dad.

   b. There are appropriate and inappropriate ways to help children learn proper behavior.

    c. Consistent use of nurturing parenting techniques helps children learn appropriate ways to behave.

10. Write the word DISCIPLINE on a piece of paper. Brainstorm with the parents what the word means.

   - To guide, lead others.
   - To establish rules and standards to follow.
   - To encourage good behavior.

11. Write the word REWARD on a piece of paper. Brainstorm with the parents what the word means.

   - A positive consequence for appropriate behavior.
   - The purpose of rewards is to increase good behavior — to help children feel good.
   - Brainstorm types of rewards parents use.

12. Write the word PUNISHMENT on a piece of paper. Brainstorm with the parents what the word means.

   - A negative consequence for misbehavior.
   - The purpose of punishment is to decrease bad behavior — not to hurt children.
   - Brainstorm types of punishments parents use.

13. Ensure that the parents fully comprehend the differences among the terms.

14. Ask parents to take turns completing the following statements:

   - The type of punishment I received from my parents when I was a child was _____.
   - After the punishment, I felt _____.
   - The type of punishment I give my children is _____.
   - Afterwards, he/she feels _____.
   - What I need to learn about punishment is _____.

15. Ask parents to take turns completing the following statements:

   - The type of rewards I received as a child were _____.
   - When I receive a reward, I feel _____.
   - The rewards I use with my children are _____.

16. Discuss the inappropriate use of punishment with infants.

   - Punishment is only used when children know right from wrong and choose to misbehave. Infants do not understand right from wrong.
   - Infants are never punished. They are not responsible for their behavior.
   - Infants need guidance, support, and security — not punishment.

17. Suggest that at the next session they will discuss different techniques of discipline, rewards, and punishments that help children learn right from wrong while helping them feel good about themselves.

1. Remind the parents that these statements are to be said seriously even though the statements are practice in experiencing touch.

2. This exercise will not be easy for many parents to express their feelings about touch and management. It may take two sessions to complete all information.

3. Be sure to share with the parents that children under two years of age should not be punished for their behavior because they are unaware of what they are doing. You will be discussing the concept of behavior management with infants and toddlers during future sessions.

PARENT ACTIVITY:	**13.3 Home Practice Exercise**
CONSTRUCT:	**Empathy**
MATERIALS:	**Parent Handbooks**

GOAL:

To reinforce nurturing touch between parents and children.

OBJECTIVES:

1. To practice positive touch.

2. To increase opportunities for good touch between parents and children.

3. To practice touch and talk statements.

4. To establish a warm and supportive atmosphere.

PROCEDURES:

1. Instruct parents to locate the Home Practice Exercise on page 140 in their Handbooks. Review the exercise with them:

   a. Practice touching yourself in a nurturing way.

   b. Practice touching and talking to your children in a nurturing way.

   c. Complete family log.

2. Tell parents that in addition to the Home Practice Exercise, they are to spend 30 minutes each day with each of their children in nurturing playtime activities. Playtime is a time with the parent and child alone – no TV, no other distractions. Playing a game or reading books are good activities. From the *Nurturing Book for Babies and Children*, have the parents practice activities listed in the following sections: Activities for Infants, Activities for Toddlers, Activities for Preschoolers, or Infant and Child Massage. Have the parents remember what they did and report the next week.

IF'S, AND'S, OR BUT'S:

Nurturing touch can be hugs, hand holding, rubbing, stroking; nurturing touch is touch that feels good. Encourage parents to practice on themselves as well.

FAMILY ACTIVITY:	13.4 Family Nurturing Time
CONSTRUCT:	Empathy, Self-Awareness
MATERIALS:	Nurturing Book for Babies and Children

ACTIVITIES FOR INFANTS (Birth to 15 months):

Utilizing the *Nurturing Book for Babies and Children*, select activities from the sections entitled Activities for Infants or Infant and Child Massage. Engage parents in practicing songs, play and stimulation activities, or massage. Vary the activities weekly to promote interest.

ACTIVITIES FOR TODDLERS (15 months to 3 years):

Utilizing the *Nurturing Book for Babies and Children*, select activities from the sections entitled Activities for Toddlers or Infant and Child Massage. Engage parents in practicing songs, play, language, and movement activities, or massage. Vary the activities weekly to promote interest.

ACTIVITIES FOR PRESCHOOLERS (3-5 years):

Use the following activities when working with preschool children and their parents. Use the activities as the basis for involving infants and toddlers if you are conducting a home visit with children ages birth to five years.

FAMILY ACTIVITY:	13.5 Hello Time: My Favorite Animal
CONSTRUCT:	Self-Awareness
MATERIALS:	None

GOAL:

To increase child's awareness of self and others.

OBJECTIVES:

1. To have children name an animal they can identify with.

2. To have children identify characteristics of the animal they see in themselves.

PROCEDURES:

1. Assemble children and adults in a circle sitting on the floor.

2. Today we are all going to get a chance to act like an animal. The rest of us will have to guess what animal we are. Then I'll ask you how you feel today. Does everyone understand how to play the game?

3. Let each child and parent have a turn. After the group guesses the animal say, "Well, Mrs. _ (monkey, cat, etc.), how are you feeling today?"

IF'S, AND'S, OR BUT'S:

Kids will love to see adults playing like animals.

FAMILY ACTIVITY: 13.6 I'm a Dynamic Doer
CONSTRUCT: Self-Awareness
MATERIALS: None

GOAL:

To increase positive self-worth and self-esteem in children.

OBJECTIVES:

1. To increase self-awareness.

2. To reinforce positive family interactions.

PROCEDURES:

1. Assemble children in a large circle, squatting on the floor.

2. Using the tune of "I'm a Little Tea Pot," conduct the following activity.

I'm a Dynamic Doer

We're dynamic doers, here we stand (Have children stand),

Next to our friends, we all shake hands (Have children shake hands with those standing on left and right),

Telling them they're as nice as they could be (Simulate saying something by cupping hands over mouth to children standing on left and right),

I wish they could come home with me (Grab a partner, skip together).

When we're in school, we all play nice (Lock arms with partner, do square dance move),

Sharing our toys, and saying thanks (Girls curtsy, boys bow to their neighbors),

When we have to go, we all feel sad (Rub eyes with fists),

We'll be back soon, and feel real glad (Smile and laugh).

3. Repeat the song.

IF'S, AND'S, OR BUT'S:

Have fun with the song, keep the action moving. Rehearse the moves with the children so they learn the exercise.

FAMILY ACTIVITY: 13.7 Circle Time: Strength Bombardment
CONSTRUCT: Empathy
MATERIALS: Puppets

GOAL:

To increase the child's ability to give and receive praise.

OBJECTIVES:

1. To bombard children with all the strengths others see in him/her.

2. To be able to accept the positive comments of others.

3. To reinforce positive parent-child communication.

PROCEDURES:

1. Have children and adults sit in a circle on the floor. Begin by explaining that a lot of people (adults and children) often have a hard time hearing others say something nice about them. This happens because we are used to hearing only bad things. We are going to practice listening to nice things said about us, and saying nice things about others.

2. Focusing on one person at a time, the group is to bombard the person with all the strengths they see in him/her. The person being bombarded should remain silent or say thank you after each compliment.

3. Try to list at least ten strengths for each person. No "put-down" statements are allowed. Only positive things are to be mentioned. At the end of the exercise ask the children to discuss how they felt giving and receiving feedback. Was one easier than the other? Which one?

IF'S, AND'S, OR BUT'S:

1. Support children in their efforts in saying nice things about others. Reinforce the concept of praise.

2. Even though there may be a lot of repetition, that's OK. The practice in saying something nice is important.

3. It's OK for the children to say something nice to the parents. In fact, it's ideal.

GOAL:

To increase positive regard for touch.

OBJECTIVES:

1. To experience a successful task completion.

2. To experience a positive tactile sensation.

3. To express self-creativity using art materials.

4. To increase positive parent-child interactions.

5. To reinforce comfort in using nurturing touch.

PROCEDURES:

1. Motivate children's interest by having them help make the soap clay using the following recipe:

   In bowl mix: 1 part water
   3 parts Ivory Flakes
   (optional food coloring may
   be added to water, if desired)

2. Give each child a small portion of soap clay and encourage them to handle it and form it into an animal or other shape.

3. Finger painting with the soap clay is a permissible use of the activity.

FAMILY HUG:

1. End each home visit with a family hug. Everyone get in a circle and put your arms around the people next to you. During the family hug time, anyone can say anything they like. It is a time for free expression.

2. At a natural time, close the activities for the day.

IF'S, AND'S, OR BUT'S:

1. Ivory Snow may be used if Ivory Flakes are not available; however, Ivory Flakes give a nice, slippery texture.

2. Finished sculptures may be wrapped as gifts or bathroom decorations. Sculptures work well as hand soap.

NURTURING PROGRAM FOR PARENTS AND CHILDREN BIRTH TO FIVE YEARS
SESSION 14

BEHAVIOR CONSTRUCT:	Behavior Management
SESSION CONCEPT:	Behavior Management
BRIEF DESCRIPTION:	Parents learn how to administer alternatives to corporal punishment. Children learn what time-out is and how to take a quiet time-out.
INTENDED USE:	For parents of children 2½ to 5 years
PREREQUISITE KNOWLEDGE:	Behavior Management, Family Rules, Praise, Hurting Touch

AGENDA

Parent Activities	**Materials**
14.1 Icebreaker and Home Practice Check In	*Parent Handbooks*
14.2 Punishing Behavior	*Parent Handbooks*, **Time-Out** AV presentation, AV equipment
14.3 Home Practice Exercise	*Parent Handbooks*

Family Activities*	**Materials**
14.4 Family Nurturing Time	*Nurturing Book for Babies and Children*
14.5 Hello Time: I Spy	None
14.6 Streamer Dance	Cassette player and cassettes or record player and records, streamers
14.7 Circle Time: Time-Out	Chair, puppets
14.8 Air Painting and Family Hug	Tempera paints, straws, butcher block paper

*For parents with infants or toddlers, use activities presented in *Nurturing Book for Babies and Children*. For parents with preschoolers (ages 3-5), use the activities listed below Family Nurturing Time.

PARENT ACTIVITY: 14.1 Icebreaker and Home Practice Check In
CONSTRUCT: Empathy
MATERIALS: Parent Handbooks

GOAL:

To reinforce parents' awareness of the value of alternatives to hitting children.

OBJECTIVES:

1. To increase parental empathy toward childrens' needs.

2. To increase the value of not hitting children.

3. To continue to establish group cohesion.

PROCEDURES:

1. Begin today's parent activities by having each adult respond to the following:

   • Right now my biggest concern about my child's behavior is _____ .

   • If my child could tell me the most effective way for his/her behavior to be punished, s/he would say to _____ .

2. After each parent has had an opportunity to respond to the statements above, review the Home Practice Exercise from the previous meeting. Also discuss perceived changes in family members and their interactions as reported in the family log.

IF'S, AND'S, OR BUT'S:

Increasing empathy is the key to reducing the likelihood that parents would choose not to use hitting. The second important factor to reducing hitting is a technique to substitute for hitting. Time-out presented in the following activity is a valid, nonabusive technique for punishing children's behavior.

PARENT ACTIVITY: 14.2 Punishing Behavior
CONSTRUCT: Behavior Management
MATERIALS: Parent Handbooks, Time-Out AV presentation, AV equipment

GOAL:

To increase parents' knowledge of appropriate behavior management techniques for administering punishment.

OBJECTIVES:

1. To increase parents' knowledge of the following: loss of privilege, parental disappointment, and being grounded.

2. To increase parents' ability to implement time-out.

PROCEDURES:

1. Explain that during the next hour, you will be discussing various techniques that parents can utilize as forms of punishment in place of hitting and yelling. Instruct parents to locate the information entitled **Behavior Management** on pages 5-8 in their Handbooks.

2. Review the concepts of punishment, discipline, and rewards:

   - Discipline—to guide children by helping them learn right from wrong.

   - Punishment—a consequence for undesirable, purposeful misbehavior.

   - Reward—a consequence for desirable, appropriate behavior.

3. Remind the parents that praise is the most powerful technique to help children learn to do the right things. Praise children for who they are (being) or what they do (doing).

4. Write down on a piece of paper the word INFANTS (birth to 1 1/2 years). Under the word, discuss the inappropriateness of punishing infants for their behavior.

   - Infants do not understand cause and effect (if something happens, something else will happen).

   - Infants do not perform misdeeds or misbehavior on purpose. They are only exploring their environment, and need to be protected from being hurt.

   - Baby-proofing, redirection, and praise are three good strategies to utilize in helping infants manage their environment.

   - Infants do not have the cognitive skills to know the difference between right and wrong.

   - Infants need love, protection, and support—not punishment.

   - If you become frustrated with what your infant is doing, rather than punish the infant, find a quiet place to calm down.

5. Introduce and discuss the following four types of management techniques. Stress the age-appropriateness of the strategy:

   a. **Loss of Privilege:** Appropriate for three years and older. A privilege is a right granted by the parent. Privileges are watching TV, playing with a toy, riding a bicycle, etc. If a child misuses the object or misuses the privilege, he/she loses it for a while. A toy or a privilege is taken away only when it is misused (thrown, broken, child riding bicycle outside boundary, etc.). Brainstorm with the parents what a privilege is and when it should be taken away.

   b. **Being Grounded:** Appropriate for child 3 1/2 years and older. When a child leaves a yard or an area purposefully, without permission, an appropriate punishment would be being grounded to the yard or house. The child must know it wasn't appropriate to leave the yard before being grounded can be used as a form of punishment. Brainstorm with the parent examples of when being grounded could be used.

c. **Parental Disappointment:** Appropriate for child 2 1/2 years and older. Parental disappointment is a simple statement which expresses the disappointment a parent has in a behavior the child has chosen to perform. The intent is to build some caring and an awareness in the child of the parent's disappointment. An example of the use of parental disappointment is:

"Son, I want you to know how disappointed I am that you chose to hit your brother (or whatever the misdeed). I'm sure the next time you're upset, you won't hit your brother and you will tell him not to take your toys. But right now, I feel disappointed."

Brainstorm instances when the parent can use disappointment. Discuss the overuse of expressing "disappointment" for every misbehavior.

d. **Time-Out:** Appropriate for a child three years and older. Instruct parents to locate the information entitled **Time-out** on pages 44-47 in their Handbooks. Time-out is a systematic removal of a child to a quiet area. Use time-out as a punishment for seriously violating family rules. Before using time-out:

- Make sure the child understands what time-out is.
- Establish rules that will warrant time-out.
- Pick a time-out place.
- Establish how long time-out will last.
- Ignore all promises designed to avoid going to time-out.
- Tell the child how long time-out will last.
- Remind the child time-out starts when he/she is quiet.
- After time-out, praise and redirect the child to appropriate behavior.

Time-out can be initiated by the parent or child.

6. If you are using the audio-visual programs, present the AV entitled **Time-Out** only if the parent has children three years of age and older. Afterwards, role play time-out; you be the 3-year-old child. Role play giving a time-out. Use the steps identified in the handbook for using time-out. Switch roles. You be the parent and let the parent be the child.

7. Mention to the parents that when they feel stressed out, taking some quiet time for themselves would be very appropriate.

IF'S, AND'S, OR BUT'S:

Providing parents with alternatives to hitting is a primary goal in the program. Get them to practice all the techniques and reinforce their use.

GOAL:

To reinforce parents' use of appropriate management and disciplinary techniques.

OBJECTIVES:

1. To practice use of time-out.

2. To ensure parents practice skills developed in the program.

3. To help parents learn new ways to resolve problem situations.

4. To practice praise as a form of behavior management.

5. To establish a warm and supportive atmosphere.

PROCEDURES:

1. Instruct parents to locate the Home Practice Exercise on page 140 in their Handbooks. Review the exercise with them:

   a. Use time-out at least twice when rules are broken.

   b. Praise child two times; self one time.

   c. Do one thing to reinforce your positive feelings of self.

   d. Complete family log.

2. Tell parents that in addition to the Home Practice Exercise, they are to spend 30 minutes each day with each of their children in nurturing playtime activities. Playtime is a time with the parent and child alone—no TV, no other distractions. Playing a game or reading books are good activities. From the *Nurturing Book for Babies and Children*, have the parents practice activities listed in the following sections: Activities for Infants, Activities for Toddlers, Activities for Preschoolers, or Infant and Child Massage. Have the parents remember what they did and report the next week.

IF'S, AND'S, OR BUT'S:

Parents will need a bit of encouragement to use time-out. Remind parents that using time-out is an effective means of punishing inappropriate behavior.

FAMILY ACTIVITY: 14.4 Family Nurturing Time
CONSTRUCT: Empathy, Self-Awareness
MATERIALS: Nurturing Book for Babies and Children

ACTIVITIES FOR INFANTS (Birth to 15 months):

Utilizing the *Nurturing Book for Babies and Children*, select activities from the sections entitled Activities for Infants or Infant and Child Massage. Engage parents in practicing songs, play and stimulation activities, or massage. Vary the activities weekly to promote interest.

ACTIVITIES FOR TODDLERS (15 months to 3 years):

Utilizing the *Nurturing Book for Babies and Children*, select activities from the sections entitled Activities for Toddlers or Infant and Child Massage. Engage parents in practicing songs, play, language, and movement activities, or massage. Vary the activities weekly to promote interest.

ACTIVITIES FOR PRESCHOOLERS (3-5 years):

Use the following activities when working with preschool children and their parents. Use the activities as the basis for involving infants and toddlers if you are conducting a home visit with children ages birth to five years.

FAMILY ACTIVITY: 14.5 Hello Time: I Spy
CONSTRUCT: Empathy
MATERIALS: None

GOAL:

To describe simple, tangible characteristics of both self and others.

OBJECTIVES:

1. To increase children's awareness of self.
2. To increase children's awareness of others.

PROCEDURES:

1. Have children and adults sit in a circle on the floor.
2. Explain that today we will be playing a guessing game called "I Spy." We all take turns describing something someone has in the room, and everyone else tries to guess who it is. For example, I say, "I spy someone wearing glasses," and everyone else has to guess who I spy.

IF'S, AND'S, OR BUT'S:

If a child is having difficulty describing another child, give a prompt.

FAMILY ACTIVITY: 14.6 Streamer Dance
CONSTRUCT: Age-Appropriate Developmental Expectations
MATERIALS: Cassette player and cassettes or record player and records, streamers

GOAL:

To express self through creative expression.

OBJECTIVES:

1. To increase positive adult-child interactions through music and dance.

2. To help children express themselves through positive play.

PROCEDURES:

1. Tie streamers to the wrists of everyone and tell the children that they are going to dance or move slow when the music is slow and dance or move fast when the music is fast. Set boundaries in terms of the area of rooms where children may dance.

2. Play the music and have the adults demonstrate fast and slow dancing with the streamers.

IF'S, AND'S, OR BUT'S:

1. Children who are reluctant to dance or respond to music with their bodies may feel less apprehensive since their attention is placed on the movements of the streamers.

2. Streamers may be attached to ankles, fingers, or around waists for variation.

3. A reluctant child may not want the streamer tied to him, and should be allowed to hold it in his/her hands. S/he may change his/her mind after observing others.

FAMILY ACTIVITY: 14.7 Circle Time: Time-Out
CONSTRUCT: Behavior Management
MATERIALS: Chair, puppets

GOAL:

To increase children's understanding of time-out.

OBJECTIVES:

1. To increase children's abilities to take a time-out.

2. To practice taking appropriate time-out.

3. To increase family's use of time-out.

PROCEDURES:

1. Assemble family members in a circle. Explain to them that this is a special time called Circle Time. During Circle Time children and adults get to talk about all different things.

2. The key to conducting Circle Time is MANAGEMENT. Without group management, this activity will not be successful. One way to successfully manage the group is to control the talking. If talking out of turn occurs, you might make it a home visit rule.

3. Utilize the following steps to teach the concept of time-out:

   a. Ask the children if anyone knows what time-out is.

   b. Why do children take time-out? (Breaking rules on purpose, throwing and breaking something as opposed to dropping something and breaking it.)

   c. How are children supposed to take a time-out? (Go to the chair/corner and sit/stand quietly for the period of time teacher/aide/parent tells you.)

4. Role play the appropriate way to take a time-out. Pretend you are a child who has been told to take a 2 minute time-out. Go to the chair in the corner and sit quietly. Ask for children to volunteer to role play going to time-out.

5. An important part in teaching a concept is to show a non-example of the concept (discrimination). Using the "fooler approach" explain to the children that you will try to trick them and see if they really know how to take a time-out. Act out the following, asking afterwards if that was the right way to take a time-out.

   a. Complain going to the chair, be noisy in the chair, kneel/stand/lean on the chair, complain you want to get out, etc. Ask children if that was the right way to take a time-out.

   b. Again, get volunteers to model how to take an appropriate time-out.

6. Play act situations taken from the rules utilizing the puppets. Some examples may be:

   a. Illustrate a situation where one puppet hits another puppet. Ask the children what should be done to the puppet who was hitting. Reinforce the concept of time-out.

   b. Illustrate a situation where two puppets are yelling. Reinforce time-out concept.

   c. Illustrate a situation where one puppet throws something. Reinforce concept of time-out.

   d. Illustrate one puppet teasing another. Reinforce concept of time-out.

IF'S, AND'S, OR BUT'S:

1. While play acting with puppets, encourage responses from the children as to what kind of punishment the child should receive. Attempt to get at their fears of physical punishment or extended periods of isolation.

2. Make sure the puppets play act the correct way to take a time-out.

3. Make sure you understand the concept of time-out and the procedures for implementing time-out. A detailed description of time-out is presented in the *Parent Handbook*.

4. Let the parents role play with the children how to take an appropriate time-out.

GOAL:

To gain creative expression through the use of a gross motor developmental skill.

OBJECTIVES:

1. To increase child's gross motor ability to blow through a straw.

2. To increase child's creative expression.

3. To reinforce comfort in using nurturing touch.

PROCEDURES:

1. Use paints that are somewhat runny. Adding a little water to tempera paints will provide a desired consistency.

2. Assemble children and adults standing in a circle around a table. Place sheets of paper on the table with open paint containers.

3. Place straws in the paint. Hold the top of the straw so that the paint stays in the straw.

4. Hold the top of the straw on the paper and let the paint run out.

5. Have the child blow through the straw at the paint, spreading the paint all over the paper. The more the child continues to blow at the paint, the further it will spread around the paper.

6. Have the child develop his/her own creative picture. Use different straws for different colors.

FAMILY HUG:

1. End each home visit with a family hug. Everyone get in a circle and put your arms around the people next to you. During the family hug time, anyone can say anything they like. It is a time for free expression.

2. At a natural time, close the activities for the day.

IF'S, AND'S, OR BUT'S:

1. Because the children are using paint, keep the handling of the open paint container to a minimum. You may want to put the paint on the paper and let the child blow it around.

2. Do not allow children to walk away from the table with the paint or straws.

3. Watch for children who may want to blow the paint through the straw at some other object or person.

NURTURING PROGRAM FOR PARENTS AND CHILDREN BIRTH TO FIVE YEARS

SESSION 15

BEHAVIOR CONSTRUCT: Child Development

SESSION CONCEPT: Ages and Stages

BRIEF DESCRIPTION: Parents will discuss the importance inappropriate expectations have on a child's self-esteem and self-concept and will review developmental abilities at various time during childhood. Children will review how to take a time-out and will have fun moving to music.

INTENDED USE: For parents of children birth to 5 years

PREREQUISITE KNOWLEDGE: Praise

AGENDA

Parent Activities	Materials
15.1 Icebreaker and Home Practice Check In	*Parent Handbooks*
15.2 Ages and Stages	*Parent Handbooks*, **Ages and Stages** AV presentation, AV equipment
15.3 Home Practice Exercise	*Parent Handbooks*

Family Activities*	Materials
15.4 Family Nurturing Time	*Nurturing Book for Babies and Children*
15.5 Hello Time: Guess How I Feel	Feeling Faces
15.6 Shake Your Booty	Scarf
15.7 Circle Time: Time-Out Review	Puppets
15.8 Marble Painting and Family Hug	Marbles, shoe boxes, white paper, tempera paint

*For parents with infants or toddlers, use activities presented in *Nurturing Book for Babies and Children*. For parents with preschoolers (ages 3-5), use the activities listed below Family Nurturing Time.

PARENT ACTIVITY: 15.1 Icebreaker and Home Practice Check In
CONSTRUCT: Empathy, Self-Awareness, Child Development
MATERIALS: Parent Handbooks

GOAL:

To increase parents' awareness of the impact of developmental characteristics on self.

OBJECTIVES:

1. To identify developmental differences.

2. To enable parents to recall developmental differences between themselves and their peers.

PROCEDURES:

1. Begin today's parent activities by having each adult respond to the following:

    • Right now I am feeling _____ .

    • I was ahead of my friends/peers in _____ and it felt _____ .

    • I was behind my friends/peers in _____ and it felt _____ .

2. After each parent has had an opportunity to respond to the statements above, review the Home Practice Exercise from the previous meeting. Also discuss perceived changes in family members and their interactions as reported in the family log.

IF'S, AND'S, OR BUT'S:

Being an early or late bloomer has its advantages and disadvantages. Help parents focus on how they felt at the time.

PARENT ACTIVITY: 15.2 Ages and Stages
CONSTRUCT: Child Development
MATERIALS: Parent Handbooks, Ages and Stages AV presentation, AV equipment

GOAL:

To increase parents' understanding of stages and appropriate developmental expectations.

OBJECTIVES:

1. To help parents accept that development takes place throughout lifetime stages.

2. To enable parents to learn what they can and/or cannot expect from their children.

3. To help parents understand the appropriateness of refusing tasks which are developmentally beyond the capabilities of the person — adult or child.

4. To help parents understand the relationship between a child's self-concept and parental expectations.

PROCEDURES:

1. If you are using the audio-visual programs, present the AV entitled **Ages and Stages**.

2. Instruct parents to locate the information entitled **Ages and Stages** on pages 48-51 in their Handbooks. Utilize the information presented to discuss the following:

    a. Developmental stages are periods of time children grow and learn new things.

    b. Four kinds of developmental stages:

      - Physical

      - Intellectual

      - Language

      - Social and emotional

    c. Everyone goes through stages of growth throughout life.

    d. Knowing what to expect at various stages of growth is important for children to develop a positive self-concept and self-esteem.

    e. Parents who place inappropriate developmental expectations on their children encourage them to feel inadequate.

3. Select the resource material on Child Development in the *Parent Handbook* that is appropriate to the age of the child(ren) in the family, and review the material with the parents.

IF'S, AND'S, OR BUT'S:

1. Expectations do have an effect on children, on their self-concept and performance. As teachers and parents we need to be aware of how we can program our children for success by having positive and reasonable expectations.

2. This activity may need more time to complete. Don't hesitate in coming back to the information for continued instruction.

PARENT ACTIVITY:	**15.3 Home Practice Exercise**
CONSTRUCT:	**Self-Awareness**
MATERIALS:	**Parent Handbooks**

GOAL:

To increase parents' knowledge of age appropriate expectations.

OBJECTIVES:

1. To help parents learn more appropriate developmental expectations for their kids.

2. To continue to allow parents to experience success through completing tasks.

3. To increase parents' awareness of their children's capabilities.

4. To establish a warm and supportive atmosphere.

PROCEDURES:

1. Instruct parents to locate the Home Practice Exercise on page 140 in their Handbooks. Review the exercise with them:

   a. Review the information on development.

   b. Note at least one thing you learned which you didn't know before about each of your children.

   c. Praise yourself and your children.

   d. Complete family log.

2. Tell parents that in addition to the Home Practice Exercise, they are to spend 30 minutes each day with each of their children in nurturing playtime activities. Playtime is a time with the parent and child alone — no TV, no other distractions. Playing a game or reading books are good activities. From the *Nurturing Book for Babies and Children*, have the parents practice activities listed in the following sections: Activities for Infants, Activities for Toddlers, Activities for Preschoolers, or Infant and Child Massage. Have the parents remember what they did and report the next week.

IF'S, AND'S, OR BUT'S:

Parents may express some anxiety about reading the material. Have them focus on the ages of their child(ren) only.

FAMILY ACTIVITY:	**15.4 Family Nurturing Time**
CONSTRUCT:	**Empathy, Self-Awareness**
MATERIALS:	**Nurturing Book for Babies and Children**

ACTIVITIES FOR INFANTS (Birth to 15 months):

Utilizing the *Nurturing Book for Babies and Children*, select activities from the sections entitled Activities for Infants or Infant and Child Massage. Engage parents in practicing songs, play and stimulation activities, or massage. Vary the activities weekly to sustain interest.

ACTIVITIES FOR TODDLERS (15 months to 3 years):

Utilizing the *Nurturing Book for Babies and Children*, select activities from the sections entitled Activities for Toddlers or Infant and Child Massage. Engage parents in practicing songs, play, language, and movement activities, or massage. Vary the activities weekly to sustain interest.

ACTIVITIES FOR PRESCHOOLERS (3-5 years):

Use the following activities when working with preschool children and their parents. Use the activities as the basis for involving infants and toddlers if you are conducting a home visit with children ages birth to five years.

FAMILY ACTIVITY: 15.5 Hello Time: Guess How I Feel
CONSTRUCT: Empathy
MATERIALS: Feeling Faces

GOAL:

To increase awareness of facial expressions of feelings.

OBJECTIVES:

1. To allow children to recognize feelings with appropriate facial expression.

2. To encourage recognition of feelings in others.

3. To increase children's awareness of their own feelings.

PROCEDURES:

1. Assemble children and adults in a circle seated on the floor.

2. Begin by saying that today we are going to talk about feelings. Using the feeling faces, hold up a face and ask who can identify the feeling.

3. Have children suggest why the child may be feeling the way he/she is.

4. Ask the children and adults if anyone has recently felt the identified feeling.

IF'S, AND'S, OR BUT'S:

Feeling recognition and awareness are important prerequisites for managing one's behavior.

FAMILY ACTIVITY: 15.6 Shake Your Booty
CONSTRUCT: Behavior Management
MATERIALS: Scarf

GOAL:

To give children experience in leading and following.

OBJECTIVES:

1. To increase child's ability to follow commands.

2. To allow children opportunity to lead family activities.

PROCEDURES:

1. Have children and adults sit in a circle on the floor.

2. Explain the activity. I am going to see how well we follow directions. I am going to drop this scarf from as high as I can reach. While it is in the air, you are to hum, but only while it is in the air. When the scarf reaches the floor, I want you to be as quiet as you can.

3. Drop the scarf two times for the children to catch on.

4. This time, when I drop the scarf, I want you to wiggle all over while the scarf is in the air. When the scarf reaches the floor, I want you stand at attention.

5. Have children take turns dropping the scarf. Before dropping the scarf, the home visitor is to tell the family what they are to do while the scarf is in the air.

IF'S, AND'S, OR BUT'S:

Permit each child to drop the scarf several times. Notice not only how each leader commands the family, but also the nature of the response.

FAMILY ACTIVITY:	**15.7 Circle Time: Time-Out Review**
CONSTRUCT:	**Behavior Management**
MATERIALS:	**Puppets**

GOAL:

To reinforce concepts of time-out through role-play.

OBJECTIVES:

1. To reinforce knowledge of appropriate time-out concepts.

2. To challenge children using a "fooler" technique.

PROCEDURES:

1. Have children and adults sit in a circle on the floor.

2. Remind them that this is Circle Time: a time to talk about things and pay attention.

3. Explain to the children that you are going to see if they remember how to take a time-out correctly. To do that, you will attempt to fool them.

4. Role play various concepts of time-out with both correct and incorrect ways and try to fool the children. For example, you may say to the children: "I bet I can fool you guys. I bet nobody here knows how to sit in the time-out chair. Is this the way?" (Act nutty.) Response is "No." "Is this the way?" (Put chair on head.) Response is "No." "Well then, who can show me the right way?" (Bet child to demonstrate the correct way.)

5. Repeat activity using other steps: going to time-out/refusing to go; sitting nicely/making faces; leaving time-out nicely/knocking over chair.

6. Play act the following home situations utilizing the puppets:

   a. Illustrate a situation where a child puppet throws something at home. Ask children for suggestions for punishment. Reinforce the parent puppet telling child to take a time-out.

   b. Same characters as above, only child puppet is hitting brother/sister. Time-out is reinforced.

c. Illustrate situation where child puppet hurts the dog, is required to take a time-out but he doesn't. Parent forcibly escorts child to time-out without excessive abusive/force.

d. Illustrate a situation where a child gets angry at a parent for not allowing the child to have a snack just before dinner. The child throws a glass (any object), and it crashes to the floor. The child is sent to time-out.

IF'S, AND'S, OR BUT'S:

1. While using the puppets, encourage children to respond as to what kind of punishment the child should receive. Get at their fears of physical punishment or extended periods of isolation.

2. Make sure the puppets play act the correct way to take a time-out.

FAMILY ACTIVITY:	**15.8 Marble Painting and Family Hug**
CONSTRUCT:	**Appropriate Developmental Expectations**
MATERIALS:	**Marbles, shoe boxes, white paper, tempera paint**

GOAL:

To reinforce creative expression through art.

OBJECTIVES:

1. To foster creativity in children.

2. To enhance social interactions.

3. To reinforce comfort in using nurturing touch.

PROCEDURES:

1. Do this activity at tables. It may be easier to have children and adults work in pairs.

2. Children drop marbles into paint and then into a shoe box or a shallow dish with paper cut to fit the bottom. By moving the box or plate, the children can roll the marbles from side to side and from top to bottom to make a design. Using different colors gives an exciting contrast.

FAMILY HUG:

1. End each home visit with a family hug. Everyone get in a circle and put your arms around the people next to you. During the family hug time, anyone can say anything they like.

2. At a natural time, close the activities for the day.

IF'S, AND'S, OR BUT'S:

1. Good for physically handicapped child because even the slightest movement produces a design.

2. Use different sizes of boxes and different sizes of marbles to get various effects.

3. The finished product could be used as greeting cards or wrapping paper.

NURTURING PROGRAM FOR PARENTS AND CHILDREN BIRTH TO FIVE YEARS

SESSION 16

BEHAVIOR CONSTRUCT: Child Development

SESSION CONCEPT: Skill Strips

BRIEF DESCRIPTION: Parents review child growth and development. Children engage their tactile sense by playing with shaving cream.

INTENDED USE: For parents of children birth to 5 years

PREREQUISITE KNOWLEDGE: None

AGENDA

Parent Activities	Materials
16.1 Icebreaker and Home Practice Check In	*Parent Handbooks*
16.2 Skill Strips	*Parent Handbooks*
16.3 Home Practice Exercise	*Parent Handbooks*

Family Activities*	Materials
16.4 Family Nurturing Time	*Nurturing Book for Babies and Children*
16.5 Hello Time: Good Morning To You	None
16.6 Circle Time: Row, Row, Row Your Boat	None
16.7 Shaving Cream and Family Hug	Shaving cream, food coloring

*For parents with infants or toddlers, use activities presented in *Nurturing Book for Babies and Children*. For parents with preschoolers (ages 3-5), use the activities listed below Family Nurturing Time.

PARENT ACTIVITY: 16.1 Icebreaker and Home Practice Check In
CONSTRUCT: Empathy
MATERIALS: Parent Handbooks

GOAL:

To increase parents' awareness and sensitivity to the developmental limitations of others.

OBJECTIVES:

1. To increase parents' empathy toward the needs of their children.

2. To provide parents with a positive direction toward helping their child develop skills and abilities.

PROCEDURES:

1. Begin today's parent activities by having each adult respond to the following:

   • One thing I wish I was able to do when I was my child's age is _____ .

   • One thing I hope my child(ren) will be able to do when they get to my age is _____ .

2. After each parent has had an opportunity to respond to the statements above, review the Home Practice Exercise from the previous meeting. Also discuss perceived changes in family members and their interactions as reported in the family log.

IF'S, AND'S, OR BUT'S:

If the child of the parent is an infant, have the parent fantasize what ability the parent would like to have if he/she were an infant.

PARENT ACTIVITY: 16.2 Skill Strips
CONSTRUCT: Child Development
MATERIALS: Parent Handbooks

GOAL:

To reinforce knowledge of age-appropriate skills and abilities of children.

OBJECTIVES:

1. To increase parents' awareness of the relationship between feelings of self-worth and parental expectations.

2. To review child growth and development.

PROCEDURES:

1. Have each adult respond to the following statements:

   - One expectation my parent(s) had for me that I never met was _____ and it led me to feel _____.

   - One expectation my parent(s) had for me that I did achieve was _____ and it led me to feel _____.

2. Instruct parents to locate the information entitled **Skill Strips** on pages 67-69 in their Handbooks. Inform the parents that they are to circle the age they think children should begin to perform the behavior.

3. Review the responses of the parents with the responses provided here:

Developmental Skills Answer Sheet*

Behaviors	0-12 months A	12-24 months B	24-36 months C	36-48 months D	48-60 months E
Takes a few steps without support	(A)	B	C	D	E
Repeats same syllable 2-3 times	(A)	B	C	D	E
Builds tower of 3 blocks	A	(B)	C	D	E
Says 5 different words	A	(B)	C	D	E
Points to 3 body parts on self	A	(B)	C	D	E
Uses pincer grasp to pick up object	(A)	B	C	D	E
Imitates peek-a-boo	(A)	B	C	D	E
Pulls off socks	A	(B)	C	D	E
Holds and drinks from cup using 2 hands	(A)	B	C	D	E
Follows rules by imitating actions of other children	A	B	C	(D)	E
Snaps or hooks clothing	A	B	C	(D)	E
Pedals tricycle 5 feet	A	B	C	(D)	E
Attempts to help parent with tasks by doing part of a chore (e.g. hold dust pan)	A	B	(C)	D	E
Walks backwards	A	B	(C)	D	E
Will attend for 5 minutes while a story is read	A	B	C	(D)	E
Sucks liquid from glass using a straw	A	B	(C)	D	E
Imitates counting to 3	A	B	C	(D)	E
Puts on mittens	A	B	C	(D)	E
Holds up fingers to tell age	A	B	(C)	D	E
Uses word for bathroom need	A	B	(C)	D	E
Stands on one foot for 4-8 seconds	A	B	C	D	(E)
Uses words: sister, brother, grandmother, grandfather	A	B	C	D	(E)
Stays dry all night	A	B	C	D	(E)
Takes turns with 8-9 other children	A	B	C	D	(E)
Draws a man (head, trunk, 4 limbs)	A	B	C	D	(E)
Engages in socially acceptable behavior in public	A	B	C	D	(E)

*Taken from Portage Guide to Early Education Checklist of Developmental Skills.

IF'S, AND'S, OR BUT'S:

The goal is to increase parents' knowledge and awareness of developmental capabilities of children. If either one is lacking in the parent, the child is more apt to have inappropriate demands placed on him/her. Work with the parent to achieve a level of practical knowledge and awareness.

PARENT ACTIVITY: 16.3 Home Practice Exercise
CONSTRUCT: Child Development, Empathy
MATERIALS: Parent Handbooks

GOAL:

To increase parents' knowledge of age appropriate expectations of children.

OBJECTIVES:

1. To reinforce parents' feelings of competence as a knowledgeable caregiver.

2. To reinforce the positive self-esteem and self-concept of children.

3. To establish a warm and supportive atmosphere.

PROCEDURES:

1. Instruct parents to locate the Home Practice Exercise on page 141 in their Handbooks. Review the exercise with them:

   a. Pay close attention to the skills and abilities of your child(ren). Note one thing that you observe that you weren't aware of before.

   b. Upon task accomplishment or effort, praise your child for doing.

   c. Tonight, praise your child for doing.

   d. Complete family log.

2. Tell parents that in addition to the Home Practice Exercise, they are to spend 30 minutes each day with each of their children in nurturing playtime activities. Playtime is a time with the parent and child alone — no TV, no other distractions. Playing a game or reading books are good activities. From the *Nurturing Book for Babies and Children*, have the parents practice activities listed in the following sections: Activities for Infants, Activities for Toddlers, Activities for Preschoolers, or Infant and Child Massage. Have the parents remember what they did and report the next week.

IF'S, AND'S, OR BUT'S:

Praise is a concept that simply cannot be stressed too often.

ACTIVITIES FOR INFANTS (Birth to 15 months):

Utilizing the *Nurturing Book for Babies and Children*, select activities from the sections entitled Activities for Infants or Infant and Child Massage. Engage parents in practicing songs, play and stimulation activities, or massage. Vary the activities weekly to sustain interest.

ACTIVITIES FOR TODDLERS (15 months to 3 years):

Utilizing the *Nurturing Book for Babies and Children*, select activities from the sections entitled Activities for Toddlers or Infant and Child Massage. Engage parents in practicing songs, play, language, and movement activities, or massage. Vary the activities weekly to sustain interest.

ACTIVITIES FOR PRESCHOOLERS (3-5 years):

Use the following activities when working with preschool children and their parents. Use the activities as the basis for involving infants and toddlers if you are conducting a home visit with children ages birth to five years.

FAMILY ACTIVITY: 16.5 Hello Time: Good Morning to You
CONSTRUCT: Empathy
MATERIALS: None

GOAL:

To increase children's awareness of the presence and feelings of others.

OBJECTIVES:

1. To increase children's self-awareness.

2. To allow children to share how they feel.

3. To increase listening skills.

PROCEDURES:

1. Begin this activity with children and adults seated on the floor in a circle.

2. Take turns singing the following song to each child, to the tune of "Happy Birthday."

    Good Morning to you, Good Morning to you,
    Good Morning to___(child's name)___, How are you today?

3. Each child should be encouraged to tell how he/she is feeling or he/she may choose to sing his/her response, to the tune of "Happy Birthday."

I'm happy today, I'm happy today,
I'm happy today, I'm happy today.

(Other feeling words may be used: grumpy, sleepy, sad, silly, lonely, etc.)

4. An adult may choose to model the sung response for the children, but allow them to choose how they express their feelings to the group.

5. Be sure to focus the attention on the person being greeted; i.e., "Where's Adam? Let's all sing to him."

IF'S, AND'S, OR BUT'S:

If a chid does not respond by saying how he feels, try to elicit from others how they think he may be feeling; i.e., "Look at Adam. How do you think he may be feeling? I see a smile. Do you think he's happy or sad?"

FAMILY ACTIVITY:	**16.6 Circle Time: Row, Row, Row Your Boat**
CONSTRUCT:	**Empathy**
MATERIALS:	**None**

GOAL:

To increase positive social interactions through play.

OBJECTIVES:

1. To involve children and adults in active and cooperative musical activities.

2. To foster creative expression through music.

PROCEDURES:

1. Request children and adults to sit in a circle with their legs spread apart so an adult or another child can sit between them.

2. Explain to the group that we are all going to pretend that we are in a boat and we have to row to get to shore.

3. Have the children hold the arms of the person in front of them. When the song begins, everyone will make a rowing movement with their hands.

Row, Row, Row Your Boat

Row, row, row your boat gently down the stream,
Merrily, merrily, merrily, merrily,
Life is but a dream.

4. To add variety, move slow when casually rowing, fast when being chased by a shark, etc.

IF'S, AND'S, OR BUT'S:

Ask a child if he or she wants to lead the activity.

FAMILY ACTIVITY: 16.7 Shaving Cream and Family Hug
CONSTRUCT: Self-Awareness
MATERIALS: Shaving cream, food coloring

GOAL:

To participate in creative artistic expression involving tactile stimulation.

OBJECTIVES:

1. To participate in an art activity involving physical and tactile sensory experience.

2. To engage parents and children in creative, original self-expression.

3. To increase parents' ability to foster creative expression in their children.

4. To reinforce comfort in using nurturing touch.

PROCEDURES:

1. Get everyone to stand around the kitchen table. Introduce the activity by holding up and shaking a can of shaving cream.

2. Inform parents that children and adults simply do not get enough time to have fun with touch. This activity is designed to experience positive touch and to promote positive touch with your children.

3. (*PLEASE NOTE:* We recommend covering your table with a nonabsorbent material such as plastic garbage bags cut open or butcher block paper. Tape edges down to prevent movement during smearing.) Demonstrate painting with shaving cream by squirting it onto the table and smearing it around.

4. Squirt some shaving cream on the table for each person. Encourage parents and children to finger paint with the shaving cream on the table.

5. Add interest to the activity by adding a bit of food coloring to various piles of shaving cream. Encourage everyone to share their piles of shaving cream blending the colors.

FAMILY HUG:

1. End each home visit with a family hug. Everyone get in a circle and put your arms around the people next to you. During the family hug time, anyone can say anything they like. It is a time for free expression.

2. At a natural time, close the activities for the day.

IF'S, AND'S, OR BUT'S:

1. Parents will feel a bit awkward "playing" like children. Encourage parents to participate by suggesting to them that knowing how to play like a child will encourage them to play with their children.

2. Children might get really excited. Help them manage their behavior but remain nurturing.

NURTURING PROGRAM FOR PARENTS AND CHILDREN BIRTH TO FIVE YEARS

SESSION 17

BEHAVIOR CONSTRUCT: Self-Awareness

SESSION CONCEPT: Troublesome Feelings

BRIEF DESCRIPTION: Parents will discuss how to handle feelings and the payoffs for not being able to handle certain feelings. Parents will also experience a visualization called Yellow Balloon. Family members will play the Nurturing Game to enhance self-awareness, touch, praise, and feelings.

INTENDED USE: For parents of children birth to 5 years

PREREQUISITE KNOWLEDGE: Behavior Payoffs, Parent's Needs

AGENDA

Parent Activities	Materials
17.1 Icebreaker and Home Practice Check In	*Parent Handbooks*
17.2 Troublesome Feelings	*Parent Handbooks*
17.3 Yellow Balloon Visualization	None
17.4 Home Practice Exercise	*Parent Handbooks*

Family Activities*	Materials
17.5 Family Nurturing Time	*Nurturing Book for Babies and Children*
17.6 Hello Time: Happy to See You	None
17.7 Circle Time: Here's One Foot	None
17.8 Nurturing Game and Family Hug	Nurturing Game

*For parents with infants or toddlers, use activities presented in *Nurturing Book for Babies and Children*. For parents with preschoolers (ages 3-5), use the activities listed below Family Nurturing Time.

PARENT ACTIVITY: 17.1 Icebreaker and Home Practice Check In
CONSTRUCT: Self-Awareness
MATERIALS: Parent Handbooks

GOAL:

To reinforce parents' use of their personal power to positively influence their lives.

OBJECTIVES:

1. To identify areas in parents' lives that need change.

2. To activate parents' personal power to enhance their life.

PROCEDURES:

1. Begin today's parent activities by having each adult respond to the following:

   • Today I'm feeling _____ .

   • Three ways my life could be fuller and happier are: _____, _____, and _____.

2. After each parent has had an opportunity to respond to the statements above, review the Home Practice Exercise from the previous meeting. Also discuss perceived changes in family members and their interactions as reported in the family log.

IF'S, AND'S, OR BUT'S:

Listen to the ideas parents express. Perhaps many of the ideas are unrealistic, which, in turn, could lead to higher frustration and continued failure. Maybe you need to help parents by challenging the utility of seemingly unrealistic hopes.

PARENT ACTIVITY: 17.2 Troublesome Feelings
CONSTRUCT: Self-Awareness
MATERIALS: Parent Handbooks

GOAL:

To develop parents' confidence in their ability to handle their feelings.

OBJECTIVES:

1. To reinforce parents' ability to identify their feelings.

2. To increase understanding of payoffs of feelings.

3. To increase parents' handling or preventing of troublesome feelings.

4. To identify predictors of troublesome feelings.

PROCEDURES:

1. Explain to the parents that it is very important to be aware of their feelings and to express them. Ask them to think of every feeling they have as a giant spring. When they do not express feelings, they have to hide them. Tell them to think of having to step on a giant spring to keep it down. It takes a lot of energy to keep the spring (their hidden feelings) down — energy they could use for something else. People often keep painful and scary feelings down.

2. Get some examples of how and when people keep scary and painful feelings hidden. Remind them that it is healthy to recognize all feelings, even the painful and scary ones. Once feelings are allowed expression, they do not hurt as much and are not as scary.

3. Instruct parents to locate the information entitled **Handling Troublesome Feelings** on pages 70-71 in their Handbooks. Ask parents to respond to the following statement first by writing the response in their handbook and then by sharing their response.

   - The feeling I have the most trouble handling is _____ .

4. Then discuss that although negative feelings do cause pain, etc., there must be some payoff in it or we wouldn't have them. Ask parents to respond to the following statement by writing the response in their handbook and then sharing their responses.

   - When I feel _____ , my payoff is that I _____ , or I don't have to _____ , or other people _____ .

5. Have parents locate the two statements in their handbook labelled MOST and LEAST. Ask parents to respond to the following:

   - I am most apt to have trouble with my troublesome feelings when _____ .
   - I am least apt to have trouble with my troublesome feelings when _____ .

6. Review the earlier conversation on parents' needs. Are you getting stimulation and enough stroking in each of these areas? How is your "stroke" bank? Do you have a safety net, a savings account or are you getting low in reserves?

7. Are you being nice to yourself? Or when you get to feeling "down," are you the first one to heap on the criticism? Are you realistic?

8. Instruct parents to locate the information entitled **Misery Making Beliefs and Better Choices** on pages 72-73 in their Handbooks. Review each of the beliefs and better choices. Are parents holding onto beliefs in their lives that cause misery? Ask each parent to identify the one that is most common to them.

9. Do a Suggestion Circle for handling troublesome feelings. Each person give his or her best suggestion about what to do to handle that troublesome feeling. List three things each parent can do.

IF'S, AND'S, OR BUT'S:

1. Have parents focus on all six areas of needs as a solution to their troublesome feelings.

2. This is a long exercise with many important concepts. Spend the time necessary to ensure understanding.

PARENT ACTIVITY:	17.3 Yellow Balloon Visualization
CONSTRUCT:	Self-Awareness
MATERIALS:	None

GOAL:

To reduce parents' attachment from the memory of a troublesome feeling.

OBJECTIVES:

1. To provide parents with a technique they can use to reduce stress/frustration.

2. To provide parents additional insight into their relationship with troublesome feelings or situations.

PROCEDURES:

1. Leader read the following visualization:

Yellow Balloon

First find a comfortable position for your body to be in while I talk to you a little. Lie on the floor if you can. If you are not comfortable on the floor, wiggle around in your chair until you find a position that is comfortable. Close your eyes. (Pause) Now pay attention to your breathing for a few breaths. Pay attention to how your breath moves into your nose and fills your chest with cool, fresh air and then how your breath moves out of you in warm, most air filled with the leftovers from your living process. You are nourishing yourself at all times with fresh air whether or not you are aware of it.

Now think for a moment about that troublesome feeling you have been working with this session. Name it again inside of yourself and feel your stomach tense up as you prepare to do battle with it again, but this time you won't fight it. Now think for another moment of one or two terrible situations this feeling has gotten you into. Think of a few times you have tried to forget, that you would rather not be bothered with anymore, that you would like to be free of, that you deserve to be free of. Now, when they are clear in your mind (pause), envision a trash can. See clearly before you a trash can, see its color, see its shape. A large trash can it is. And now I'd like you to see yourself picking up those situations which caused you so much pain and putting them into the trash can. And now the lid—you are putting on the lid and fastening it into place. Now envision yourself attaching several hooks to the trash can, hooks along the rim of the trash can. You are surprised at how smoothly it is going. The hooks are now all attached so you can hook on the strings which hold the balloon, the big yellow balloon, and it is much bigger than the trash can. You hook all of the string on it so easily. The strings at the edge of the trash can are now getting tight as you let the balloon go out of your hands softly. The balloon rises up slowly. It begins to float upward. The strings are all taut, and the balloon is rising. The trash can is wobbling a little, and now it starts off the ground. It is rising clearly and powerfully into the air. It is up to the tree tops now, and it is still rising so strongly; it's now above the trees and high in the sky. You can still see it quite well, but it is getting smaller and smaller as it rises higher and higher. The yellow balloon is floating so high you can hardly see it anymore, except as a small speck of yellow, and still it rises. You watch and watch until it gets smaller and smaller and then finally (pause), it disappears (pause).

Now begin to be conscious of your body again, and wiggle around until you feel like opening your eyes. Then open your eyes and sit up and, (pause) smile!

IF'S, AND'S, OR BUT'S:

The Yellow Balloon exercise will help parents reduce levels of stress and frustration regarding a particular feeling.

PARENT ACTIVITY:	**17.4 Home Practice Exercise**
CONSTRUCT:	**Behavior Management, Self-Awareness, Empathy**
MATERIALS:	**Parent Handbooks**

GOAL:

To increase parents' abilities in handling troublesome feelings.

OBJECTIVES:

1. To provide parents with practice in managing troublesome feelings.

2. To allow parents to practice their personal power.

3. To establish a warm and supportive atmosphere.

PROCEDURES:

1. Instruct parents to locate the Home Practice Exercise on page 141 in their Handbooks. Review the exercise with them:

   a. Deal with troublesome feelings with new awareness.

   b. Be aware of misery-making beliefs when they arise and think of better choices.

   c. Complete family log.

2. Tell parents that in addition to the Home Practice Exercise, they are to spend 30 minutes each day with each of their children in nurturing playtime activities. Playtime is a time with the parent and child alone—no TV, no other distractions. Playing a game or reading books are good activities. From the *Nurturing Book for Babies and Children*, have the parents practice activities listed in the following sections: Activities for Infants, Activities for Toddlers, Activities for Preschoolers, or Infant and Child Massage. Have the parents remember what they did and report the next week.

IF'S, AND'S, OR BUT'S:

Handling troublesome feelings in a positive way reflects a strong sense of personal power.

FAMILY ACTIVITY: 17.5 Family Nurturing Time
CONSTRUCT: Empathy, Self-Awareness
MATERIALS: Nurturing Book for Babies and Children

ACTIVITIES FOR INFANTS (Birth to 15 months):

Utilizing the *Nurturing Book for Babies and Children*, select activities from the sections entitled Activities for Infants or Infant and Child Massage. Engage parents in practicing songs, play and stimulation activities, or massage. Vary the activities weekly to sustain interest.

ACTIVITIES FOR TODDLERS (15 months to 3 years):

Utilizing the *Nurturing Book for Babies and Children*, select activities from the sections entitled Activities for Toddlers or Infant and Child Massage. Engage parents in practicing songs, play, language, and movement activities, or massage. Vary the activities weekly to sustain interest.

ACTIVITIES FOR PRESCHOOLERS (3-5 years):

Use the following activities when working with preschool children and their parents. Use the activities as the basis for involving infants and toddlers if you are conducting a home visit with children ages birth to five years.

FAMILY ACTIVITY: 17.6 Hello Time: Happy to See You
CONSTRUCT: Empathy
MATERIALS: None

GOAL:

To reinforce family cohesion.

OBJECTIVES:

1. To personally greet each child and parent.

2. To experience successful interactions in a family setting.

3. To get parents and children to have fun.

PROCEDURES:

1. Have everyone sit on the floor in a circle.

2. Explain that we will take turns singing a song to each person in the group.

3. Go around the circle and sing the following song to each person (to the tune of "This is the Way We Wash Our Clothes").

> We're happy to see you here today,
> Here today, here today,
>
> We're happy to see you here today,
> Happy to see you, __(name)__ .

4. After the name, ask the person, "How are you today?"

5. All children and adults should be sung to and asked how they are.

IF'S, AND'S, OR BUT'S:

1. After a person has been sung to, he or she may choose the next person for the group to sing to.

2. Touch each person in some way when they are being greeted (e.g., shake hands, touch their arm, pat their shoulder), but do not force this if a person is uncomfortable. Ask the person how they would like to be touched.

3. In a family setting, parents may be called by their first name or by their role (mom, dad, pop, mother, etc.). Check with the parent to see which they prefer prior to beginning the activity.

FAMILY ACTIVITY:	17.7 Circle Time: Here's One Foot
CONSTRUCT:	Empathy
MATERIALS:	None

GOAL:

To increase positive parent-child interactions through play.

OBJECTIVES:

1. To involve children and parents in active and cooperative musical activities.

2. To foster creative expression through music.

PROCEDURES:

1. Request parents and children to stand in a circle to participate in this activity.

2. Ask everyone if they know the song "This Old Man." Sing a few bars so they know the melody.

3. Tell them that we are all going to pretend to be an old man who is going to do a variety of things.

4. Demonstrate what you want to do using the following verse:

Here's One Foot (This Old Man)

> Here's one foot, here are two.
> Each is wearing one new shoe.
> So I'll stand up, turn around,
> Dance around the floor,
> Dancing is what feet are for.

5. Alter the movement by suggesting or requesting from group the desired change. Some suggested movements: walk, run, tip toe, skip, march, etc.

IF'S, AND'S, OR BUT'S:

See if one of the parents wants to lead the activity.

FAMILY ACTIVITY:	**17.8 Nurturing Game and Family Hug**
CONSTRUCT:	**Behavior Management**
MATERIALS:	**Nurturing Game**

GOAL:

To reinforce appropriate social interactions through cooperative play.

OBJECTIVES:

1. To reinforce concepts of behavior management.

2. To increase self-awareness.

3. To foster positive touch interactions.

4. To reinforce comfort in using nurturing touch.

PROCEDURES:

1. Assemble children and adults in a circle sitting on the floor.

2. The goal of the game is to all begin at start and end up at "home." To get home, each player has to roll one die and move his/her game piece the appropriate number of squares.

3. Players land on colored squares that correspond to the following:

> **Orange** squares represent **self-awareness**.
>
> **Green** squares represent **behavior management**.
>
> **Pink** squares represent **touch**.
>
> **Yellow** squares represent **praise**.
>
> **Blue** squares represent **feelings**.

4. When a player lands on a square s/he has to pick up a card and complete the activity. There are no cards for pink and yellow squares. Each time a player (adult or child) lands on a pink square, s/he has to hug or touch someone in a nice way. Each time a player lands on a yellow square, s/he has to praise someone else.

5. The behavior management cards indicate a particular behavior occurred appropriately. The player may be rewarded by moving ahead one to three squares or penalized one to three squares for inappropriate behavior. Chance dictates behavior management.

6. Blue feeling cards and orange self-awareness cards are action cards that the players have to respond to. When the behavior is completed, the next person rolls the die.

FAMILY HUG:

1. End each home visit with a family hug. Everyone get in a circle and put your arms around the people next to you. During the family hug time, anyone can say anything they like. It is a time for free expression.

2. At a natural time, close the activities for the day.

IF'S, AND'S, OR BUT'S:

1. The goal is to encourage interactions between children and adults. The game is based on the programs' constructs and reinforces concepts presented throughout the program.

2. Younger children will need help playing the game and should be encouraged to play.

NURTURING PROGRAM FOR PARENTS AND CHILDREN BIRTH TO FIVE YEARS

SESSION 18

BEHAVIOR CONSTRUCT: Self-Awareness

SESSION CONCEPT: Handling Stress

BRIEF DESCRIPTION: Parents will discuss the concept of stress, complete a brief life stress measure, and experience the Sanctuary Visualization. Children and parents will engage in play and work together on a family collage.

INTENDED USE: For parents of children birth to 5 years

PREREQUISITE KNOWLEDGE: None

AGENDA

Parent Activities

		Materials
18.1	Icebreaker and Home Practice Check In	*Parent Handbooks*
18.2	Handling Stress	*Parent Handbooks*
18.3	Sanctuary Visualization	None
18.4	Home Practice Exercise	*Parent Handbooks*

Family Activities*

		Materials
18.5	Family Nurturing Time	*Nurturing Book for Babies and Children*
18.6	Hello Time: The Farmer in the Dell	None
18.7	Red Light, Green Light	Large area free of obstacles
18.8	Circle Time: Play	None
18.9	Family Collage and Family Hug	Magic markers, scissors, magazines, glue/tape, crayons, butcher block paper

*For parents with infants or toddlers, use activities presented in *Nurturing Book for Babies and Children*. For parents with preschoolers (ages 3-5), use the activities listed below Family Nurturing Time.

PARENT ACTIVITY: 18.1 Icebreaker and Home Practice Check In
CONSTRUCT: Self-Awareness
MATERIALS: Parent Handbooks

GOAL:

To increase parents' personal awareness of stress and its management.

OBJECTIVES:

1. To increase parents' understanding of stress.

2. To share stressful life situations.

3. To share ways of coping.

PROCEDURES:

1. Begin today's parent activities by having each adult respond to the following:

   ● One thing that creates a lot of stress in my life is _____ .

   ● One way I handle this stress is by _____ .

2. After each parent has had an opportunity to respond to the statements above, review the Home Practice Exercise from the previous meeting. Also discuss perceived changes in family members and their interactions as reported in the family log.

IF'S, AND'S, OR BUT'S:

Stress management is a good activity to discuss near holiday times.

PARENT ACTIVITY: 18.2 Handling Stress
CONSTRUCT: Self-Awareness
MATERIALS: Parent Handbooks

GOAL:

To gain a greater understanding of stress and how it impacts on lives.

OBJECTIVES:

1. To increase parents' ability to assess stress in their lives.

2. To increase parents' alternatives in handling stress.

3. To provide parents support in coping with stressful events.

4. To identify stressors in life and work on coping skills.

PROCEDURES:

1. Ask each parent to respond to the statement: Stress is. Get their reactions, perceptions, and beliefs of stress. Parents don't need to identify the causes of stress at this time.

2. Next ask parents to focus on how they create their own personal stress and how they can use their personal power to reduce stress. Have parents respond to the following:

   - One way I can use my personal power to reduce stress is by _____ .

3. Instruct parents to locate the information entitled **Life Stress Measure** on page 75 in their Handbooks. This measure is designed to assess the likelihood of an individual becoming ill or the probability that stress will effect a person's health. Ask each parent to complete the measure by:

   a. Circling the number before each life event that has occurred in the past 12 months.

   b. Filling in the number of points for each of the identified life events in the right hand column.

   c. Adding up the number of points and placing the total on the Total line.

4. After each parent has completed the measure, discuss the interpretation of the point total:

   a. Less than 150 points: There is less than 37% probability of becoming ill within two years.

   b. 150 to 300 points: There is 51% probability of becoming ill within two years.

   c. Over 300 points: There is 80% probability of becoming ill within two years.

5. Instruct parents to locate the information entitled **Stress Management Techniques** on page 76 in their Handbooks. To help parents reduce and manage stress, discuss the five major techniques:

   a. Organization: Spend less time on nonessentials: plan what you want to accomplish and when; schedule the day and pace yourself accordingly.

   b. Change your environment: Establish supporting relationships; change the furniture layout of your house or apartment.

   c. Improve communication skills: Practice assertiveness skills; learn to fight fairly or to gracefully retreat.

   d. Adopt a new attitude: Let go of the past and learn to live within the limits set down; learn to laugh; choose a more positive attitude.

   e. Build your stamina: Get regular exercise; improve your diet; learn relaxation skills.

IF'S, AND'S, OR BUT'S:

1. Taking responsibility for personal stress is one way to use personal power. Help parents understand they can do much to reduce their stress by identifying how they contribute to their own stress and taking actions to reduce the stress.

2. Stress recognition is the first step to handling stress. Management techniques are the answer to stress reduction.

GOAL:

To reinforce internal feelings of success in replacing the internal feelings of failure.

OBJECTIVES:

1. To relax parents.

2. To give parents confidence in their ability to handle situations.

3. To provide parents with a successful relaxation experience.

PROCEDURES:

1. Instruct the parents to get comfortable. Read the following to the parents:

Sanctuary

Imagine being outside in your own special space. Place anything in it you want: a lake, a beach, a river, a meadow, trees, flowers, birds . . . anything you want.

And now imagine a wall around this space. This wall is a safe wall to keep this special place totally safe. You can make this wall as tall as you want or as low as you want. It is your wall, and it is your own special place. There is one strong gate to this safe place and the gate is locked and you have the only key with you.

Enjoy the feeling of being in your own safe place. Enjoy the sunlight and the sky, enjoy the quiet and soft sounds. If you want to add anything or change anything, you can. You can have a spiritual guide keep you and your sanctuary free from all evil thoughts, to keep the evil thoughts out. If you want, you can do it yourself by always focusing on the good parts of the sanctuary. It is your own sanctuary.

Look around you again. See the wall, and see all the beauty in your sanctuary. Select the place you will go to the next time you come, or perhaps you will come back to the place you are right now. It is a beautiful and safe place, and now it's time to take your key out and walk towards the gate. You are going to unlock the gate of your sanctuary, and then lock it again behind you, so it will stay just as you left it, until you come again. Now, wiggle around a little, open your eyes, and sit up, whenever you're ready.

IF'S, AND'S, OR BUT'S:

It is important to read slowly and in a calm, reassuring voice for the visualization to be effective. Practice before you read to the group.

PARENT ACTIVITY: 18.4 Home Practice Exercise
CONSTRUCT: Self-Awareness, Empathy
MATERIALS: Parent Handbooks

GOAL:

To increase parents' ability to recognize and handle stress in self and children.

OBJECTIVES:

1. To become aware of stressors in life.

2. To practice new coping mechanisms.

3. To help children recognize and handle stress.

4. To establish a warm and supportive atmosphere.

PROCEDURES:

1. Instruct parents to locate the Home Practice Exercise on page 141 in their Handbooks. Review the exercise with them:

   a. Write down the number of times you felt stress, what caused the stress, and how you handled it.

   b. Practice handling stress with one of the new techniques learned.

   c. Complete family log.

2. Tell parents that in addition to the Home Practice Exercise, they are to spend 30 minutes each day with each of their children in nurturing playtime activities. Playtime is a time with the parent and child alone—no TV, no other distractions. Playing a game or reading books are good activities. From the *Nurturing Book for Babies and Children*, have the parents practice activities listed in the following sections: Activities for Infants, Activities for Toddlers, Activities for Preschoolers, or Infant and Child Massage. Have the parents remember what they did and report the next week.

IF'S, AND'S, OR BUT'S:

Reinforce the concept of personal power and how it can be used to reduce stress.

FAMILY ACTIVITY:	18.5 Family Nurturing Time
CONSTRUCT:	Empathy, Self-Awareness
MATERIALS:	Nurturing Book for Babies and Children

ACTIVITIES FOR INFANTS (Birth to 15 months):

Utilizing the *Nurturing Book for Babies and Children*, select activities from the sections entitled Activities for Infants or Infant and Child Massage. Engage parents in practicing songs, play and stimulation activities, or massage. Vary the activities weekly to sustain interest.

ACTIVITIES FOR TODDLERS (15 months to 3 years):

Utilizing the *Nurturing Book for Babies and Children*, select activities from the sections entitled Activities for Toddlers or Infant and Child Massage. Engage parents in practicing songs, play, language, and movement activities, or massage. Vary the activities weekly to sustain interest.

ACTIVITIES FOR PRESCHOOLERS (3-5 years):

Use the following activities when working with preschool children and their parents. Use the activities as the basis for involving infants and toddlers if you are conducting a home visit with children ages birth to five years.

FAMILY ACTIVITY:	18.6 Hello Time: The Farmer in the Dell
CONSTRUCT:	Empathy
MATERIALS:	None

GOAL:

To build positive parent-child interactions.

OBJECTIVES:

1. To help parents and children relate in a positive, nurturing way.

2. To help parents learn to enjoy their children.

PROCEDURES:

1. This is the traditional version of the Farmer in the Dell circle game.

2. Assemble children and adults holding hands in a circle.

3. Choose one child to stand in the center of the circle and be the "farmer."

4. The group moves in a circle around the "farmer" while singing. As the song calls for the farmer to "take a wife," have the child in the center of the circle choose another child or adult to join him inside the circle.

5. Continue in the same way until the verse "the cheese stands alone." Have the "cheese" stand in the center of the circle while the children sing that verse.

6. If the game is repeated, the person who was the "cheese" becomes the "farmer" for the new game.

The Farmer in the Dell

The farmer in the dell, the farmer in the dell,
Hi ho the dairy-o, the farmer in the dell.

The farmer takes a wife, the farmer takes a wife,
Hi ho the dairy-o, the farmer takes a wife.

The wife takes a child, the wife takes a child,
Hi ho the dairy-o, the wife takes a child.

The child takes a nurse, the child takes a nurse,
Hi ho the dairy-o, the child takes a nurse.

The nurse takes a dog, the nurse takes a dog,
Hi ho the dairy-o, the nurse takes a dog.

The dog takes a cat, the dog takes a cat,
Hi ho the dairy-o, the dog takes a cat.

The cat takes a rat, the cat takes a rat,
Hi ho the dairy-o, the cat takes a rat.

The rat takes the cheese, the rat takes the cheese,
Hi ho the dairy-o, the rat takes the cheese.

The cheese stands alone, the cheese stands alone,
Hi ho the dairy-o, the cheese stands alone.

IF'S, AND'S, OR BUT'S:

In small families you may to use objects such as dolls or pets to participate in the game.

FAMILY ACTIVITY:	**18.7 Red Light, Green Light**
CONSTRUCT:	**Behavior Management**
MATERIALS:	**Large area free of obstacles**

GOAL:

To reinforce behavior control.

OBJECTIVES:

1. To reinforce concept of natural consequences to behavior.

2. To reinforce family interactions.

PROCEDURES:

1. Have all family members seated on the floor in a semicircle prior to starting the activity.

2. Explain the rules of the game. One person stands in front of the group with his/her back toward the group. The remaining group members are standing behind. The goal is to sneak up on the person in front without being caught. The person in front says "Green Light," which gives the others permission to sneak up. At any time the person in front may yell "Red Light" and quickly turn around. If anyone is caught moving, he or she must return to the rear of the group and start over. The game ends when the person in front is touched by another. That person then gets to stand in front of the group. The game begins again.

3. Repeat the game for others to get a chance to be leader.

IF'S, AND'S, OR BUT'S:

1. Remind children to touch the one in front lightly.

2. Controversy may arise regarding whether a person was caught moving or not. You may have to act as the game official, whose job is to settle disputes.

3. A reminder: It is always wise to have people seated in a semicircle prior to the beginning of each activity. Such action serves to reduce inattentive behaviors and reinforces group cohesiveness.

FAMILY ACTIVITY:	**18.8 Circle Time: Play**
CONSTRUCT:	**Empathy**
MATERIALS:	**None**

GOAL:

To increase parents' knowledge of and ability to play.

OBJECTIVES:

1. To provide play experiences for parents and children.

2. To enable parents and children to experience games which are non-competitive, non-threatening, and fun.

PROCEDURES:

1. Define what play is, the importance of play, its relationship to fantasy, and how play differs from work.

2. Being able to play is a skill that people have to learn. Suggest that the best way to learn about play is by doing it.

3. Knots

   a. Everyone stand in a circle, shoulder to shoulder, and place your hands in the center.

   b. Join hands with others in the cirlce.

   c. If you ever want to get out of this (and we do), make sure no one holds the hands of a person right next to him/her.

   d. Now—the true test—get out.

   e. When at last the knot is unravelled, you'll find yourselves in one large circle or occasionally to interconnected ones.

   f. If there is one tangle which stops it all, you may administer knot-aid, a momentary break in hands.

   g. You could shake hands to celebrate successful completion and maybe you'll end up back in another knot.

4. Stand Up

   a. Sit on the floor, back-to-back, knees bent and elbows linked.

   b. Now—simply stand up.

   c. To achieve standing up, start by sitting close and firmly packed. Then all stand up quickly at precisely the same moment. Hopefully everyone will be able to discover this on his/her own and won't need directions.

5. Lap Sit

   a. Everyone stand in a circle shoulder-to-shoulder.

   b. Now turn to the right.

   c. Now, very gently everybody sit down in the lap of the person behind them.

   d. The largest number to do this was 1,468!

   e. Now wave your arms out to the sides. If you fly, you'll be the first. If you fall over, you'll be in good company.

IF'S, AND'S, OR BUT'S:

The size difference between adults and children should encourage more cooperation for the games to be played.

FAMILY ACTIVITY: 18.9 Family Collage and Family Hug
CONSTRUCT: Empathy
MATERIALS: Magic markers, scissors, magazines, glue/tape, crayons, butcher block paper

GOAL:

To facilitate family interactions through cooperative art activity.

OBJECTIVES:

1. To have children and parents work cooperatively on an art activity.

2. To continue building family cohesiveness through cooperative activity.

3. To reinforce comfort in using nurturing touch.

PROCEDURES:

1. Have one large sheet of butcher block paper. Assign each person of the family a section of the paper to draw, color, and paste pictures on.

2. Children and parents can put anything they want on the collage.

3. At the end, hang the collage and invite all to admire the art work.

FAMILY HUG:

1. End each home visit with a family hug. Everyone get in a circle and put your arms around the people next to you. During the family hug time, anyone can say anything they like. It is a time for free expression.

2. At a natural time, close the activities for the day.

IF'S, AND'S, OR BUT'S:

1. If you're working with children only, assign each to a large enough section of paper to work on to reduce any possible conflicts.

2. Make sure you have plenty of markers and crayons for them to use to draw.

NURTURING PROGRAM FOR PARENTS AND CHILDREN BIRTH TO FIVE YEARS
SESSION 19

BEHAVIOR CONSTRUCT: Empathy

SESSION CONCEPT: Establishing a Nurturing Diapering and Dressing Routine

BRIEF DESCRIPTION: Parents will learn about nurturing routines and how to establish a nurturing routine during times they have to diaper and dress their children. Children will discuss the concept fear and will engage in finger painting.

INTENDED USE: For parents of children birth to 5 years

PREREQUISITE KNOWLEDGE: Praise

AGENDA

Parent Activities

		Materials
19.1	Icebreaker and Home Practice Check In	*Parent Handbooks*
19.2	Nurturing Routines	*Parent Handbooks*, **Nurturing Routines/Diapering and Dressing Your Child** AV presentation, AV equipment
19.3	Diapering and Dressing Nurturing Routines	Same as listed for 19.2
19.4	Home Practice Exercise	*Parent Handbooks*

Family Activities*

		Materials
19.5	Family Nurturing Time	*Nurturing Book for Babies and Children*
19.6	Hello Time: I Get Scared When	None
19.7	Duck, Duck, Goose	None
19.8	Circle Time: Fear	Puppets
19.9	Finger Painting and Family Hug	Finger paint, paint smocks, finger paint paper

*For parents with infants or toddlers, use activities presented in *Nurturing Book for Babies and Children*. For parents with preschoolers (ages 3-5), use the activities listed below Family Nurturing Time.

PARENT ACTIVITY: 19.1 Icebreaker and Home Practice Check In
CONSTRUCT: Empathy
MATERIALS: Parent Handbooks

GOAL:

To reinforce parents' ability to be empathic to the feelings of others.

OBJECTIVES:

1. To increase parents' attempts to communicate their feelings to others.

2. To encourage parents to facilitate communication.

PROCEDURES:

1. Begin today's parent activities by having each adult respond to the following:

    *   Something I once said to someone that I wish I could take back is _____ .

    *   What I would like to say instead is _____ .

2. After each parent has had an opportunity to respond to the statements above, review the Home Practice Exercise from the previous meeting. Also discuss perceived changes in family members and their interactions as reported in the family log.

IF'S, AND'S, OR BUT'S:

Continued emphasis on empathy, the ability to be aware of the feelings and needs of others, will serve to solidify desired parenting behaviors.

PARENT ACTIVITY: 19.2 Nurturing Routines
CONSTRUCT: Empathy
MATERIALS: Parent Handbooks, Nurturing Routines/Diapering and Dressing
                   Your Child AV presentation, AV equipment

GOAL:

To increase parents' ability to establish nurturing routines with their children.

OBJECTIVES:

1. To increase parents' awareness of nurturing routines.

2. To identify parent-child interactions where nurturing routines could be established.

3. To discuss the value of establishing nurturing routines.

PROCEDURES:

1. If you are using the audio-visual programs, present the AV entitled **Nurturing Routines**. Stop the filmstrip or video before **Diapering and Dressing Your Child** begins.

2. Instruct parents to locate the information entitled **Establishing Nurturing Routines** on pages 77-79 in their Handbooks. Utilize the information presented to discuss the following major concepts with the parents:

   a. A routine is a consistent way of doing things.

   b. A nurturing routine is a consistent way of doing things that enhances a child's self-esteem and self-concept.

   c. Nurturing routines help establish:

   - Consistency
   - Empathy
   - Positive Self-Esteem
   - Positive Self-Concept

   d. Nurturing routines consist of:

   - Gentle positive touch
   - Praise for being and doing
   - Pleasant expressions and tone of voice
   - Empathic caregivers
   - Fun
   - Consistency

   e. Nurturing routines should be established for:

   - Diapering and Dressing Times
   - Feeding Times
   - Bath Time
   - Bedtime

IF'S, AND'S, OR BUT'S:

The nurturing routine concept embodies all the major goals of the program into action. Discussing the concept is necessary before teaching the parents how to implement the behavior.

GOAL:

To increase parents' ability to establish a nurturing parenting routine during diapering and dressing times.

OBJECTIVES:

1. To increase parents' awareness of the relationship between learning to dress and independence.

2. To increase parents' perception of diapering and dressing as a partnership.

3. To help parents implement a nurturing diapering and dressing routine.

PROCEDURES:

1. If you are using the audio-visual programs, present the AV entitled **Diapering and Dressing Your Child**.

2. Instruct parents to locate the information entitled **Nurturing Diapering and Dressing Routines** on pages 80-82 in their Handbooks. Utilize the information presented to discuss the following major concepts with the parents:

   a. Children like to do things for themselves.

      - Children develop autonomy.

      - Children develop a sense of independence.

   b. Dressing and diapering children is a partnership.

   c. In establishing a nurturing routine during diapering and dressing:

      - **Step 1.** Let your children have input into what they are going to wear.

      - **Step 2.** Allow your children to do the things they can do by themselves without any help from you.

      - **Step 3.** Assist your children in getting dressed but allow them to still have the lead.

      - **Step 4.** Take the lead and do the things for them that they can't do themselves.

   d. Knowing when to use the steps:

      - Observe your children closely and notice what they can do by themselves.

      - On the tasks they can't do, break them down into smaller steps and support their attempts and accomplishments.

      - The partnership method of diapering and dressing should begin in infancy and continue through childhood.

Not wanting to do everything for a child will be very difficult for many parents. Parents in this role generally perceive themselves as "knowing more and being more capable" than children or fostering feelings of dependency. The issue at hand is not supremacy or dependency, but rather empathy and encouraging the development of autonomy.

PARENT ACTIVITY: 19.4 Home Practice Exercise
CONSTRUCT: Empathy
MATERIALS: Parent Handbooks

GOAL:

To provide parents with practice in implementing a nurturing routine during dressing and diapering.

OBJECTIVES:

1. To promote empathic parent-child interactions.

2. To enhance child development.

3. To promote a positive self-concept and self-esteem in parents and children.

4. To establish a warm and supportive atmosphere.

PROCEDURES:

1. Instruct parents to locate the Home Practice Exercise on page 141 in their Handbooks. Review the exercise with them:

   a. Practice implementing the nurturing diapering and dressing routine with each of your children.

   b. Complete family log.

2. Tell parents that in addition to the Home Practice Exercise, they are to spend 30 minutes each day with each of their children in nurturing playtime activities. Playtime is a time with the parent and child alone — no TV, no other distractions. Playing a game or reading books are good activities. From the *Nurturing Book for Babies and Children*, have the parents practice activities listed in the following sections: Activities for Infants, Activities for Toddlers, Activities for Preschoolers, or Infant and Child Massage. Have the parents remember what they did and report the next week.

IF'S, AND'S, OR BUT'S:

Effectively using the routine will take some practice. Keep referring back to this exercise throughout the program to monitor progress.

FAMILY ACTIVITY:	19.5 Family Nurturing Time
CONSTRUCT:	Empathy, Self-Awareness
MATERIALS:	Nurturing Book for Babies and Children

ACTIVITIES FOR INFANTS (Birth to 15 months):

Utilizing the *Nurturing Book for Babies and Children*, select activities from the sections entitled Activities for Infants or Infant and Child Massage. Engage parents in practicing songs, play and stimulation activities, or massage. Vary the activities weekly to sustain interest.

ACTIVITIES FOR TODDLERS (15 months to 3 years):

Utilizing the *Nurturing Book for Babies and Children*, select activities from the sections entitled Activities for Toddlers or Infant and Child Massage. Engage parents in practicing songs, play, language, and movement activities, or massage. Vary the activities weekly to sustain interest.

ACTIVITIES FOR PRESCHOOLERS (3-5 years):

Use the following activities when working with preschool children and their parents. Use the activities as the basis for involving infants and toddlers if you are conducting a home visit with children ages birth to five years.

FAMILY ACTIVITY:	19.6 Hello Time: I Get Scared When
CONSTRUCT:	Self-Awareness
MATERIALS:	None

GOAL:

To increase children's awareness of feelings of being scared.

OBJECTIVES:

1. To identify feelings of "scared."

2. To become aware of scary situations.

PROCEDURES:

1. Assemble children and adults in a circle sitting on the floor.

2. Briefly discuss the feeling "scared."

3. Have everyone respond to the following statements:

    - Today I'm feeling _____ .

    - I get scared when _____ .

Children will generally respond that they feel scared when left alone, at night, when they see monsters, etc. Listen for the responses that suggest extreme or unusual fears, or feelings of being scared when with a particular person. The child may be hinting about possible sexual or physical abuse.

FAMILY ACTIVITY:	**19.7 Duck, Duck, Goose**
CONSTRUCT:	**Developmental**
MATERIALS:	**None**

GOAL:

To increase positive social interactions among children and parents.

OBJECTIVES:

1. To increase children's ability to follow simple rules.

2. To use big and small muscle movements.

3. To play cooperatively in structured activity.

4. To have fun.

PROCEDURES:

1. Have children and adults sit in a circle. Remove obstacles in immediate area for room to run around circle.

2. Select one child who will be "It." "It" walks around the circle tapping each child and adult on the shoulder saying, "Duck."

3. After tapping several people, "It" must tap someone saying, "Goose!" and then "Goose" chases "It" back to the empty spot in the circle.

4. If "It" is tagged by "Goose" before sitting down, the person remains "It." If not, "Goose" becomes "It" and Steps 2 and 3 are repeated.

IF'S, AND'S, OR BUT'S:

This is a very popular game among children. Although it serves as a nice gross motor exercise, caution the overuse of the game.

GOAL:

To increase the children's ability to identify and respond with judgments appropriate to social, emotional, and physical developmental issues.

OBJECTIVES:

1. To increase child's understanding of the concept of fear.

2. To increase child's ability to recognize feelings of fear.

3. To increase child's ability to effectively manage feelings of fear.

PROCEDURES:

1. Today we are going to talk about fear. Can someone tell me what fear means? (Wait for response and reinforce.) Does anyone here ever get scared or have fears? (Wait for response and reinforce.) Fear is a feeling that we can use our personal power to help control. We control fear by doing something to help us feel less afraid. I will read you some statements, and you tell us if you would be scared, and then tell us after each statement how you could use your personal power to stop being scared. (You may choose to use puppets to act out the following.)

   a. Watching a TV movie with ghosts and monsters. (Watch with someone; turn set off; look for funny things.)

   b. Being all alone at night in your bedroom. (Sleep with light on.)

   c. Being lost. (Ask police officer for help.)

   d. Strange noises in your home. (Tell parents and investigate.)

   e. A big dog comes by you. (Call for help; walk away.)

IF'S, AND'S, OR BUT'S:

When talking about fear, the anxiety some children have may be exhibited in acting out, silly behavior. Confront child by asking if _____ is scary to talk about. Help the child understand his/her anxieties.

FAMILY ACTIVITY: 19.9 Finger Painting and Family Hug
CONSTRUCT: Self-Awareness
MATERIALS: Finger paint, paint smocks, finger paint paper

GOAL:

To participate in creative artistic expression involving tactile stimulation.

OBJECTIVES:

1. To participate in an art activity involving physical and tactile sensory experience.

2. To engage in creative, original self-expression that is appropriate to each child's individual social and developmental level.

3. To give and accept nurturing physical contact appropriately as part of self-help activities.

4. To reinforce comfort in using nurturing touch.

PROCEDURES:

1. Tell the children that today they will be doing finger painting during art. It's best to use something to protect the table or floor from the paint.

2. Demonstrate finger painting with emphasis on various ways of painting: painting with the whole hand, individual fingers, fist, elbow, etc. Encourage exploration.

3. Allow the children time to put their hands into the paint unassisted. If a child does not respond, encourage him/her individually in order to get some type of involvement.

4. Talk about the texture and feel of the paint.

5. Finger painting may be done either directly on the table top (or on oilcloth to protect the table) or on finger paint paper. Paper should be wet before painting.

6. Paintings on the tabletop may be saved by placing a piece of paper over the painted surface and rubbing the paper to transfer the design.

FAMILY HUG:

1. End each home visit with a family hug. Everyone get in a circle and put your arms around the people next to you. During the family hug time, anyone can say anything they like. It is a time for free expression.

9. At a natural time, close the activities for the day.

IF'S, AND'S, OR BUT'S:

Should be a fun activity. Utilize cleanup time to provide nurturing physical contact.

NURTURING PROGRAM FOR PARENTS AND CHILDREN BIRTH TO FIVE YEARS

SESSION 20

BEHAVIOR CONSTRUCT:	Empathy
SESSION CONCEPT:	Establishing a Nurturing Feeding Routine
BRIEF DESCRIPTION:	Parents learn how to establish a nurturing parent-child routine during feeding times. Children discuss who is a stranger and how to respond to strangers.
INTENDED USE:	For parents of children birth to 5 years
PREREQUISITE KNOWLEDGE:	Nurturing Routines, Diapering and Dressing, Praise

AGENDA

Parent Activities

	Materials
20.1 Icebreaker and Home Practice Check In	*Parent Handbooks*
20.2 Nurturing Feeding Routine	*Parent Handbooks*, **Yum Yum Eat 'Em Up** AV presentation, AV equipment
20.3 Home Practice Exercise	*Parent Handbooks*

Family Activities*

	Materials
20.4 Family Nurturing Time	*Nurturing Book for Babies and Children*
20.5 Hello Time: Where is _____ ?	None
20.6 Tall and Small	None
20.7 Circle Time Strangers	Puppets
20.8 I'm Someone Special and Family Hug	Construction paper, string, safety pins, magic markers, scissors

*For parents with infants or toddlers, use activities presented in *Nurturing Book for Babies and Children*. For parents with preschoolers (ages 3-5), use the activities listed below Family Nurturing Time.

PARENT ACTIVITY: 20.1 Icebreaker and Home Practice Check In
CONSTRUCT: Self-Awareness
MATERIALS: Parent Handbooks

GOAL:

To increase parents' awareness of accomplishments and mistakes made during life.

OBJECTIVES:

1. To encourage parents to look at the good and not solely the bad.

2. To reinforce self-introspection.

PROCEDURES:

1. Begin today's parent activities by having each adult respond to the following:

   - The single biggest accomplishment of my life so far is _____ .

   - The single biggest mistake I ever made was _____ .

2. After each parent has had an opportunity to respond to the statements above, review the Home Practice Exercise from the previous meeting. Also discuss perceived changes in family members and their interactions as reported in the family log.

IF'S, AND'S, OR BUT'S:

Ask parents to explain the contributing factors associated with their major accomplishment and mistake. Check for patterns; important ingredients that may not be present now.

PARENT ACTIVITY: 20.2 Nurturing Feeding Routine
CONSTRUCT: Empathy
MATERIALS: Parent Handbooks, Yum Yum Eat 'Em Up AV presentation, AV equipment

GOAL:

To increase parents' ability to establish a nurturing parenting routine during feeding times.

OBJECTIVES:

1. To discuss why feeding time goes from a purely enjoyable experience to one of frustration for both parents and children.

2. To increase parents' knowledge of the importance of feeding times.

3. To increase parents' ability to establish a nurturing feeding time routine.

PROCEDURES:

1. If you are using the audio-visual programs, present the AV entitled **Yum Yum Eat 'Em Up**.

2. Instruct parents to locate the information entitled **Nurturing Feeding Time Routine** on pages 83-88 in their Handbooks. Utilize the information presented to discuss the following major concepts with the parents:

   a. The importance of feeding times:

      - Babies know how much they need to eat.

      - Babies learn a lot about themselves through their earliest experiences in eating.

      - Babies lose weight initially, then double their weight in the first 3 to 5 months.

      - Around one year of age, babies become more choosy and less hungry.

      - Teething often takes away a child's appetite.

   b. Establishing a nurturing feeding time routine:

      - Provide your child with a comfortable eating environment.

      - Allow your child the opportunity to reject food.

      - Reinforce personal choice in eating.

      - Allow children to eat larger than usual amounts of one wholesome food than others.

      - Encourage children to begin to feed themselves beginning around 12 to 15 months.

      - Encourage children to use a spoon to eat with.

      - Expect feeding to be a messy experience.

      - Praise your child for his efforts in eating.

IF'S, AND'S, OR BUT'S:

The thought of allowing young children to feed themselves with all the resulting messiness will probably be the biggest concern many parents have. Explore the issue with them. Encourage parents to practice having children feed themselves while you are there.

PARENT ACTIVITY:	**20.3 Home Practice Exercise**
CONSTRUCT:	**Empathy**
MATERIALS:	**Parent Handbooks**

GOAL:

To provide parents with practice in implementing a nurturing routine during feeding times.

OBJECTIVES:

1. To promote empathic parent-child interactions.

2. To enhance child development.

3. To promote a positive self-concept and self-esteem in parents and children.

4. To establish a warm and supportive atmosphere.

PROCEDURES:

1. Instruct parents to locate the Home Practice Exercise on page 141 in their Handbooks. Review the exercise with them:

   a. Practice implementing the nurturing feeding routine with each of your children.

   b. Continue implementing the nurturing routine during diapering and dressing.

   c. Complete family log.

2. Tell parents that in addition to the Home Practice Exercise, they are to spend 30 minutes each day with each of their children in nurturing playtime activities. Playtime is a time with the parent and child alone — no TV, no other distractions. Playing a game or reading books are good activities. From the *Nurturing Book for Babies and Children*, have the parents practice activities listed in the following sections: Activities for Infants, Activities for Toddlers, Activities for Preschoolers, or Infant and Child Massage. Have the parents remember what they did and report the next week.

IF'S, AND'S, OR BUT'S:

Two routines may be overwhelming for some families. Offer your support and encouragement to try.

FAMILY ACTIVITY: 20.4 Family Nurturing Time
CONSTRUCT: Empathy, Self-Awareness
MATERIALS: Nurturing Book for Babies and Children

ACTIVITIES FOR INFANTS (Birth to 15 months):

Utilizing the *Nurturing Book for Babies and Children*, select activities from the sections entitled Activities for Infants or Infant and Child Massage. Engage parents in practicing songs, play and stimulation activities, or massage. Vary the activities weekly to sustain interest.

ACTIVITIES FOR TODDLERS (15 months to 3 years):

Utilizing the *Nurturing Book for Babies and Children*, select activities from the sections entitled Activities for Toddlers or Infant and Child Massage. Engage parents in practicing songs, play, language, and movement activities, or massage. Vary the activities weekly to sustain interest.

ACTIVITIES FOR PRESCHOOLERS (3-5 years):

Use the following activities when working with preschool children and their parents. Use the activities as the basis for involving infants and toddlers if you are conducting a home visit with children ages birth to five years.

FAMILY ACTIVITY: 20.5 Hello Time: Where is _____?
CONSTRUCT: Empathy
MATERIALS: None

GOAL:

To have children gain an awareness of others in the group.

OBJECTIVES:

1. To greet each child and adult by their first name.

2. To increase recognition of the needs of others.

3. To have fun in family interactions.

PROCEDURES:

1. Children and adults should be seated in a circle on the floor.

2. Ask everyone if they know the tune "Frere Jacques." Hum the tune and see if they recognize the melody. It is a good idea to have the children hum or sing the tune with you without any words a couple of times to ensure they know the song.

3. Using the tune of "Frere Jacques," sing the following words, first alone, and then once with the group. Use your first name (or the name of a parent) and identify an activity (suggest running or hopping).

   Where is _____?

   Where is __(name)__ ? Where is __(name)__ ?
   Please stand up, please stand up.

   (Dance, hop, run, etc.) around the group __(name)__ .
   (Dance, hop, run, etc.) around the group __(name)__ .

   Then sit down, then sit down.

4. Explain that everyone will have a chance to get up and move when it is their turn.

5. Choose a child to begin. Sing the song, inserting the movement. Allow the child to choose the next person, or the adult may choose who is next.

IF'S, AND'S, OR BUT'S:

1. For variation, ask for movement suggestions from the group. Children especially like to choose movements for adults and view this as a good joke. The response of the adult to this teasing provides a good model for behavior.

2. Noncompliant children may be encouraged if they are allowed to take a turn with a friend. Vary the song to include two people. Example: "Where are Jesse and Chad?"

FAMILY ACTIVITY:	20.6 Tall and Small
CONSTRUCT:	Self-Awareness
MATERIALS:	None

GOAL:

To increase family cohesion through movement activities.

OBJECTIVES:

1. To use large muscles.

2. To increase language and cognition.

3. To experience success through participation and repetition.

4. To reinforce patience (appropriate need delay).

PROCEDURES:

1. Children and adults are seated in a circle on the floor.

2. Introduce activity by demonstrating the exercise. Children should watch during this time.

> *Words:* Now I'm small.
> *Movement:* Squat or crouch position on floor.
>
> *Words:* But now I'm tall.
> *Movement:* Jump up and reach up with arms.
>
> *Words:* Now I'm so little you can't see me at all.
> *Movement:* Crouch on floor and hide face with hands.
>
> *Words:* See me grow, grow, grow.
> *Movement:* Slowly stand up and reach arms up.
>
> *Words:* Now I'm a giant with a ho-ho-ho.
> *Movement:* Stand on tip-toes and pat stomach while saying "ho-ho-ho."

3. Repeat activity and encourage children to participate. Proceed slowly so that all children in the group can keep up with the pace.

4. Repeat the activity 2 or 3 times until children are able to perform the actions with the accompanying words.

IF'S, AND'S, OR BUT'S:

With a very young child, or a child who is reluctant to participate, an adult may attempt to assist the child by gently, physically prompting the child through the movements.

FAMILY ACTIVITY: 20.7 Circle Time: Strangers
CONSTRUCT: Developmental
MATERIALS: Puppets

GOAL:

To increase the children's ability to identify and respond with judgments appropriate to social, emotional, and physical developmental issues.

OBJECTIVES:

1. To increase the child's understanding of interactions with strangers.

2. To increase the child's ability to effectively manage his or her own behavior related to interactions with strangers.

3. To understand the cautions associated with interactions with strangers.

PROCEDURES:

1. Today we are going to talk about strangers. Can someone tell me who a stranger is? (Wait for response and reinforce.) Why should we be concerned about talking to strangers? (Wait for response and reinforce.) What might happen if you talk to strangers? (Wait for response and, if necessary, discuss.) I will read you some stories and you tell me what you should do. (You may want to use the puppets to tell the stories.)

   a. You are walking home from your friend's, or from school, and a car pulls up next to the curb. The man driving the car says your mom sent him to pick you up and take you home. You don't know the man. What should you do?

   b. You are having fun at the playground when a stranger asks you if he/she can play with you. As he/she pushes you on a swing, he/she tells you he/she would like to go for a walk with you. What should you do?

   c. Has anyone ever been frightened by a stranger?

   d. Has anyone ever been helped by a stranger?

   e. Should we ever ask for help from strangers? (Yes, from police, teachers, doctors, etc.).

IF'S, AND'S, OR BUT'S:

1. Open the discussion by asking if relatives or parents of friends can also be strangers.

2. Discuss how strangers are often nice people who can help you when you're lost, open doors, or help carry packages.

3. Discuss how to recognize strangers from professionals (police, fire person, social worker, etc.).

FAMILY ACTIVITY: 20.8 I'm Someone Special and Family Hug
CONSTRUCT: Self-Awareness, Developmental
MATERIALS: Construction paper, string, safety pins, magic markers, scissors

GOAL:

To reinforce feelings of self-esteem and self-concept.

OBJECTIVES:

1. To reinforce positive feelings of self.

2. To demonstrate support for self.

3. To remind children of positive experiences in program.

4. To reinforce comfort in using nurturing touch.

PROCEDURES:

1. Have parents and children sit in a circle on the floor.

2. Explain that we are going to make ourselves special badges that shows everyone how special we really are.

3. The special badges can say anything that indicates something positive of themselves. Brainstorm some ideas for badges: I'm me, I'm special, I like me, etc.

4. Help the children design their badges in the shape of a circle or heart.

5. Have everyone cut badge out and pin to shirt, or put string through both ends and encourage everyone to wear badges around their necks.

FAMILY HUG:

1. End each home visit with a family hug. Everyone get in a circle and put your arms around the people next to you. During the family hug time, anyone can say anything they like. It is a time for free expression.

2. At a natural time, close the activities for the day.

IF'S, AND'S, OR BUT'S:

Badges are encouragement for children to remember how special they are.

NURTURING PROGRAM FOR PARENTS AND CHILDREN BIRTH TO FIVE YEARS

SESSION 21

BEHAVIOR CONSTRUCT: Child Development

SESSION CONCEPT: Nutrition and Dinner Time

BRIEF DESCRIPTION: Parents discuss important facts about proper nutrition and ways to make dinner time more fun. Children identify who their favorite friend is and learn to talk to a friend when they need help or feel badly.

INTENDED USE: For parents of children birth to 5 years

PREREQUISITE KNOWLEDGE: Establishing a Nurturing Feeding Routine

---

AGENDA

Parent Activities	Materials
21.1 Icebreaker and Home Practice Check In	*Parent Handbooks*
21.2 Nutrition and Dinner Time	*Parent Handbooks*
21.3 Home Practice Exercise	*Parent Handbooks*

Family Activities*	Materials
21.4 Family Nurturing Time	*Nurturing Book for Babies and Children*
21.5 Hello Time: My Favorite Friend	None
21.6 Over and Under	Small objects to pass
21.7 Circle Time: Telling A Friend	Puppets
21.8 Hand Mural and Family Hug	4-5 large pie plates, aluminum foil, tempera paints, (4-5 colors), long sheets of butcher block paper

*For parents with infants or toddlers, use activities presented in *Nurturing Book for Babies and Children*. For parents with preschoolers (ages 3-5), use the activities listed below Family Nurturing Time.

PARENT ACTIVITY: 21.1 Icebreaker and Home Practice Check In
CONSTRUCT: Child Development
MATERIALS: Parent Handbooks

GOAL:

To increase parents' awareness of their feelings and attitudes about dinner time.

OBJECTIVES:

1. To help parents become aware of their family interaction patterns during eating times.

2. To begin discussion of how dinner times can be more pleasant.

PROCEDURES:

1. Begin today's parent activities by having each adult respond to the following:

   - Dinner time when I was a kid was _____ .

   - Dinner time in my house now is _____ .

   - One way I can make dinner time more pleasant is by _____ .

2. After each parent has had an opportunity to respond to the statements above, review the Home Practice Exercise from the previous meeting. Also discuss perceived changes in family members and their interactions as reported in the family log.

IF'S, AND'S, OR BUT'S:

1. Dinner time is often remembered as a time of strict, harsh rules for many parents when they were kids. It's not surprising that many families still express old harsh attitudes. Dinner time and eating should be fun times. Listen for parents who express troubles getting kids to eat. Eating is one area where children can display autonomy and rebel.

2. When parents describe dinner time when they were kids, ask them to focus on the conversation, manners, food, attitudes, etc.

PARENT ACTIVITY: 21.2 Nutrition and Dinner Time
CONSTRUCT: Child Development
MATERIALS: Parent Handbooks

GOAL:

To increase parents' ability to make judgments about appropriate diet and mealtime behavior.

OBJECTIVES:

1. To increase parents' knowledge of general nutrition facts.

2. To increase parents' awareness of their feelings about food and eating.

3. To increase parents' skills in handling mealtime behaviors.

PROCEDURES:

1. Write on paper or say the word: FOOD.

2. Have parents freely associate other words: "What is it, how do you like it, when do you want it, what's your fantasy food, what will it do for you?"

3. Instruct parents to locate the information entitled **Nurturing Feeding Time Routine** on pages 83-88 in their Handbooks. Discuss with the parents the diet habits of their children and themselves. Do parents model eating the right foods? Are children hearing mom telling them to eat nutritious foods but seeing mom eating junk food?

4. Review each of the suggestions to get kids to acquire proper eating habits.

IF'S, AND'S, OR BUT'S:

1. Help parents brainstorm ways to get children to eat more nutritious foods if the discussion begins to go in that direction. Suggesting to eat proper foods may only be half the problem; getting the kids to eat the food may be as important an issue.

2. Mealtimes can be very unpleasant for some families. Tie in earlier exercises regarding family rules and behavior management to assist parents in this exercise.

PARENT ACTIVITY: **21.3 Home Practice Exercise**
CONSTRUCT: **Child Development**
MATERIALS: **Parent Handbooks**

GOAL:

To encourage more pleasant mealtime experiences.

OBJECTIVES:

1. To practice new ways to make mealtime more pleasant.

2. To encourage the use of appropriate nutrition.

3. To establish a warm and supportive atmosphere.

PROCEDURES:

1. Instruct parents to locate the Home Practice Exercise on page 141 in their Handbooks. Review the exercise with them:

    a. Do one thing to make family dinner time nicer.

    b. Serve a nutritious snack.

    c. Practice Nurturing Routines.

    d. Complete family log.

---

2. Tell parents that in addition to the Home Practice Exercise, they are to spend 30 minutes each day with each of their children in nurturing playtime activities. Playtime is a time with the parent and child alone—no TV, no other distractions. Playing a game or reading books are good activities. From the *Nurturing Book for Babies and Children*, have the parents practice activities listed in the following sections: Activities for Infants, Activities for Toddlers, Activities for Preschoolers, or Infant and Child Massage. Have the parents remember what they did and report the next week.

IF'S, AND'S, OR BUT'S:

Praise parents' efforts in completing the Home Practice Exercise.

FAMILY ACTIVITY:	**21.4 Family Nurturing Time**
CONSTRUCT:	**Empathy, Self-Awareness**
MATERIALS:	**Nurturing Book for Babies and Children**

ACTIVITIES FOR INFANTS (Birth to 15 months):

Utilizing the *Nurturing Book for Babies and Children*, select activities from the sections entitled Activities for Infants or Infant and Child Massage. Engage parents in practicing songs, play and stimulation activities, or massage. Vary the activities weekly to sustain interest.

ACTIVITIES FOR TODDLERS (15 months to 3 years):

Utilizing the *Nurturing Book for Babies and Children*, select activities from the sections entitled Activities for Toddlers or Infant and Child Massage. Engage parents in practicing songs, play, language, and movement activities, or massage. Vary the activities weekly to sustain interest.

ACTIVITIES FOR PRESCHOOLERS (3-5 years):

Use the following activities when working with preschool children and their parents. Use the activities as the basis for involving infants and toddlers if you are conducting a home visit with children ages birth to five years.

FAMILY ACTIVITY:	**21.5 Hello Time: My Favorite Friend**
CONSTRUCT:	**Empathy**
MATERIALS:	**None**

GOAL:

To increase social interactions among children in program.

OBJECTIVES:

1. To identify friendships.

2. To reinforce social relationships.

PROCEDURES:

1. Have children and adults sit in a circle on the floor.

2. Have each child and adult respond to the following statements:

   • Right now I am feeling _____ .

   • My favorite friend is _____ .

IF'S, AND'S, OR BUT'S:

1. If children can respond why the person is their favorite friend, pursue the issue.

2. You may need to clarify for the children what a "friend" is.

FAMILY ACTIVITY:	**21.6 Over and Under**
CONSTRUCT:	**Developmental**
MATERIALS:	**Small objects to pass**

GOAL:

To facilitate group interactions through play.

OBJECTIVES:

1. To help children play cooperatively with others.

2. To increase children's appropriate social interactions.

3. To increase children's fine and gross motor coordination.

PROCEDURES:

Listed below is a game that requires adults and children to cooperate.

Over and Under

Have children and adults line up with their legs apart.

The first person passes an object (ball, eraser, etc.) over his/her head to the second person, who passes it through his/her legs to the third person, who passes it over his/her head, and so on.

The last person runs to the beginning of the line and starts the object over his/her head again.

When the first person returns to the head of the line, the relay is finished.

1. If you have enough people for two teams, you can have a friendly race.

2. Add some excitement to the game by requiring speed — the faster you pass the object, the better.

FAMILY ACTIVITY:	**21.7 Circle Time: Telling a Friend**
CONSTRUCT:	**Developmental Expectations**
MATERIALS:	**Puppets**

GOAL:

To increase the children's ability to identify and respond with judgments appropriate to social, emotional, and physical developmental issues.

OBJECTIVES:

1. To increase the child's understanding of the concept of asking for help.

2. To increase the child's ability to effectively communicate to others their fears, concerns, and problems.

PROCEDURES:

1. Today we are going to talk about telling others your problems and how you feel. Does anybody here ever tell anyone their problems, or how they feel? Who is your favorite person to tell things to? I'm going to read some stories and let's see if anyone can tell me how they can use their personal power to solve a problem.

   a. Your best friend has just hurt herself and you feel real sad. She is your best friend and you can't see her for several days and can't play with her for several weeks. You're sad and you go home and your mom asks you what's wrong. You look sad. You say loudly, "Nothing is wrong!" What would be better to say?

   b. There is a guy you know who is a bully. Does everyone know what a bully is? (Wait for response.) This bully likes to hit other kids and threaten them. He picks on you every day and says he is going to beat you up. Since the bully is bigger and older than you, he scares you. What should you do? (Reinforce concept of telling others and asking for help.)

2. Calling puppets by their names, act out the following situations:

   Two puppets are sitting talking to each other. Puppet #2 has bruises and a bandage on his/her head. Puppet #1 is asking Puppet #2 where and how s/he got hurt.

   Puppet #1: Puppet #2, you look a mess. You have scratches on your arms and a bandage on your head. Did you fall down?

   Puppet #2: No, Puppet #1. I didn't fall down. I got hurt another way but I can't tell you. I'm too embarrassed.

Puppet #1: You mean you didn't fall down? Did someone hit you or push you down?

Puppet #2: Yes, but I can't tell you. I just can't.

Leader: Why do you think Puppet #2 can't tell anyone?

Puppet #1: Why?

Puppet #2: Because, if I tell you then I'm going to be in big trouble. I might even be hit again.

Puppet #1: That sounds real bad.

Puppet #2: I'll only tell you if you promise not to tell anyone.

Puppet #1: You can't tell anyone, not even your parents?

Puppet #2: Yesterday my (mom, dad, brother, uncle, etc.) got real angry at me and hit me.

Leader: Ask the children, "How do you suppose Puppet #2 is feeling?"

Puppet #1: Your (mom, dad, brother, uncle, etc.) must have been real mad at you.

Puppet #2: _____ was and now I'm afraid.

Puppet #1: I would be afraid, too. What should we do?

Leader: Ask the children, What should Puppets #1 and #2 do?"

Elicit suggestions from the children. Try to elicit suggestions that encourage Puppets #1 and #2 to tell someone, perhaps a teacher or a grandmother, or other favorite family friend or relative. When the discussion leads to telling someone, reinforce the earlier session regarding communication.

Puppet #1: I have an idea. Let's tell ____ (teacher, grandmother, mom, etc.) S/he can help.

Puppet #2: Oh, I don't know. I'm pretty scared. Do you think _____ can help?

Puppet #1: Yes! Let's tell _____. I'll go with you.

IF'S, AND'S, OR BUT'S:

1. Identify others that children can tell if they have a problem.

2. Encourage the concept of telling someone when you have a problem. Keep bringing in the concept of personal power. Personal power is telling someone how you feel, telling someone your problem, and asking for help.

3. You may need to clarify the term "problem."

FAMILY ACTIVITY: 21.8 Hand Mural and Family Hug
CONSTRUCT: Self-Awareness
MATERIALS: 4-5 large pie plates, aluminum foil, tempera paints (4-5 colors), long sheets of butcher block paper

GOAL:

Spontaneous creative expression through exploration of color and design.

OBJECTIVES:

1. To increase tactile stimulation.

2. To increase group cohesion.

3. To have fun.

4. To reinforce comfort in using nurturing touch.

PROCEDURES:

1. Line the bottom of pie pans with aluminum foil.

2. Pour enough of the tempera paints to cover the bottoms of the various pie pans. Place a large sheet of butcher paper close by.

3. Have each child and adult place their hands in a color of choice and print their hands on a sheet of butcher block paper.

4. Encourage creative designs of hand prints.

5. After everyone has placed their hand prints on paper, have family try to identify who the hand prints belong to.

FAMILY HUG:

1. End each home visit with a family hug. Everyone get in a circle and put your arms around the people next to you. During the family hug time, anyone can say anything they like. It is a time for free expression.

2. At a natural time, close the activities for the day.

IF'S, AND'S, OR BUT'S:

Manage the use of the paints.

NURTURING PROGRAM FOR PARENTS AND CHILDREN BIRTH TO FIVE YEARS

SESSION 22

BEHAVIOR CONSTRUCT:	Empathy
SESSION CONCEPT:	Establishing a Nurturing Bath Time Routine
BRIEF DESCRIPTION:	Parents will learn how to establish a nurturing routine during bath times. Children will discuss the good and bad things about taking a bath.
INTENDED USE:	For parents of children birth to 5 years
PREREQUISITE KNOWLEDGE:	Praise, Nurturing Routines

AGENDA

Parent Activities — Materials

Parent Activities	Materials
22.1 Icebreaker and Home Practice Check In	*Parent Handbooks*
22.2 Establishing a Nurturing Tubby Time Routine	*Parent Handbooks*, **Tubby Time** AV presentation, AV equipment
22.3 Home Practice Exercise	*Parent Handbooks*

Family Activities* — Materials

Family Activities*	Materials
22.4 Family Nurturing Time	*Nurturing Book for Babies and Children*
22.5 Hello Time: This is the Way	None
22.6 Dancercise	Cassette player and cassettes or record player and records
22.7 Circle Time: Taking a Bath	None
22.8 Picture Painting and Family Hug	Tempera paints, paint brushes, butcher block paper

*For parents with infants or toddlers, use activities presented in *Nurturing Book for Babies and Children*. For parents with preschoolers (ages 3-5), use the activities listed below Family Nurturing Time.

GOAL:

To increase parents' awareness of how bath time is now and the way it was in childhood.

OBJECTIVES:

1. To encourage parents to view bath time as a nurturing family time.

2. To alert parents to the similarities and differences in bath time as a child and as an adult.

PROCEDURES:

1. Begin today's parent activities by having each adult respond to the following:

   • The fondest memory I have of taking a bath when I was a child is _____ .

   • The best part about bath time now as an adult is _____ .

2. After each parent has had an opportunity to respond to the statements above, review the Home Practice Exercise from the previous meeting. Also discuss perceived changes in family members and their interactions as reported in the family log.

IF'S, AND'S, OR BUT'S:

See how similar bath times are now for the family and how they were when the parent was a child. Any patterns? Discuss the issue with the parents a little.

FAMILY ACTIVITY: 22.2 Establishing a Nurturing Tubby Time Routine
CONSTRUCT: Empathy
MATERIALS: Parent Handbooks, Tubby Time AV presentation, AV equipment

---

GOAL:

To increase parents' ability to establish a nurturing parenting routine during bath times.

OBJECTIVES:

1. To discuss problems children have in wanting to take a bath.

2. To review steps necessary in establishing a nurturing bed time routine.

PROCEDURES:

1. If you are using the audio-visual programs, present the AV entitled **Tubby Time**.

2. Instruct parents to locate the information entitled **Nurturing Bath Time Routine** on pages 89-91 in their Handbooks. Utilize the information to discuss the following major concepts:

   a. Why is bath time a bad time?

      - Baths come at the end of the day when parents and children are anxious.

      - Bed time usually follows bath time and a lot of children don't like going to bed.

      - Bath time in many families is a chore, not fun.

      - Bath time is an on-again, off-again activity which only tends to increase anxiety.

      - Some children may have had a bad experience during a bath and associate all bath times with the bad experience.

   b. How to make bath time fun:

      - Make it sound like more fun.

      - Let your child help in preparing the bath.

      - Encourage your child to play in the tub.

      - Encourage body exploration.

      - Take a bath with your child(ren).

      - Make tubby time more enjoyable.

      - Make tubby time a daily routine.

   c. Never leave young children in the tub unattended.

   d. Keep all electrical appliances away from water.

IF'S, AND'S, OR BUT'S:

Some parents may shy away from taking a bath with their children. The issue may be related to embarrassment with nudity or possibly previous sexual abuse. Explore their feelings a little.

PARENT ACTIVITY:	22.3 Home Practice Exercise
CONSTRUCT:	Empathy
MATERIALS:	Parent Handbooks

GOAL:

To provide parents with practice in implementing a nurturing routine during bath times.

OBJECTIVES:

1. To promote empathic parent-child interactions.

2. To enhance child development.

3. To promote a positive self-concept and self-esteem in parents and children.

4. To establish a warm and supportive atmosphere.

PROCEDURES:

1. Instruct parents to locate the Home Practice Exercise on page 141 in their Handbooks. Review the exercise with them:

   a. Practice implementing the nurturing bath time routine with each of your children.

   b. Continue to practice the other nurturing routines during feeding times, and diapering and dressing times.

   c. Complete family log.

2. Tell parents that in addition to the Home Practice Exercise, they are to spend 30 minutes each day with each of their children in nurturing playtime activities. Playtime is a time with the parent and child alone — no TV, no other distractions. Playing a game or reading books are good activities. From the *Nurturing Book for Babies and Children*, have the parents practice activities listed in the following sections: Activities for Infants, Activities for Toddlers, Activities for Preschoolers, or Infant and Child Massage. Have the parents remember what they did and report the next week.

IF'S, AND'S, OR BUT'S:

Offer support to parents and children for their efforts in trying all the nurturing routines.

FAMILY ACTIVITY:	**22.4 Family Nurturing Time**
CONSTRUCT:	**Empathy, Self-Awareness**
MATERIALS:	**Nurturing Book for Babies and Children**

ACTIVITIES FOR INFANTS (Birth to 15 months):

Utilizing the *Nurturing Book for Babies and Children*, select activities from the sections entitled Activities for Infants or Infant and Child Massage. Engage parents in practicing songs, play and stimulation activities, or massage. Vary the activities weekly to sustain interest.

ACTIVITIES FOR TODDLERS (15 months to 3 years):

Utilizing the *Nurturing Book for Babies and Children*, select activities from the sections entitled Activities for Toddlers or Infant and Child Massage. Engage parents in practicing songs, play, language, and movement activities, or massage. Vary the activities weekly to sustain interest.

ACTIVITIES FOR PRESCHOOLERS (3-5 years):

Use the following activities when working with preschool children and their parents. Use the activities as the basis for involving infants and toddlers if you are conducting a home visit with children ages birth to five years.

FAMILY ACTIVITY: 22.5 Hello Time: This is the Way
CONSTRUCT: Behavior Management
MATERIALS: None

GOAL:

To build positive social interactions among family members.

OBJECTIVES:

1. To increase children's ability to communicate.

2. To reinforce positive peer interactions.

PROCEDURES:

1. Have children and adults stand in a circle.

2. Explain to them that today we are going to sing hello. Sing the following song to the tune of "This is the Way We Wash Our Clothes," and demonstrate the actions to the children.

This is the Way

This is the way we say hello (wave open hand-fingers pointing up),
Say hello (continue waving), say hello (continue waving).
This is the way we say hello, early in the morning.

This is the way we greet our friends (bow to one another),
Greet our friends, greet our friends.
This is the way we greet our friends, happy to see you here today.

3. Continue with "This is the way we . . .(smile and laugh, shake other's hands, dance and sing).

IF'S, AND'S, OR BUT'S:

Have a good time with the song. Be creative and add your own lyrics.

FAMILY ACTIVITY: 22.6 Dancercise
CONSTRUCT: Developmental
MATERIALS: Cassette player and cassettes or record player and records

GOAL:

To increase family interactions through music.

OBJECTIVES:

1. To involve children and parents in group cooperative musical activities.

2. To use large muscle movements.

3. To foster creative expression through dance.

4. To enhance self-awareness through dance.

5. To have fun.

PROCEDURES:

1. This activity will serve as a mini-dancercise movement. Have children and adults assemble in a circle.

2. Play music on a cassette player or a record player.

3. Demonstrate easy dance activities that generally use gross motor movements. The movements should change every 30 seconds to one minute to keep the interest going. Some gross motor movements may include the following:

    30 seconds, jumping jacks
    30 seconds, standing leg lifts (bending leg at hip and knee to form right angle)
    30 seconds, body twisting (turning at waist with hands on hips)
    The intent is to create gross motor movement to music.

IF'S, AND'S, OR BUT'S:

1. Some parents may feel silly dancing around. Have patience and encourage the parents to participate. Soon they will see it's fun.

2. Select music that will encourage movement. You may want to ask one of the children to pick out their favorite song to dance to.

FAMILY ACTIVITY: 22.7 Circle Time: Taking a Bath
CONSTRUCT: Developmental, Empathy
MATERIALS: None

GOAL:

To increase nurturing parent-child interactions during bath time.

OBJECTIVES:

1. Children will be able to share good and bad aspects related to taking a bath.

2. Children will be able to offer suggestions on how bath time can be more fun.

PROCEDURES:

1. Have children and adults in a circle sitting on the floor.

2. Explain that today we are going to talk about bath time. Ask parents and children to respond to the following questions:

    Children:

    • What I like best about taking a bath is _____ .

    Parent:

    • What I like best about giving my child a bath is _____ .

    Children:

    • What I don't like most of all about bath time is _____ .

    Parent:

    • What I don't like most of all about giving my child a bath is _____ .

    Children:

    • Taking a bath would be more fun if _____ .

    Parent:

    • Giving my child a bath would be more fun if _____ .

    Children:

    • One thing I could do to make my bath time more pleasant for mom/dad is _____ .

    Parent:

    • One thing I could do to make bath time more pleasant for my child is _____ .

IF'S, AND'S, OR BUT'S:

The goal is to discuss how bath time can be better for both kids and parents. The important nurturing concept being practiced is communication: getting parents and their children talking.

FAMILY ACTIVITY: 22.8 Picture Painting and Family Hug
CONSTRUCT: Developmental
MATERIALS: Tempera paints, paint brushes, butcher block paper

GOAL:

To increase children's self-concept and self-esteem through accomplishment of age appropriate tasks.

OBJECTIVES:

1. To foster creative expression through art.

2. To increase fine motor skills.

3. To reinforce comfort in using nurturing touch.

PROCEDURES:

1. Assemble children around a table.

2. Instruct children to paint a picture. Place no other requirements on the content of the activity.

3. Display the picture(s) for viewing.

FAMILY HUG:

1. End each home visit with a family hug. Everyone get in a circle and put your arms around the people next to you. During the family hug time, anyone can say anything they like. It is a time for free expression.

2. At a natural time, close the activities for the day.

IF'S, AND'S, OR BUT'S:

1. Keeping the content of the picture entirely up to the child will reduce anxieties related to expectations of adults. Make sure you offer plenty of praise for the effort and picture.

2. Make sure parents get a chance to paint a picture as well.

NURTURING PROGRAM FOR PARENTS AND CHILDREN BIRTH TO FIVE YEARS

SESSION 23

BEHAVIOR CONSTRUCT: Empathy

SESSION CONCEPT: Establishing a Bed Time Nurturing Routine

BRIEF DESCRIPTION: Parents will learn ways to make bed time for children more enjoyable and nurturing. Children will discuss their likes and dislikes of bed time and will be active in art.

INTENDED USE: For parents of children birth to 5 years

PREREQUISITE KNOWLEDGE: Praise, Nurturing Routines, Nurturing Bath Time Routine

AGENDA

Parent Activities	Materials
23.1 Icebreaker and Home Practice Check In	*Parent Handbooks*
23.2 Establishing a Nurturing Bedtime Routine	*Parent Handbooks*, **Night Night** AV presentation, AV equipment
23.3 Home Practice Exercise	*Parent Handbooks*

Family Activities*	Materials
23.4 Family Nurturing Time	*Nurturing Book for Babies and Children*
23.5 Hello Time: Loud and Soft	None
23.6 Feeling Song	None
23.7 Circle Time: Going to Bed	None
23.8 Dippy Do and Family Hug	Food colors or tempera paints, paper towels, 4 small containers, newspapers

*For parents with infants or toddlers, use activities presented in *Nurturing Book for Babies and Children*. For parents with preschoolers (ages 3-5), use the activities listed below Family Nurturing Time.

PARENT ACTIVITY: 23.1 Icebreaker and Home Practice Check In
CONSTRUCT: Self-Awareness
MATERIALS: Parent Handbooks

GOAL:

To increase parents' awareness of how bedtime was as a child.

OBJECTIVES:

1. To encourage parents to view bedtime as a nurturing family time.

2. To increase parents' awareness of what their children may need for a more peaceful bedtime experience.

PROCEDURES:

1. Begin today's parent activities by having each adult respond to the following:

   - What I remember most about bedtime as a child is _____ .

   - What I really needed from my parents at bedtime was ____ ; what I got instead was ____ .

2. After each parent has had an opportunity to respond to the statements above, review the Home Practice Exercise from the previous meeting. Also discuss perceived changes in family members and their interactions as reported in the family log.

IF'S, AND'S, OR BUT'S:

Bedtime may have been a scary time for many adults when they were children. Keep a sharp ear open for any sexual or physical abuse that may have occurred. If sexual abuse was an experience the parent had, encourage her/him to share the feelings. If it still seems to be a very difficult problem for the parent, maybe a referral to a professional counselor would help.

PARENT ACTIVITY: 23.2 Establishing a Nurturing Bedtime Routine
CONSTRUCT: Empathy
MATERIALS: Parent Handbooks, Night Night AV presentation, AV equipment

GOAL:

To increase parents' ability to establish a nurturing parenting routine during bed time.

OBJECTIVES:

1. To discuss problems children have in going to bed.

2. To review steps necessary in establishing a nurturing bedtime routine.

3. To discuss bedtime parenting myths and facts.

PROCEDURES:

1. If you are using the audio-visual programs, present the AV entitled **Night Night**.

2. Instruct parents to locate the information entitled **Nurturing Bedtime Routine** on pages 92-95 in their Handbooks. Utilize the information to discuss the following major concepts with the parents:

   a. All children experience some difficulty in going to bed. Some of the problems they experience are:

      • Separation anxiety from mom.

      • Night time hunger.

      • Night time fears.

      • Night time activities of other family members.

      • Sleeping in a room previously used as a place of punishment.

   b. Building a nurturing bedtime routine:

      • Identify a consistent time for bedtime.

      • Make bath time a part of the bedtime routine.

      • Select clothes children will wear to bed.

      • Help your children put on their bedtime clothes in the bedroom, not in other rooms of the house.

      • Brush teeth as a part of the bedtime routine.

      • Read stories with your children before they go to sleep.

      • Choose pleasant, not scary, books to read.

      • Put children in bed before they fall asleep.

      • Tuck your children in and praise them for being or doing.

      • If they awaken during the night, investigate to determine their needs.

   c. Bedtime myths and facts:

      • **Myth**: Paying attention to crying children will spoil them.
        Fact: Children become spoiled through inconsistent rules and feelings of insecurity.

      • **Myth**: Children who occasionally sleep in the parents' bed will never want to leave.
        Fact: Wanting to sleep with mom and dad is probably a need for children to feel secure. When feelings of security are felt, the need for sleeping with mom and dad is lessened.

IF'S, AND'S, OR BUT'S:

Probably the most important of all the nurturing routines is the bedtime routine, but it is probably the most controversial. Picking up crying children, reading night time stories and allowing children to occasionally sleep in the parents' bed are all bound to make some parents uneasy. Stick to your guns and don't back off. Support all parents' efforts.

PARENT ACTIVITY: 23.3 Home Practice Exercise
CONSTRUCT: Empathy
MATERIALS: Parent Handbooks

GOAL:

To provide parents with practice in implementing a nurturing bed time routine.

OBJECTIVES:

1. To promote empathic parent-child interactions.

2. To enhance child development.

3. To promote a positive self-concept and self-esteem in parents and children.

4. To establish a warm and supportive atmosphere.

PROCEDURES:

1. Instruct parents to locate the Home Practice Exercise on page 141 in their Handbooks. Review the exercise with them:

   a. Practice implementing the nurturing bed time routine with each of your children.

   b. Continue to practice other nurturing routines during feeding times, diapering and dressing times, and bath times.

   c. Complete family log.

2. Tell parents that in addition to the Home Practice Exercise, they are to spend 30 minutes each day with each of their children in nurturing playtime activities. Playtime is a time with the parent and child alone – no TV, no other distractions. Playing a game or reading books are good activities. From the *Nurturing Book for Babies and Children*, have the parents practice activities listed in the following sections: Activities for Infants, Activities for Toddlers, Activities for Preschoolers, or Infant and Child Massage. Have the parents remember what they did and report the next week.

IF'S, AND'S, OR BUT'S:

Keep encouraging and praising parents' efforts in completing the Home Practice Exercise.

FAMILY ACTIVITY: 23.4 Family Nurturing Time
CONSTRUCT: Empathy, Self-Awareness
MATERIALS: Nurturing Book for Babies and Children

ACTIVITIES FOR INFANTS (Birth to 15 months):

Utilizing the *Nurturing Book for Babies and Children*, select activities from the sections entitled Activities for Infants or Infant and Child Massage. Engage parents in practicing songs, play and stimulation activities, or massage. Vary the activities weekly to sustain interest.

ACTIVITIES FOR TODDLERS (15 months to 3 years):

Utilizing the *Nurturing Book for Babies and Children*, select activities from the sections entitled Activities for Toddlers or Infant and Child Massage. Engage parents in practicing songs, play, language, and movement activities, or massage. Vary the activities weekly to sustain interest.

ACTIVITIES FOR PRESCHOOLERS (3-5 years):

Use the following activities when working with preschool children and their parents. Use the activities as the basis for involving infants and toddlers if you are conducting a home visit with children ages birth to five years.

FAMILY ACTIVITY: 23.5 Hello Time: Loud and Soft
CONSTRUCT: Self-Awareness
MATERIALS: None

GOAL:

To have family members become aware of their self and others through selected verbal expression of feelings.

OBJECTIVES:

1. To greet each child and adult by first name.

2. To gain sensitivity to the feelings of others.

3. To encourage self-expression and ownership of feelings.

PROCEDURES:

1. Children and adults should be seated in a circle on the floor. A parent or home visitor should act as the leader of the activity.

2. The adult leading the activity explains the rules of the game. Rules: The group will take turns saying hello to everyone individually in either a loud or soft voice. The adult may say, "When it is your turn, you can tell us if you want us to say hello in a loud voice or a soft voice. When we ask, 'how are you?' you can answer in a loud or soft voice. After your turn, you can choose the next person for us to say hello to."

3. The adult chooses a child and asks whether they'd like a loud or soft voice. After the child indicates his choice, the group responds in a loud or soft voice by saying, "Hello ."

4. The adult asks, "How are you?" and the child is encouraged to respond. The adult may remark that the child appears happy, sad, etc., in response to the child's feeling.

5. The child chooses the next person to be greeted, and Steps 3 and 4 are repeated.

IF'S, AND'S, OR BUT'S:

1. Remind children that loud voices are for outside use but that it is okay to yell during this special activity.

2. When a child doesn't respond to "How are you?" or "Do you want loud or soft?" the group may be enlisted to interpret how the child is feeling and how they should talk to them.

> **Example:** "Are you feeling sad, happy, etc."
>
> How does Chad look? How do you think he feels? How do you think he'd like us to say hello?

FAMILY ACTIVITY:	**23.6 Feeling Song**
CONSTRUCT:	**Empathy**
MATERIALS:	**None**

GOAL:

To reinforce appropriate adult/child interactions.

OBJECTIVES:

1. To help parents and children learn to enjoy each other.

2. To provide an opportunity for the children to be with the parents in a safe atmosphere.

3. To physically and emotionally nourish children and parents.

4. To increase awareness of feelings.

PROCEDURES:

1. Have adults and children stand in a circle.

2. Explain the activity. We are going to sing a song that has lots of feelings. The song goes like this:

Feeling Song

When you're happy and you know it, clap your hands,
When you're happy and you know it, clap your hands,
When you're happy and you know it, then your face will surely show it,
When you're happy and you know it, clap your hands.

---

3. Repeat singing the song with the children clapping their hands.

4. Repeat the song with the following stanzas:

> When you're mad...stamp your feet.
> When you're sad...wipe your eyes.
> When you're scared...scream out loud (Ahhh!).
> When you're cold...shake and shiver (shake body).
> When you're hot...sweat and faint (bend to knees).

IF'S, AND'S, OR BUT'S:

1. Encourage everyone to participate even though some may feel somewhat hesitant.

2. Ask children for suggestions for additional activities.

FAMILY ACTIVITY:	**23.7 Circle Time: Going to Bed**
CONSTRUCT:	**Developmental, Empathy**
MATERIALS:	**None**

GOAL:

To increase nurturing parent-child interactions during bed time.

OBJECTIVES:

1. To enable children to share good and bad aspects related to going to bed.

2. To enable children to offer suggestions on how going to bed can be more pleasant.

PROCEDURES:

1. Have children and adults sit in a circle on the floor.

2. Explain that today we are going to talk about getting ready and going to bed. Ask parents and children to respond to the following questions:

Children:

● What I like best about getting ready and going to bed is ____ .

Parent:

● What I like best about getting my child ready for bed is ____ .

Children:

● What I don't like most of all about getting ready and going to bed is _____ .

Parent:

● What I don't like most of all about getting my child ready for bed is _____ .

Children:

- Going to bed would be more fun if _____ .

Parent:

- Getting my child ready for bed would be more fun if _____ .

Children:

- One thing I could do to make getting ready for bed more pleasant for Mom/Dad is _____ .

Parent:

- One thing I could do to make bed time more pleasant for my child is _____ .

IF'S, AND'S, OR BUT'S:

The goal is to discuss how bed time can be more pleasant for parents and kids. The most important nurturing concept being practiced is communication: getting parents and their children talking.

FAMILY ACTIVITY:	**23.8 Dippy Do and Family Hug**
CONSTRUCT:	**Appropriate Developmental Expectations**
MATERIALS:	**Food colors or tempera paints, paper towels, 4 small containers, newspapers**

GOAL:

To increase children's self-concept and self-esteem through accomplishment of age appropriate tasks.

OBJECTIVES:

1. To foster creative expression through art.

2. To increase fine motor skills.

3. To reinforce comfort in using nurturing touch.

PROCEDURES:

1. Assemble children and parents around a table.

2. Fill 4 small containers with various liquid colors (food colors or watered down tempera paints).

3. Each child should receive a fan-folded paper towel (either fan-fold them before activity or have children fan-fold the towels). The folds should be approximately 1 inch wide, running lengthwise along the paper towel.

4. Start at one end of the fan and fold across 1 1/2 inches up. Repeat folding over and over to the end, ending with a square.

5. Dip each corner in a different color allowing it to soak on the corner. Leave some white in the middle.

6. Unfold carefully and lay out to dry on newspapers.

FAMILY HUG:

1. End each home visit with a family hug. Everyone get in a circle and put your arms around the people next to you. During the family hug time, anyone can say anything they like. It is a time for free expression.

2. At a natural time, close the activities for the day.

IF'S, AND'S, OR BUT'S:

1. Children will love to do several designs. Hang up for all to see.

2. Make sure parents also complete their own design.

3. Family hugs should be a very common and comfortable experience for parents and children. At this stage in the program, feelings of defensiveness, hostility, and anxiety should have been replaced with comfort and openness.

NURTURING PROGRAM FOR PARENTS AND CHILDREN BIRTH TO FIVE YEARS

SESSION 24

BEHAVIOR CONSTRUCT: Self-Awareness

SESSION CONCEPT: Anger

BRIEF DESCRIPTION: Parents and children discuss anger and ways to express and control it.

INTENDED USE: For parents of children birth to 5 years

PREREQUISITE KNOWLEDGE: Stress Management

AGENDA

Parent Activities	Materials
24.1 Icebreaker and Home Practice Check In	*Parent Handbooks*
24.2 Handling My Anger	*Parent Handbooks*
24.3 Home Practice Exercise	*Parent Handbooks*

Family Activities*	Materials
24.4 Family Nurturing Time	*Nurturing Book for Babies and Children*
24.5 Hello Time: I Get Mad When	None
24.6 Simon Says	None
24.7 Circle Time: Controlling My Anger	Puppets
24.8 Tissue Art and Family Hug	White paper, pieces of different colored tissue, glue

*For parents with infants or toddlers, use activities presented in *Nurturing Book for Babies and Children*. For parents with preschoolers (ages 3-5), use the activities listed below Family Nurturing Time.

FAMILY ACTIVITY: 24.1 Icebreaker and Home Practice Check In
CONSTRUCT: Self-Awareness
MATERIALS: Parent Handbooks

GOAL:

To increase parents' awareness of how we learn anger but fail to act on expressing feelings of anger.

OBJECTIVES:

1. To help parents identify fears related to expressing anger.

2. To increase parents' awareness of early models they witnessed in handling anger.

PROCEDURES:

1. Begin today's parent activities by having each adult respond to the following:

   • As a child, I can remember my parent(s) expressing their anger by _____ .

   • The biggest fear I have in expressing my anger is _____.

2. After each parent has had an opportunity to respond to the statements above, review the Home Practice Exercise from the previous meeting. Also discuss perceived changes in family members and their interactions as reported in the family log.

IF'S, AND'S, OR BUT'S:

Often parents' fears about expressing anger are related to anger situations they experienced as children. How our parents handled their anger is probably pretty close to the way we handle our anger. To change that reaction might be too scary. These statements will help clarify the fears.

PARENT ACTIVITY: 24.2 Handling My Anger
CONSTRUCT: Self-Awareness
MATERIALS: Parent Handbooks

GOAL:

To identify appropriate ways to express anger.

OBJECTIVES:

1. To increase parents' ability to express anger.

2. To develop alternatives to release anger.

3. To become aware of how the manner in which anger is expressed influences others.

PROCEDURES:

1. Instruct the family that today's visit will focus on identifying and expressing anger. Share with the parents that there is a relationship between feeling hurt and feeling angry. People get angry when they have been hurt. They often react with anger because they believe feelings of hurt show vulnerability or weakness. When people withhold their anger, they always make their life more complicated. The way to maintain a healthy perspective is to keep up-to-date with all their emotions. When people hold any emotion inside, they cease to be their own master.

2. Instruct parents to locate the information entitled **Handling My Anger** on pages 96-97 in their Handbooks. Have parents respond to the following statements:

   • One situation that occurs at home that often results in my getting angry is _____ .

   • When I am angry, I am apt to _____ . When this occurs, I feel _____ , and those around me feel _____ .

   • One way I would like to handle my anger is _____ .

3. Share information regarding the purpose of anger. Anger lets you know that a need of yours is going unrecognized. As with all feelings it is important to express your anger, not suppress it. There are two reason to express it: to let the anger out and to recognize and meet the underlying need. When you are angry, you must **think**, as well as **feel**. Count to ten, give yourself time to think. If you need something now, use an I statement to ask for what you want. If you need something later, redirect your anger to get out anger energy. Then think of a strategy for asking for what you want to meet your unmet need using an I statement. Today we will focus on anger redirection techniques to help you release anger energy in positive, non-destructive ways.

4. Review some of the ways parents could express anger appropriately that are listed below:

   a. Angry Letter — Write a short letter to each person you are angry with. Tell them that you are angry with them for what they did or did not do. Put the letter in its own envelope and place it where you can easily see it. When you feel the anger again, open it up and read it. Add how you are feeling to the end of it. Keep the letter for a few weeks or as long as you feel relief when you look at it. After you no longer have the need to look at the letter, get rid of it. Dispose of the letter with a ceremony. Make it a meaningful occasion.

   b. Anger Cry and Scream — Close yourself in a room away from everyone. Scream out your worst opinion of this person. The louder you scream the better. It's okay if you begin to cry. When you're done, wash your hands and face and go for a walk.

   c. Anger Role Play — Imagine the person you're angry with is sitting across from you in an empty chair. Tell this person how angry you are with him/her. Then, move to the empty chair and speak as he/she would speak to you. Then jump back to your chair and discredit the person's argument and logic. Tear it to shreds. Go back and forth, playing yourself and the other person as long and as often as you need.

   d. Physical Exercise Activities — Go jogging, do sit-ups, run up and down a flight of stairs, exert yourself in exercise. When you begin feeling exhausted, do ten more, each time calling out the person's name in anger.

e. Angry Shreds — Write the name of the person you're angry with in large letters on a piece of paper. Tear the paper into as many pieces as you can. The quicker you tear, the better. Burn the scraps or flush them in a toilet bowl. While you are doing this, think "You deserve my anger." It really works.

f. Ridiculous Imagery — Exaggerate personal aspects of the person with whom you are angry. It could be their physical appearance, name, professional role, or profession.

IF'S, AND'S, OR BUT'S:

The important issue in this exercise is the recognition of anger and ways to handle anger. Focus on appropriate alternatives.

PARENT ACTIVITY: **24.3 Home Practice Exercise**
CONSTRUCT: **Self-Awareness**
MATERIALS: **Parent Handbooks**

GOAL:

To give parents an opportunity to recognize and appropriately handle feelings of anger.

OBJECTIVES:

1. To encourage parents to use their positive personal power.

2. To reinforce alternatives to hitting.

3. To maintain a warm and supportive atmosphere.

PROCEDURES:

1. Instruct parents to locate the Home Practice Exercise on page 142 in their Handbooks. Review the exercise with them:

   a. Practice handling anger by using one of the three alternatives identified.

   b. Pay attention to the times you get angry and to the issues related to your anger. Is there a pattern? Are certain needs you have not being given a chance for fulfillment?

   c. Complete family log.

2. Tell parents that in addition to the Home Practice Exercise, they are to spend 30 minutes each day with each of their children in nurturing playtime activities. Playtime is a time with the parent and child alone — no TV, no other distractions. Playing a game or reading books are good activities. From the *Nurturing Book for Babies and Children*, have the parents practice activities listed in the following sections: Activities for Infants, Activities for Toddlers, Activities for Preschoolers, or Infant and Child Massage. Have the parents remember what they did and report the next week.

IF'S, AND'S, OR BUT'S:

Anger awareness and its management are vital issues to discuss and to help parents adopt. Some anger may be directed at children because certain parents' needs are not reaching fulfillment. Encourage parents to recognize patterns.

FAMILY ACTIVITY: 24.4 Family Nurturing Time
CONSTRUCT: Empathy, Self-Awareness
MATERIALS: Nurturing Book for Babies and Children

ACTIVITIES FOR INFANTS (Birth to 15 months):

Utilizing the *Nurturing Book for Babies and Children*, select activities from the sections entitled Activities for Infants or Infant and Child Massage. Engage parents in practicing songs, play and stimulation activities, or massage. Vary the activities weekly to sustain interest.

ACTIVITIES FOR TODDLERS (15 months to 3 years):

Utilizing the *Nurturing Book for Babies and Children*, select activities from the sections entitled Activities for Toddlers or Infant and Child Massage. Engage parents in practicing songs, play, language, and movement activities, or massage. Vary the activities weekly to sustain interest.

ACTIVITIES FOR PRESCHOOLERS (3-5 years):

Use the following activities when working with preschool children and their parents. Use the activities as the basis for involving infants and toddlers if you are conducting a home visit with children ages birth to five years.

FAMILY ACTIVITY: 24.5 Hello Time: I Get Mad When
CONSTRUCT: Self-Awareness
MATERIALS: None

GOAL:

To increase children's awareness of situations which precipitate feelings of anger.

OBJECTIVES:

1. To increase recognition of feelings of anger.
2. To share feeling of anger.

1. Have children and adults sit in a circle on the floor.

2. Have each child and adult respond to the following:

   - Right now I am feeling _____ .
   - What makes me mad is _____ .

IF'S, AND'S, OR BUT'S:

Tell children feelings of anger/mad are okay to have. It is how we handle our feelings that counts.

FAMILY ACTIVITY: **24.6 Simon Says**
CONSTRUCT: **Behavior Management**
MATERIALS: **None**

GOAL:

To increase child's ability to respond to behavior management.

OBJECTIVES:

1. To increase child's ability to follow directions.

2. To increase child's ability to identify body parts.

3. To increase child's auditory memory.

4. To give the child an opportunity to give commands.

PROCEDURES:

1. Explain the rules of "Simon Says." When Simon says to do something, the players must follow the command.

2. Two versions of the game can occur:

   a. Adult is Simon giving children commands. Commands can be gross motor movements (hopping, jumping,etc.), fine motor movements (writing, cuttings, etc.), or identification of body parts (touch ears, eyes, etc.).

   b. Children can be Simon taking turns giving the adult and other children commands.

IF'S, AND'S, OR BUT'S:

1. You may want to change the name "Simon Says" to the name of the person giving the commands; e.g., "Billy says."

2. Make sure everyone gets a turn.

3. Kids will love giving adults commands.

FAMILY ACTIVITY: 24.7 Circle Time: Controlling my Anger
CONSTRUCT: Self-Awareness
MATERIALS: Puppets

GOAL:

To help children learn ways to manage their anger.

OBJECTIVES:

1. To help children recognize times they get angry.

2. To discuss ways to handle angry feelings.

PROCEDURES:

1. Have children and adults sit in a circle on the floor.

2. Today we will talk about ways to handle our anger. Ask each person when they get mad (refer to Hello Time) and what they do when they get angry.

3. Ask each person if there is a better way to handle angry feelings instead of doing what they do.

4. Ask children what the consequences are when they choose to get angry.

5. Use the puppets to role play how children handle their anger. Role play both good and bad examples.

IF'S, AND'S, OR BUT'S:

Remind everyone that getting angry is okay. What is not okay is the way we sometimes express our anger.

FAMILY ACTIVITY: 24.8 Tissue Art and Family Hug
CONSTRUCT: Developmental
MATERIALS: White paper, pieces of different colored tissue, glue

GOAL:

To increase children's self-concept and self-esteem through accomplishment of age appropriate tasks.

OBJECTIVES:

1. To foster creative expression through art.

2. To increase fine motor skills.

3. To reinforce comfort in using nurturing touch.

PROCEDURES:

1. Assemble children around a table.

2. Fill a large container with various shapes and sizes of different colored tissue.

3. Provide each child with his/her own sheet of white paper.

4. Instruct the children that they are to glue the different sizes and colors of tissue onto the sheet of white paper, making a mosaic. The tissue should overlap each other creating different colors and patterns.

FAMILY HUG:

1. End each home visit with a family hug. Everyone get in a circle and put your arms around the people next to you. During the family hug time, anyone can say anything they like. It is a time for free expression.

2. At a natural time, close the activities for the day.

IF'S, AND'S, OR BUT'S:

1. You will need to cut the tissue in various shapes and sizes before beginning the activity.

2. Have children display their works of art by hanging them on a wall.

NURTURING PROGRAM FOR PARENTS AND CHILDREN BIRTH TO FIVE YEARS

SESSION 25

BEHAVIOR CONSTRUCT: Behavior Management

SESSION CONCEPT: Choices and Consequences

BRIEF DESCRIPTION: Parents and children learn and practice the concept of making/giving a choice; taking the consequences.

INTENDED USE: For parents of children birth to 5 years

PREREQUISITE KNOWLEDGE: Behavior Management, Family Rules, Praise, Time-Out

AGENDA

Parent Activities

		Materials
25.1	Icebreaker and Home Practice Check In	*Parent Handbooks*
25.2	Helping Children Manage Their Behavior	*Parent Handbooks*, **Choices and Consequences** AV presentation, AV equipment
25.3	Home Practice Exercise	*Parent Handbooks*

Family Activities*

		Materials
25.4	Family Nurturing Time	*Nurturing Book for Babies and Children*
25.5	Hello Time: Good Morning to You	None
25.6	Hopping Song	None
25.7	Circle Time: Choices and Consequences	Puppets
25.8	Clay and Family Hug	Clay, newspaper, water

*For parents with infants or toddlers, use activities presented in *Nurturing Book for Babies and Children*. For parents with preschoolers (ages 3-5), use the activities listed below Family Nurturing Time.

PARENT ACTIVITY: 25.1 Icebreaker and Home Practice Check In
CONSTRUCT: Self-Awareness
MATERIALS: Parent Handbooks

GOAL:

To increase parental awareness of the value in making decisions from anticipated consequences.

OBJECTIVES:

1. To introduce the concept of giving children choices.

2. To increase parental awareness of the process of making decisions.

3. To continue to establish group cohesion.

PROCEDURES:

1. Begin today's parent activities by having each adult respond to the following:

   • Right now I am feeling _____ .

   • When faced with several choices regarding a situation, I generally tend to choose _____ .

2. After each parent has had an opportunity to respond to the statements above, review the Home Practice Exercise from the previous meeting. Also discuss perceived changes in family members and their interactions as reported in the family log.

IF'S, AND'S, OR BUT'S:

A critical skill in helping children learn to become responsible for their behavior is allowing them to make choices. With choices comes decision making; with decision making comes responsibility. When parents become aware of how they make choices in their lives, they can begin to foster decision making in their children.

PARENT ACTIVITY: 25.2 Helping Children Manage Their Behavior
CONSTRUCT: Behavior Management
MATERIALS: Parent Handbooks, Choices and Consequences AV presentation, AV equipment

GOAL:

To increase parents' knowledge of choices and consequences as a behavior management technique.

OBJECTIVES:

1. To increase parents' ability to use choices and consequences.

2. To focus on alternatives to corporal punishment.

3. To provide children the opportunity to become responsible for their behavior.

4. To provide parents an opportunity to practice choices and consequences.

PROCEDURES:

1. Mention to the parents that they are going to focus on learning to give children power by giving them choices. Begin by saying the word POWER. Review with the parents the meaning of this word and the term "personal power." Remind the parents that children desire to have personal power and want to express it. Personal power is a good thing. Without it, people (children) would be vulnerable to all kinds of hurts, pains, and unwanted touch. When children feel they don't have power, they fight to get it.

2. Brainstorm with the parents for positive and negative ways children use their personal power. Some examples are:

   - Positive use of personal power — cooperating, coming to meals on time, following rules, etc.

   - Negative use of personal power — temper tantrums, being uncooperative, holding their breath, etc.

3. Mention that when children feel they don't have any power that's when they use their personal power in a negative way. It's their way of showing their parents that they are powerful.

   a. **Giving children choices.** One way to provide children with power and to reduce power struggles is to give them choices. Giving children choices provides them with a good way to use their power. Choices help children learn to manage their own behavior. Choices also let children know that they have power and can defuse potential power struggles. Choices help children take responsibility for their behaviors.

   Giving children choices can begin at birth. Choices can be given in the following areas: dressing, eating, bath time, and playtime. Brainstorm with the parents other areas and situations where they can provide children with choices.

   b. **Choices and Consequences.** If you are using the audio-visual programs, present the AV entitled **Choices and Consequences.** Instruct parents to locate the information entitled **Choices and Consequences** on pages 100-103 in their Handbooks. Utilize the information presented to discuss the following major concepts with the parents:

   - Choices and consequences is a technique used by parents to help children take responsibility for their behavior.

   - There are two kinds of consequences: natural and logical.
     Natural consequences happen by themselves.
     Logical consequences are planned.

   - Children learn best through choices.

   - If you promise a particular consequence or reward, you'd better deliver.

   - Threats are not consequences.

   - Consequences must be related to the behavior.

4. Break into pairs and have the parent play the parent; the home visitor play the child. Have the "parent" select a problem situation s/he faces at home. Role play the situation using choices and consequences. Instruct parents to use the following format:

> _(name of child)_ , you are _(undesirable behavior)_ . You have a choice. You can either _(choice #1)_ , or _(choice #2)_ . However, if you continue to _(undesirable behavior)_, you will _(consequence)_ . It's your choice.

IF'S, AND'S, OR BUT'S:

1. While parents are practicing choices and consequences, note the behaviors, choices and consequences for appropriateness.

2. You may encourage the parents to ask themselves: "Is the behavior I'm focusing on a real problem? Have I given appropriate and acceptable choices? Are the consequences appropriate and nonabusive?"

3. Consequences that are appropriate and desirable to use are time-out, loss of privilege, or restitution (paying back).

PARENT ACTIVITY: 25.3 Home Practice Exercise
CONSTRUCT: Behavior Management, Self-Awareness
MATERIALS: Parent Handbooks

GOAL:

To increase parents' ability in using choices and consequences as a behavior management technique.

OBJECTIVES:

1. To increase parents' awareness of opportunities to use choices and consequences.

2. To increase parents' success in managing children's behavior.

3. To learn appropriate disciplinary techniques.

4. To discuss changes in family interactions.

5. To maintain a warm and supportive atmosphere.

PROCEDURES:

1. Instruct parents to locate the Home Practice Exercise on page 142 in their Handbooks. Review the exercise with them:

   a. Use choices and consequences at least three times.

   b. Praise child(ren) twice and self once.

   c. Continue to use time-out for misbehavior.

   d. Complete family log.

2. Tell parents that in addition to the Home Practice Exercise, they are to spend 30 minutes each day with each of their children in nurturing playtime activities. Playtime is a time with the parent and child alone—no TV, no other distractions. Playing a game or reading books are good activities. From the *Nurturing Book for Babies and Children*, have the parents practice activities listed in the following sections: Activities for Infants, Activities for Toddlers, Activities for Preschoolers, or Infant and Child Massage. Have the parents remember what they did and report the next week.

IF'S, AND'S, OR BUT'S:

Remind parents to define success as attempting the Home Practice Exercise as well as completing the exercise.

FAMILY ACTIVITY:	**25.4 Family Nurturing Time**
CONSTRUCT:	**Empathy, Self-Awareness**
MATERIALS:	**Nurturing Book for Babies and Children**

ACTIVITIES FOR INFANTS (Birth to 15 months):

Utilizing the *Nurturing Book for Babies and Children*, select activities from the sections entitled Activities for Infants or Infant and Child Massage. Engage parents in practicing songs, play and stimulation activities, or massage. Vary the activities weekly to sustain interest.

ACTIVITIES FOR TODDLERS (15 months to 3 years):

Utilizing the *Nurturing Book for Babies and Children*, select activities from the sections entitled Activities for Toddlers or Infant and Child Massage. Engage parents in practicing songs, play, language, and movement activities, or massage. Vary the activities weekly to sustain interest.

ACTIVITIES FOR PRESCHOOLERS (3-5 years):

Use the following activities when working with preschool children and their parents. Use the activities as the basis for involving infants and toddlers if you are conducting a home visit with children ages birth to five years.

GOAL:

To increase children's awareness of the presence and feelings of others.

OBJECTIVES:

1. To increase children's self-awareness.

2. To allow children to share how they feel.

3. To increase listening skills.

PROCEDURES:

1. Begin this activity with children and adults seated on the floor in a circle.

2. Take turns singing the following song to each child, to the tune of "Happy Birthday."

   Good Morning to __(child's name)__ , Good Morning to __(child's name)__ ,
   Good morning to__(child's name)__ , How are you today?

3. Each child should be encouraged to tell how he/she is feeling or he/she may choose to sing his/her response, to the tune of "Happy Birthday."

   I'm happy today, I'm happy today,
   I'm happy today, I'm happy today.

   Other feeling words may be used: grumpy, sleepy, sad, silly, lonely, etc.

4. An adult may choose to model the sung response for the children, but allow them to choose how they express their feelings to the group.

5. Be sure to focus the attention on the person being greeted; i.e., "Where's Adam? Let's all sing to him."

IF'S, AND'S, OR BUT'S:

If a child does not respond by saying how he feels, try to elicit from others how they think he may be feeling; i.e., "Look at Adam. How do you think he may be feeling? I see a smile. Do you think he's happy or sad?"

FAMILY ACTIVITY: 25.6 Hopping Song
CONSTRUCT: Empathy
MATERIALS: None

GOAL:

To increase positive family interactions through music.

OBJECTIVES:

1. To involve children in active and cooperative musical activities.

2. To foster creative expression through music.

PROCEDURES:

1. Assemble children and adults in a circle to participate in the song activity.

2. Sing words to the tune of "99 Bottles of Beer."

> There is one person hopping, hopping all around,
> Hopping, hopping, hopping,
> Hopping hopping all around.

> **Movement:** Kids hop and increase to 2 kids, 3 kids, etc. OR have everyone participate at the same time. Ask the children what activity should be performed.

> *Example:* There is one family hopping, hopping all around.

IF'S, AND'S, OR BUT'S:

Use gross motor movements such as hopping, skipping, jumping, running backwards, etc. The idea is movement.

FAMILY ACTIVITY: 25.7 Circle Time: Choices and Consequences
CONSTRUCT: Behavior Management
MATERIALS: Puppets

GOAL:

To increase the child's understanding of personal power through choices and consequences.

OBJECTIVES:

1. To increase the child's understanding of choices and consequences.

2. To reinforce the concept that children make choices through their personal power.

3. To increase children's awareness that they choose to behave in a certain way based on expected consequences.

4. To increase children's responsibility for their behavior.

212

PROCEDURES:

1. Assemble children and adults in a circle.

2. Introduce the concept for discussion: choices and consequences.

3. Choices are decisions we make to do something or not to do something. Consequences are things that happen to us after we have made a choice. There are two kinds of consequences: good ones and bad ones. Have children give examples of a choice and a consequence.

4. The following examples are provided to help illustrate the concept. You may choose to have the children role play the choices/consequences. Ask children to brainstorm what could happen if they choose to perform one behavior or the other.

   a. To steal or not to steal someone's pencil.

   b. To dress warm in the winter or not.

   c. To hit or not hit someone when you are angry.

   d. To disobey mom/dad or to obey them.

   e. To look both ways when crossing the street or to run across without looking.

   f. To take a time-out quietly or to fight and make a lot of noise in time-out.

5. Play act the following situations with the puppets highlighting the concept of choosing to perform a certain behavior and the good and bad consequences of the action.

   a. Telling someone a lie.

      Example: Puppet #1 sees Puppet #2 drop a nickel from his/her pants pocket. Puppet #1 races toward the nickel, picks it up and puts it in his/her pocket.

      Puppet #1: (singing) Boy-o-boy. I found a nickel. I found a nickel.

      Puppet #2: Aren't you lucky! I have a nickel, too! (He reaches in his pants to find his nickel, but it's gone. He begins to cry.)

      Puppet #1: Well, don't look at me. This is my nickel. My mother gave it to me.

      Facilitator: What did Puppet #1 do? (he/she told a lie). How could he/she have used his/her personal power in a good way? What could he/she have done? (told the truth; given the nickel back to Puppet #2). Explain consequences with the children and what could happen as a consequence of lying. How did Puppet #1 use his/her personal power?

   b. Repeat the same sequence this time with Puppet #1 telling the truth. Ask the children to brainstorm what could happen for telling the truth. How did Puppet #1 use his/her personal power?

6. If time allows, repeat the play acting with other topics. Choose one relevant to the family. Some examples could be taking a quiet/noisy time-out, hitting others/treating others nicely, etc.

IF'S, AND'S, OR BUT'S:

1. Facilitate discussion about choices and consequences as it relates to behavior. If the children begin to understand the relationship to behavior, you have begun to accomplish your goal.

2. Use choices and consequences as a form of behavior management during your home visits. Encourage parents to use choices and consequences with their children at home.

FAMILY ACTIVITY: 25.8 Clay and Family Hug
CONSTRUCT: Self-Awareness
MATERIALS: Clay, newspaper, water

GOAL:

To provide children and parents an opportunity to experience their own creativity and sensitivity.

OBJECTIVES:

1. To allow children the opportunity to express themselves in clay.

2. To enable children to express their feelings in a nonverbal form.

3. To help children learn about themselves in new ways.

4. To reinforce comfort in using nurturing touch.

PROCEDURES:

1. Cover floor with newspapers—thick layers so water won't soak through.

2. Hand out clay to each person—allow children and adults to take more if they want more or to put some back until they have an amount which feels good in their hands. Encourage them to pay attention to how the clay feels in their own hands.

3. Tell everyone to make anything they want. It can be a lump, a ball, anything they choose.

4. When finished, ask parents and children to share their creations.

FAMILY HUG:

1. End each home visit with a family hug. Everyone get in a circle and put your arms around the people next to you. During the family hug time, anyone can say anything they like. It is a time for free expression.

2. At a natural time, close the activities for the day.

IF'S, AND'S, OR BUT'S:

A good way to begin to break down defensiveness toward touch is to encourage tactile stimulation. Over time, the word "touch" won't have such a scary sound.

NURTURING PROGRAM FOR PARENTS AND CHILDREN BIRTH TO FIVE YEARS

SESSION 26

BEHAVIOR CONSTRUCT: Behavior Management

SESSION CONCEPT: Ignoring

BRIEF DESCRIPTION: Parents learn how and when to ignore certain inappropriate behaviors. Children discuss the concept of telling someone their concerns.

INTENDED USE: For parents of children birth to 5 years

PREREQUISITE KNOWLEDGE: Behavior Management, Praise

AGENDA

Parent Activities	Materials
26.1 Icebreaker and Home Practice Check In	*Parent Handbooks*
26.2 Ignoring	*Parent Handbooks*, **Ignoring** AV presentation, AV equipment
26.3 Home Practice Exercise	*Parent Handbooks*

Family Activities*	Materials
26.4 Family Nurturing Time	*Nurturing Book for Babies and Children*
26.5 Hello Time: London Bridge	None
26.6 Are You Sleeping?	Blanket, pillow, bell, rug or mat
26.7 Circle Time: Let's Tell Someone	Puppets
26.8 Dynamic Doer Card Game and Family Hug	Dynamic Doer and Pair It Card Games

*For parents with infants or toddlers, use activities presented in *Nurturing Book for Babies and Children*. For parents with preschoolers (ages 3-5), use the activities listed below Family Nurturing Time.

PARENT ACTIVITY: 26.1 Icebreaker and Home Practice Check In
CONSTRUCT: Self-Awareness
MATERIALS: Parent Handbooks

GOAL:

To increase parental awareness of the value of ignoring behavior.

OBJECTIVES:

1. To increase awareness of difficult child behavior management issues.

2. To share the frustration involved in ignoring certain behaviors.

3. To continue to establish group cohesion.

PROCEDURES:

1. Begin today's parent activities by having each adult respond to the following:

   • One behavior my child exhibits, which is really hard for me to ignore, is _____ .

   • When s/he displays this behavior, I feel or want to _____ .

2. After each parent has had an opportunity to respond to the statements above, review the Home Practice Exercise from the previous meeting. Also discuss perceived changes in family members and their interactions as reported in the family log.

IF'S, AND'S, OR BUT'S:

Keep a list of the behaviors parents have a difficult time ignoring. Later in the session they will be practicing ignoring and those behaviors can be the ones used in the role play.

PARENT ACTIVITY: 26.2 Ignoring
CONSTRUCT: Behavior Management
MATERIALS: Parent Handbooks, Ignoring AV presentation, AV equipment

---

GOAL:

To increase parents' skill in utilizing ignoring as an alternative behavior management technique to physical punishment.

OBJECTIVES:

1. To increase parents' knowledge of the theory and techniques of ignoring.

2. To review major concepts of ignoring.

3. To encourage parents to identify one behavior with a child they can "ignore."

4. To practice ignoring behavior.

PROCEDURES:

1. If you are using the audio-visual programs, present the AV entitled **Ignoring**.

2. Instruct parents to locate the information entitled **Ignoring as Behavior Management** on pages 104-106 in their Handbooks. Utilize the information presented to discuss the following major concepts with the parents:

   a. Ignoring is a form of behavior management used to eliminate irritating behaviors.

   b. To know when to use ignoring:

      • Assess degree of potential physical harm to child or others.

      • Assess degree of potential damage to property.

   c. Ignore irritating behaviors such as whining, temper tantrums, etc.

   d. Before you use ignoring:

      • Decide what behavior you want instead.

      • Be sure you can tolerate the behavior for a while.

      • Don't remove the child from the area.

      • Ignore the behavior 100% of the time.

   e. How to ignore:

      • Pay not attention to the behavior. Dream your favorite daydream.

      • Even though behavior may get worse, don't give in.

      • When behavior stops, praise immediately.

      • Convince others to ignore the behavior.

      • Don't ignore child; ignore behavior.

3. Ask the parents to suggest specific examples of behaviors that can be ignored.

4. Ask each parent to select a child's behavior which the parent thinks can be safely ignored.

5. Break into pairs and have one parent be the "child," the other the "parent." Role play utilizing ignoring. Have the "child" perform the undesirable behavior and the "parent" practice ignoring.

6. Switch roles and continue role playing.

7. Review and discuss the concept of ignoring.

IF'S, AND'S, OR BUT'S:

1. Remind parents to: Praise behavior you like. Ignore behavior you don't like. What you stroke is what you get.

2. For parents who express a difficult time ignoring, tell them to remember a favorite time or friend and have them focus on that time or person until the ignored behavior stops.

PARENT ACTIVITY: 26.3 Home Practice Exercise
CONSTRUCT: Behavior Management, Self-Awareness
MATERIALS: Parent Handbooks

GOAL:

To encourage parents to practice appropriate behavior management.

OBJECTIVES:

1. To provide parents with practice in using ignoring with children.

2. To maintain a warm and supportive atmosphere.

PROCEDURES:

1. Instruct parents to locate the Home Practice Exercise on page 142 in their Handbooks. Review the exercise with them:

    a. Practice ignoring twice.

    b. Praise desirable behavior.

    c. Complete family log.

2. Tell parents that in addition to the Home Practice Exercise, they are to spend 30 minutes each day with each of their children in nurturing playtime activities. Playtime is a time with the parent and child alone – no TV, no other distractions. Playing a game or reading books are good activities. From the *Nurturing Book for Babies and Children*, have the parents practice activities listed in the following sections: Activities for Infants, Activities for Toddlers, Activities for Preschoolers, or Infant and Child Massage. Have the parents remember what they did and report the next week.

IF'S, AND'S, OR BUT'S:

Remind parents to ignore behaviors of children that will not result in physical or property damage, and behaviors that children can control.

FAMILY ACTIVITY: 26.4 Family Nurturing Time
CONSTRUCT: Empathy, Self-Awareness
MATERIALS: Nurturing Book for Babies and Children

ACTIVITIES FOR INFANTS (Birth to 15 months):

Utilizing the *Nurturing Book for Babies and Children*, select activities from the sections entitled Activities for Infants or Infant and Child Massage. Engage parents in practicing songs, play and stimulation activities, or massage. Vary the activities weekly to sustain interest.

ACTIVITIES FOR TODDLERS (15 months to 3 years):

Utilizing the *Nurturing Book for Babies and Children*, select activities from the sections entitled Activities for Toddlers or Infant and Child Massage. Engage parents in practicing songs, play, language, and movement activities, or massage. Vary the activities weekly to sustain interest.

ACTIVITIES FOR PRESCHOOLERS (3-5 years):

Use the following activities when working with preschool children and their parents. Use the activities as the basis for involving infants and toddlers if you are conducting a home visit with children ages birth to five years.

FAMILY ACTIVITY:	**26.5 Hello Time: London Bridge**
CONSTRUCT:	**Empathy**
MATERIALS:	**None**

GOAL:

To reinforce appropriate adult-child interactions.

OBJECTIVES:

1. To help parents and children enjoy each other.

2. To increase positive touch.

PROCEDURES:

1. Choose two persons to be the "bridge" by facing each other and holding hands with their arms lifted high enough for others to pass under.

2. Have the rest of the people form a line and pass under the bridge as everyone sings:

London Bridge

London Bridge is falling down, falling down, falling down,

London Bridge is falling down, my fair _(name)_ .

3. As the group sings "my fair _(name)_ , " the two people who are the bridge should lower their arms and "catch" someone. Have the group sing that person's name in the line "my fair __ ."

4. The person who gets "caught" in the bridge takes the place of one of the people making up the bridge and that person joins the group moving under the bridge.

IF'S, AND'S, OR BUT'S:

Allow all children a chance to be a part of the bridge.

GOAL:

To express and accept nurturing gestures appropriately among children and their parents.

OBJECTIVES:

1. To increase positive parent-child nurturing interactions.

2. To engage in cooperative activity between children and parents.

PROCEDURES:

1. Have children and parents sit in a circle on the floor.

2. Begin to discuss the concept of nurturing. Start by using examples:

    a. When they are frightened, the feeling of comfort when someone holds them.

    b. The feelings of comfort after someone helped them do a difficult task. In this instance, nurturing is being equated to the feeling of being comforted.

3. Describe the game for parents and children. One child lies down on the rug and pillow and is covered with the blanket by the parents. Appropriate nurturing-type interactions may be demonstrated such as tucking the blanket around the child, touching him/her and saying "good night" softly. The small bell should be placed near the pillow. The child on the rug pretends to sleep while the group sings softly:

Are You Sleeping?

Are you sleeping, Are you sleeping,
Brother (Sister) _____ , Brother (Sister) _____ .

4. The group sings loudly and claps:

Morning bells are ringing, Morning bells are ringing,
Ding, ding, dong; Ding, ding, dong.
(The sleeping person jumps up and rings the bell.)

5. Activity continues until all children have been tucked in by their parents.

IF'S, AND'S, OR BUT'S:

1. This is a good activity to use to provide appropriate physical contact in a nurturing way to children and their parents who may not ordinarily be receptive to it.

2. The activity allows children to experience appropriate nurturing behaviors.

3. Build up the suspense of being quiet while a child is "sleeping" and clapping and singing loudly when he/she "wakes up." This helps children wait for their turn.

4. Encourage parents who may be feeling awkward that night time nurturing behaviors have a positive impact upon the sleeping styles of young children.

GOAL:

To increase children's ability to tell others in moments of need.

OBJECTIVES:

1. To reinforce children's understanding of the concept of telling others.

2. To reinforce children's abilities to effectively communicate to others their feelings, concerns, and problems.

PROCEDURES:

1. Have children and adults sit in a circle on the floor.

2. Review the concept of telling others. Why would we want to tell others our problems or how we feel?

3. Review with the children whom they would talk to if the following situations were occurring in their lives. Play act the skits with the puppets.

   a. Somebody picking on them.

   b. Mom or Dad hurting you or your brother/sister.

   c. If they saw another child take something that wasn't theirs.

   d. When they felt scared.

   e. When they needed help.

   f. If they didn't want to go to school.

   g. If someone was hurting their mother or father.

IF'S, AND'S, OR BUT'S:

1. Remind children of the people they could talk to if one of the above situations were happening in their lives. Learning alternatives is the first step in controlling one's own behavior.

2. Reviewing the concept of telling others can never be reinforced too strongly. Children need to be told repeatedly that they can talk to others who can help them.

3. Have parents assist in the use of the puppets by role playing one of the skits.

FAMILY ACTIVITY:	26.8 Dynamic Doer Card Game and Family Hug
CONSTRUCT:	Developmental
MATERIALS:	Dynamic Doer and Pair It Card Games

GOAL:

To reinforce the value of positive family interaction.

OBJECTIVES:

1. To allow family members to play cooperatively.

2. To reinforce appropriate social interactions.

3. To reinforce appropriate behaviors in a competitive situation.

4. To reinforce comfort in using nurturing touch.

PROCEDURES:

1. This game follows the same rules as "Old Maid" except players try to end up with the Dynamic Doer Card. The objective is to get rid of all your cards while trying to keep the Dynamic Doer card.

2. Allow approximately 8 cards for each player.

3. Add the Dynamic Doer card to the deck, shuffle, and deal the cards to all players.

4. Players may hold their pairs in front of them after all cards have been dealt. The Dynamic Doer card holder must not tell that s/he has that card, in hopes that someone else will not draw it.

5. The first player then draws a card from the player on his/her right. If it is a match to one of his/her cards, the pair can be laid down in front of the player. If not, the player adds the card to his/her hand.

6. Continue drawing from the player on the right until all cards have been matched and only the Dynamic Doer card remains.

FAMILY HUG:

1. End each home visit with a family hug. Everyone get in a circle and put your arms around the people next to you. During the family hug time. anyone can say anything they like. It is a time for free expression.

2. At a natural time, close the activities for the day.

IF'S, AND'S, OR BUT'S:

Competitive games may generate feelings about losing. Some children may need support.

NURTURING PROGRAM FOR PARENTS AND CHILDREN BIRTH TO FIVE YEARS

SESSION 27

BEHAVIOR CONSTRUCT: Empathy

SESSION CONCEPT: Personal Space

BRIEF DESCRIPTION: Parents learn to identify their personal space through the body bubble exercise. Children learn and practice how to say "No" to unwanted touch.

INTENDED USE: For parents of children birth to 5 years

PREREQUISITE KNOWLEDGE: None

AGENDA

Parent Activities   Materials

27.1   Icebreaker and Home Practice Check In   *Parent Handbooks*

27.2   Body Bubble   None

27.3   Home Practice Exercise   *Parent Handbooks*

Family Activities*   Materials

27.4   Family Nurturing Time   *Nurturing Book for Babies and Children*

27.5   Hello Time: I Spy   None

27.6   Boat Song   None

27.7   Circle Time: "Saying No"   Puppets

27.8   No-Mobile and Family Hug   Scissors, glue, magazines, string, coat hangers

*For parents with infants or toddlers, use activities presented in *Nurturing Book for Babies and Children*. For parents with preschoolers (ages 3-5), use the activities listed below Family Nurturing Time.

GOAL:

To increase parents' awareness of close social contacts.

OBJECTIVES:

1. To increase parents' awareness of their conditions for closeness.

2. To identify the person the parent feels closest to.

PROCEDURES:

1. Begin today's parent activities by having each adult respond to the following:

   - To feel close to another person, I _____ .

   - The person I feel closest to right now is _____ .

2. After each parent has had an opportunity to respond to the statements above, review the Home Practice Exercise from the previous meeting. Also discuss perceived changes in family members and their interactions as reported in the family log.

IF'S, AND'S, OR BUT'S:

Being aware of the person closest to the parent should give you an indication of how social needs are currently being met. If the parents' child is the person the parent feels closest to, perhaps inappropriate expectations are being placed on the child.

PARENT ACTIVITY: 27.2 Body Bubble
CONSTRUCT: Self-Awareness
MATERIALS: None

GOAL:

To increase awareness of personal space requirements.

OBJECTIVES:

1. To increase parents' awareness of their personal space.

2. To increase parents' awareness of others' personal space.

3. To gain an understanding of the concept of the "body bubble."

4. To increase parents' ability to say "no."

5. To increase positive use of personal power.

PROCEDURES:

1. Begin by informing the parent that today's discussion on nurturing self will focus on ways to protect self against unwanted touch and sex. Form partners for this one-to-one exercise. Tell the parents that there will be no touching, to allay any anxiety engendered by title.

2. Stand about 7 to 10 feet away, facing each other. Have one person signal to his/her partner to advance forward, stopping the person at a distance of comfort. This is the body bubble.

3. The person remaining stationary will become aware of his/her comfort with the partner standing a distance away. Instruct the partner to cut the distance in half. Ask the stationary person to get in touch with his/her feelings. Instruct the partner to then double the original distance. Ask the stationary person to get in touch with his/her feelings.

4. Reverse roles and repeat the entire exercise.

5. Next, ask your partner to remain stationary while you move very close (without touching). Move to the side, back, front of the other person, look over his/her shoulders, look up their nostrils, etc.

6. Reverse roles and repeat the entire exercise.

7. Process the entire activity.

   - Were the body bubbles the same size for of each of you?

   - Was it hard when one needed to be closer or farther away than the one moving liked?

   - Which was harder? Were you surprised?

   - How did each of you feel when your space was invaded?

   - How did you feel invading the space of others?

   - How do people constantly invade your personal space?

   - How can people use their personal power to keep their body space intact?

8. Discuss with the parents that everyone has a right to their own body and that their private places are not just their genitals, but their entire body. As such, no one has a right to touch them anywhere without their permission first. This includes strangers, parents, husbands, wives, boyfriends, and girlfriends.

9. Process the concept presented on body ownership with the parent.

   - What rights do young infants and children have regarding their right not be touched?

   - What ways are young children touched that they don't like? Draw upon personal past experiences.

10. To help people learn to protect themselves from being victims of unwanted touch, they have to honor the personal space wishes of others. If someone doesn't want to be touched, kissed, held, etc., the request must be honored.

11. Role play with the parent their right to say "no" to unwanted touch. Practice saying the concept "no." Let one partner be insistent on kissing, touching, or having intercourse while the other person practices saying, "No, I don't want to (kiss, touch you, etc.)." Switch roles and repeat the activity.

12. After role play is completed, process the activity. Discuss the concept of "date rape." Attempt to define the term. Process utilizing the following questions:

- How can you tell when necking can lead to date rape?

- How might the man act? What might he say? What would be his feelings?

- What can you do if you find yourself in a situation that could lead to date rape?

IF'S, AND'S, OR BUT'S:

1. The touch exercise will not be an easy one for some. Encourage them to try.

2. Pay close attention to the parents who are having difficulty saying "no" and who look overwhelmed. They may be currently victimized and need your help.

3. Date rape discussion may bring up some old pain for some women. Pay close attention for signs of distress and offer support and perhaps a chance to talk.

PARENT ACTIVITY: 27.3 Home Practice Exercise
CONSTRUCT: Empathy, Self-Awareness
MATERIALS: Parent Handbooks

GOAL:

To increase parents' awareness of violations of personal body space.

OBJECTIVES:

1. To become aware of violations to personal body space.

2. To become aware of violations to the personal body space of their children.

3. To increase awareness of feelings resulting from body space violations.

4. To maintain a warm and supportive atmosphere.

PROCEDURES:

1. Instruct parents to locate the Home Practice Exercise on page 142 in their Handbooks. Review the exercise with them:

   a. Notice two times your personal space had been violated.

   b. Notice one time your child(ren)'s personal space was violated.

   c. Notice one time you could have violated your child(ren)'s personal space but didn't.

   d. Complete family log.

2. Tell parents that in addition to the Home Practice Exercise, they are to spend 30 minutes each day with each of their children in nurturing playtime activities. Playtime is a time with the parent and child alone—no TV, no other distractions. Playing a game or reading books are good activities. From the *Nurturing Book for Babies and Children*, have the parents practice activities listed in the following sections: Activities for Infants, Activities for Toddlers, Activities for Preschoolers, or Infant and Child Massage. Have the parents remember what they did and report the next week.

IF'S, AND'S, OR BUT'S:

Children's body space can be violated early by taking over a task the child is not performing fast enough like zipping a jacket, tying shoes, etc. Alert parents to respect personal body space of children by first asking permission to help.

FAMILY ACTIVITY: 27.4 Family Nurturing Time
CONSTRUCT: Empathy, Self-Awareness
MATERIALS: Nurturing Book for Babies and Children

ACTIVITIES FOR INFANTS (Birth to 15 months):

Utilizing the *Nurturing Book for Babies and Children*, select activities from the sections entitled Activities for Infants or Infant and Child Massage. Engage parents in practicing songs, play and stimulation activities, or massage. Vary the activities weekly to sustain interest.

ACTIVITIES FOR TODDLERS (15 months to 3 years):

Utilizing the *Nurturing Book for Babies and Children*, select activities from the sections entitled Activities for Toddlers or Infant and Child Massage. Engage parents in practicing songs, play, language, and movement activities, or massage. Vary the activities weekly to sustain interest.

ACTIVITIES FOR PRESCHOOLERS (3-5 years):

Use the following activities when working with preschool children and their parents. Use the activities as the basis for involving infants and toddlers if you are conducting a home visit with children ages birth to five years.

FAMILY ACTIVITY: 27.5 Hello Time: I Spy
CONSTRUCT: Empathy
MATERIALS: None

GOAL:

To describe simple, tangible characteristics of both self and others.

OBJECTIVES:

1. To increase children's awareness of self.

2. To increase children's awareness of others.

PROCEDURES:

1. Have children and adults sit in a circle on the floor.

2. Explain that today we will be playing a guessing game called "I Spy." We all take turns describing something someone has in the room, and everyone else tries to guess who it is. For example, I say, "I Spy someone wearing glasses," and everyone else has to guess who I spy.

IF'S, AND'S, OR BUT'S:

If a child is having difficulty describing another child, give a prompt.

FAMILY ACTIVITY: 27.6 Boat Song
CONSTRUCT: Empathy
MATERIALS: None

GOAL:

To increase positive parent-child interactions through music and touch.

OBJECTIVES:

1. To increase parents' ability to enjoy fun times with their children.

2. To have children practice gross motor coordination.

PROCEDURES:

1. This activity takes place on the floor. Adults and children pretend to be "boats" by sitting with their legs extended in front of them and spread apart. One or two children sit in each "boat" by sitting between an adult's legs, with their backs to the adult. The children hold onto the adult's hands and pretend that they are oars.

2. Sing the song "Michael, Row Your Boat Ashore" substituting each child's name for "Michael." As you sing, move your arms in a forward/backward movement stimulating rowing a boat while holding hands with the children in each boat. Repeat the song until each person's name has been used once.

IF'S, AND'S, OR BUT'S:

1. Repeat the activity with children in pairs. They can take turns being the "boat" or the "rower."

2. Emphasize taking turns by having the person whose name has been sung choose the next person to be sung about.

3. This is a good activity to provide appropriate physical contact between adults and children in a nonthreatening way. The activity also emphasizes cooperation in taking turns and waiting.

FAMILY ACTIVITY:	**27.7 Circle Time: Saying "No"**
CONSTRUCT:	**Self-Awareness**
MATERIALS:	**Puppets**

GOAL:

To help children become more assertive in saying "No."

OBJECTIVES:

1. To identify different ways to say "No."

2. To practice assertive ways to say "No."

3. To offer support to children in their attempts to be assertive.

4. To increase children's ability to discriminate situations to say no.

5. To practice the use of no to protect self.

6. To gain confidence in controlling self-behavior.

PROCEDURES:

1. Today we are going to talk about saying "No." Sometimes we have to say "NO" to other kids and adults so we don't do things we really don't want to do. Saying "NO" is not always easy.

2. Encourage children to brainstorm on all the ways they say "No."

3. Discuss with the children times when it is okay to say no. Discuss times when it might not be okay to say no.

4. Encourage group to think of verbal ways to say "No" — nonverbal ways to say "No" (body language). Discuss.

5. Role play ways to say "No" and not really mean it.

6. Role play ways to say "No" with conviction. Discuss.

7. Role play "Scared No." Discuss.

8. Role play aggressive ways to say "No." Discuss.

9. Role play assertive ways to say "No." Discuss.

10. Playact the following situations with puppets in which the puppets refuse to participate by saying "No."

   a. A stranger asking the child to go for a ride.

   b. An invitation to steal something with a friend.

   c. A stranger asking a child in the playground to go for a walk.

   d. Any relevant class situation.

11. Just after the invitation has been made to perform an unacceptable behavior, elicit from the children what the puppet should do. In all the above cases, the puppet should say no and walk away. Have the children practice saying "No" by shouting the word. After the children have shouted "No," continue with the skit and have the puppet say no and walk/run away.

IF'S, AND'S, OR BUT'S:

Follow through on the above situations by modeling the desired behavior.

FAMILY ACTIVITY: 27.8 No-Mobile and Family Hug
CONSTRUCT: Self-Awareness
MATERIALS: Scissors, glue, magazines, string, coat hangers

GOAL:

To empower children with the ability to control their own behavior and protect themselves.

OBJECTIVES:

1. To allow children to express "No" visually.

2. To increase children's ability to protect themselves.

3. To increase children's ability to choose appropriate behaviors.

4. To reinforce comfort in using nurturing touch.

PROCEDURES:

1. Explain to children that sometimes we want to say "No" to someone but we have a hard time. We are going to make a mobile that says "No."

2. Encourage children to think of all the ways they can say no. Have them cut pictures out of magazines, draw the word, etc.

3. Help them put their mobiles together using string, tape, and coat hangers.

FAMILY HUG:

1. End each home visit with a family hug. Everyone get in a circle and put your arms around the people next to you. During the family hug time, anyone can say anything they like. It is a time for free expression.

2. At a natural time, close the activities for the day.

IF'S, AND'S, OR BUT'S:

A poster of "No" to hang in the child's room would substitute for a mobile.

NURTURING PROGRAM FOR PARENTS AND CHILDREN BIRTH TO FIVE YEARS

SESSION 28

BEHAVIOR CONSTRUCT:	Self-Awareness
SESSION CONCEPT:	Bodies, Conception, and Pregnancy
BRIEF DESCRIPTION:	Parents and children discuss names given to body parts with the focus on the genitals, breasts, and buttocks.
INTENDED USE:	For parents of children birth to 5 years
PREREQUISITE KNOWLEDGE:	Personal Power

AGENDA

Parent Activities

		Materials
28.1	Icebreaker and Home Practice Check In	*Parent Handbooks*
28.2	Bodies, Conception, and Pregnancy	None
28.3	Home Practice Exercise	*Parent Handbooks*

Family Activities*

		Materials
28.4	Family Nurturing Time	*Nurturing Book for Babies and Children*
28.5	Hello Time: Guess How I Feel	Feeling Faces
28.6	Circle Time: In and Out the Window	None
28.7	Our Bodies and Family Hug	Our Bodies pictures

*For parents with infants or toddlers, use activities presented in *Nurturing Book for Babies and Children*. For parents with preschoolers (ages 3-5), use the activities listed below Family Nurturing Time.

PARENT ACTIVITY: 28.1 Icebreaker and Home Practice Check In
CONSTRUCT: Self-Awareness
MATERIALS: Parent Handbooks

GOAL:

To increase parents' awareness of attitudes and feelings towards their sexual identity.

OBJECTIVES:

1. To increase parents' awareness of their attitudes towards nudity, sexual acts, and sexual body parts.

2. To encourage parents to share the messages they received from their parents regarding sex.

PROCEDURES:

1. Begin today's parent activities by having each adult respond to the following:

   - One message I received from my parents regarding sex was _____ .

   - One anxiety I have today in teaching my children about sex is _____ .

2. After each parent has had an opportunity to respond to the statements above, review the Home Practice Exercise from the previous meeting. Also discuss perceived changes in family members and their interactions as reported in the family log.

IF'S, AND'S, OR BUT'S:

Discussions related to sex can be incredibly frightening. However, knowing where some of the anxiety comes from helps parents begin to deal with it.

PARENT ACTIVITY: 28.2 Bodies, Conception, and Pregnancy
CONSTRUCT: Self-Awareness
MATERIALS: None

GOAL:

To increase parents' ability to use appropriate language in discussing body part recognition and function.

OBJECTIVES:

1. To identify words used to describe body functions.

2. To identify body part terminology.

3. To share messages received from parents regarding nudity, genitals and sex.

4. To express anxieties regarding sexual body areas.

5. To dispel myths surrounding contraception and pregnancy.

PROCEDURES:

1. Inform the family that today's discussion on ways to nurture self will focus on discussing pregnancy and bodies.

2. Suggest that there are many myths that prevail regarding pregnancy, masturbation, and sex. Many people are completely unaware of their own anatomy. The discussion today will focus on learning about reproductive anatomy. Write the words PENIS, VAGINA, INTER-COURSE, BREASTS, BUTTOCKS, MASTURBATION on a sheet of paper. Brainstorm all the various "slang" names used to refer to them. Write the words on the paper.

3. Process the activity using the following questions:

   - As parents, what words are you teaching your children to refer to their genitals? (Reinforce the use of proper terms to describe body parts.)

   - Why are slang words used to describe sexual functions and reproductive anatomy?

   - Why do you think people are anxious when they try to discuss their sexual body parts?

4. Inform the parents that you will read a series of value statements. They are to indicate how they feel about each statement by "thumbs up" (agree), "thumbs down" (disagree), and "palms down, facing the floor or table" (no comment). After each statement, give individuals an opportunity to defend their positions. Make sure that a variety of values are represented.

   a. Birth control should be the woman's responsibility.

   b. Minors should be able to get birth control without notifying parents.

   c. Our government should pay for birth control methods for everyone who wants them.

   d. Parents should be the only ones allowed to give information about sex to their children.

   e. Birth control information should be available to all high school students.

5. Next, ask the parent to respond to the following by indicating whether the statement is a fact or a myth regarding getting pregnant:

   a. A girl who is a virgin must have an unbroken hymen. (Myth)

   b. Once a girl has had her first period, she can become pregnant. (Fact)

   c. It is unhealthy for women to bathe or swim during their periods. (Myth)

   d. The penis grows larger with frequent sexual intercourse. (Myth)

   e. An erection is caused by increased blood flow into the penis. (Fact)

   f. Females are born with unripened eggs in their ovaries. (Fact)

   g. Males are born with sperm in their testicles. (Myth)

   h. Masturbation causes insanity. (Myth)

   i. Once a boy gets an erection, he must ejaculate or he will get sick. (Myth)

   j. The only time a girl can get pregnant is when a boy ejaculates in her. (Myth)

   k. By withdrawing a penis before ejaculation, a girl cannot get pregnant. (Myth)

l. After intercourse, if a girl uses a douche, she won't get pregnant. (Myth)

m. It is quite common for people to have absolutely no symptoms with gonorrhea, especially in early stages. (Fact)

n. There are virtually no health risks associated with condoms. (Fact)

o. Menstruation in females usually begins between ages 10 to 16 years. (Fact)

p. The first time a girl has intercourse, she can't get pregnant. (Myth)

q. A girl can get pregnant from kissing. (Myth)

r. If a boy fondles a girl's breasts, they will grow larger. (Myth)

s. A girl loses her virginity the first time she uses tampons. (Myth)

6. Process discussion by utilizing the following questions as guidelines:

   • If a man and a woman choose to be sexually active, and choose not to get pregnant, whose responsibility is it to use contraception?

   • What do adults find as the single biggest problem in using contraception?

   • If you are going to be sexually active, what are some ways to ensure contraception is being used?

   • What are some risks in being sexually active?

7. Discuss the facts and instruct the parents on functional ways to use contraception. What can men use? What can women use?

IF'S, AND'S, OR BUT'S:

1. Parents may be reluctant at first to suggest words — a little coaxing and the words will begin.

2. Expect a lot of giggling and silliness. Anxiety runs high with slang words. Be patient and reinforce attempts.

3. If the children are in earshot of the conversation, whisper or write the words on paper.

PARENT ACTIVITY: 28.3 Home Practice Exercise
CONSTRUCT: Empathy
MATERIALS: Parent Handbooks

GOAL:

To encourage parents to feel comfortable using proper terminology for sexual body parts.

OBJECTIVES:

1. To reinforce communication among family members.

2. To lessen personal anxiety regarding body part recognition.

3. To maintain a warm and supportive atmosphere.

PROCEDURES:

1. Instruct parents to locate the Home Practice Exercise on page 142 in their Handbooks. Review the exercise with them:

    a. During diapering or bath times, refer to body parts using correct terminology.

    b. Complete family log.

2. Tell parents that in addition to the Home Practice Exercise, they are to spend 30 minutes each day with each of their children in nurturing playtime activities. Playtime is a time with the parent and child alone — no TV, no other distractions. Playing a game or reading books are good activities. From the *Nurturing Book for Babies and Children*, have the parents practice activities listed in the following sections: Activities for Infants, Activities for Toddlers, Activities for Preschoolers, or Infant and Child Massage. Have the parents remember what they did and report the next week.

IF'S, AND'S, OR BUT'S:

The idea of calling genitals by their proper name is likely to make a lot of parents very anxious. Helping their children refer to their genitals with the same names will surely increase anxiety. Praise parents' efforts and support them and their children for trying.

FAMILY ACTIVITY:	**28.4 Family Nurturing Time**
CONSTRUCT:	**Empathy, Self-Awareness**
MATERIALS:	**Nurturing Book for Babies and Children**

ACTIVITIES FOR INFANTS (Birth to 15 months):

Utilizing the *Nurturing Book for Babies and Children*, select activities from the sections entitled Activities for Infants or Infant and Child Massage. Engage parents in practicing songs, play and stimulation activities, or massage. Vary the activities weekly to sustain interest.

ACTIVITIES FOR TODDLERS (15 months to 3 years):

Utilizing the *Nurturing Book for Babies and Children*, select activities from the sections entitled Activities or Toddlers or Infant and Child Massage. Engage parents in practicing songs, play, language, and movement activities, or massage. Vary the activities weekly to sustain interest.

ACTIVITIES FOR PRESCHOOLERS (3-5 years):

Use the following activities when working with preschool children and their parents. Use the activities as the basis for involving infants and toddlers if you are conducting a home visit with children ages birth to five years.

FAMILY ACTIVITY: 28.5 Hello Time: Guess How I Feel
CONSTRUCT: Empathy
MATERIALS: Feeling Faces

GOAL:

To increase awareness of facial expressions of feelings.

OBJECTIVES:

1. To allow children to recognize feelings with appropriate facial expression.

2. To encourage recognition of feelings in others.

3. To increase children's awareness of their own feelings.

PROCEDURES:

1. Assemble children and adults in a circle seated on the floor.

2. Begin by saying that today we are going to talk about feelings. Using the feeling faces, hold up a face and ask who can identify the feeling.

3. Have children suggest why the child may be feeling the way he/she is.

4. Ask the children and adults if anyone has recently felt the identified feeling.

IF'S, AND'S, OR BUT'S:

Feeling recognition and awareness are important prerequisites for managing one's behavior.

FAMILY ACTIVITY: 28.6 Circle Time: In and Out the Window
CONSTRUCT: Empathy
MATERIALS: None

GOAL:

To build positive parent-child interactions.

OBJECTIVES:

1. To help parents and children relate in a positive, nurturing way.

2. To help parents learn to enjoy their children.

PROCEDURES:

1. Have all children and parents stand in a large circle without holding hands.

2. Choose one person to start the game by walking around the circle weaving behind and in front of each person as the group sings:

> Go in and out the window, go in and out the window,
> Go in and out the window, as we have done before.

3. The person stops and stands in front of someone in the circle as the group sings:

> Now stand and face your partner, now stand and face your partner,
> Now stand and face your partner, as we have done before.

4. The person takes the hands of his partner and they weave in and out of the circle as the group sings:

> Now take her off to London, now take her off to London,
> Now take her off to London, as we have done before.

5. This game continues until everyone has a turn.

IF'S, AND'S, OR BUT'S:

Have parents act as partners with each of their children.

FAMILY ACTIVITY:	**28.7 Our Bodies and Family Hug**
CONSTRUCT:	**Self-Awareness**
MATERIALS:	**Our Bodies Pictures**

GOAL:

To increase children's awareness of proper body part recognition.

OBJECTIVES:

1. To increase understanding of the proper terms used to identify genitals.

2. To increase children's ability to protect themselves from unwanted touch.

3. To empower children with knowledge regarding the ownership of their bodies.

4. To reinforce comfort in using nurturing touch.

PROCEDURES:

1. Have children and adults sit in a circle on the floor.

2. Let's begin. Today we are going to talk about our bodies and the words we use for different parts of our bodies.

3. (Hold up front view pictures of a nude boy and girl.) I want you all to take a look at these pictures. Does anyone notice something different about these pictures? (They don't have any clothes on.) When are times when you don't have any clothes on?

4. Our job today is to talk about what we call parts of our body:

   a. (Pointing to the nose) Can anyone tell me what they call this part of the body? Nose, that's right.

   b. (Pointing to the hands) How about this part? What do we call these? Hands!

   c. (Pointing to the knees) And what about this part? Knees, very good!

   d. (Pointing to the genitals) What do you call this part of the boy's body? (penis, pee-pee, dick, etc.) We call that the penis. Can everyone say the word?

   e. (Pointing to the genitals) What do you call this part of the girl's body? (vagina, pee-pee, cunt, etc.) We call this part the vagina. Let's all say the word vagina.

   f. (Pointing to the girl's breasts) What do you call this part of the girl's body? (breasts, boobs, tits, etc.) These we call breasts. Can we say the word breasts?

   g. (Pointing to both the girls' mouth and boys' mouth) Can anyone tell me what this part of the body is called? (mouth, lips, etc.) Mouth, good!

   h. (Pointing to the buttocks) Can anyone tell me what this part of the body is called? (buttocks, butt, ass, buns, etc.) Buttocks or butt is a good word for this part.

FAMILY HUG:

1. End each home visit with a family hug. Everyone get in a circle and put your arms around the people next to you. During the family hug time, anyone can say anything they like. It is a time for free expression.

2. At a natural time, close the activities for the day.

IF'S, AND'S, OR BUT'S:

1. An obvious heightened situation for children and parents, anxiety will most likely run high. Support children in their attempts to learn.

2. Let parents know of the content before the activity begins. Parents may refuse to use proper names for body parts. Check out their anxiety.

NURTURING PROGRAM FOR ADULTS AND CHILDREN BIRTH TO FIVE YEARS

SESSION 29

BEHAVIOR CONSTRUCT: Empathy

SESSION CONCEPT: Scary Touch, Love, AIDS

BRIEF DESCRIPTION: Parents and children discuss the concept of scary touch and how to protect one's body

INTENDED USE: For parents of children birth to 5 years

PREREQUISITE KNOWLEDGE: Our Bodies, Body Bubble

AGENDA

Parent Activities	Materials
29.1 Icebreaker and Home Practice Check In	*Parent Handbooks*
29.2 Scary Touch, Love, and AIDS	Paper, pen
29.3 Home Practice Exercise	*Parent Handbooks*

Family Activities*	Materials
29.4 Family Nurturing Time	*Nurturing Book for Babies and Children*
29.5 Hello Time: Happy to See You	None
29.6 Blanket Game	Large blanket or large bed sheet
29.7 Circle Time: Scary Touch	Pictures of nude children, Scary Touch dolls
29.8 Tear and Paste and Family Hug	Old magazines, phone book pages or tissue paper, glue, cardboard, paper plates, construction paper

*For parents with infants or toddlers, use activities presented in *Nurturing Book for Babies and Children*. For parents with preschoolers (ages 3-5), use the activities listed below Family Nurturing Time.

PARENT ACTIVITY: 29.1 Icebreaker and Home Practice Check In
CONSTRUCT: Self-Awareness
MATERIALS: Parent Handbooks

GOAL:

To initiate discussion regarding beliefs about our bodies.

OBJECTIVES:

1. To become aware if how perceptions of our bodies influence how we feel about ourselves.

2. To increase awareness of anxieties related to our bodies.

PROCEDURES:

1. Begin today's parent activities by having each adult respond to the following:

   • When I look at my body, I feel _____ .

   • If I could change my body, I would _____ .

2. After each parent has had an opportunity to respond to the statements above, review the Home Practice Exercise from the previous meeting. Also discuss perceived changes in family members and their interactions as reported in the family log.

IF'S, AND'S, OR BUT'S:

Most adults either don't find their bodies appealing or are reluctant to accept their physical state of being. Listen closely for negative or positive identities based solely on physical appearance.

PARENT ACTIVITY: 29.2 Scary Touch, Love, and AIDS
CONSTRUCT: Empathy
MATERIALS: Paper, pen

GOAL:

To increase parents' awareness of their need to give and receive love.

OBJECTIVES:

1. To increase parents' awareness of feelings of love.

2. To increase parents' awareness of feelings of rejection.

3. To discuss the importance of dating.

4. To identify facts and myths of AIDS.

PROCEDURES:

1. Open the activity by stating that today's discussion on nurturing self will focus on love, dating, and AIDS.

2. Share that we all have a basic need to be loved and to give love. Being in love means that two people give of themselves in an open, honest manner and feel good about themselves as a result. Many of us fear the loss of another's love, affection, support, or caring because of our statements and actions. The most important relationship we have is that with our parents. When our parents withdraw their love, we fear that we are unlovable and feel rejected. As a result, we deny or avoid our feelings of rejection. Rejection is when someone refuses to accept our love and refuses to share theirs.

3. Discuss the differences between the words LOVE and SEX. Process the discussion by encouraging the parents to respond to the following:

   - The difference between love and sex is _____.

   - A guy and a girl go out for a date for pizza and a movie. He pays for the movie and pizza and both have a good time. Afterwards, he tells the girl she owes him. His payment is intercourse. Should she "pay" him back? Should she feel obligated?

   - Can either love or sex exist without the other?

   - How do parents feel about their children being sexually active? Why?

4. Mention that if adults choose to be sexually active, then they need to practice safe sex. Begin the discussion of AIDS by asking parents to complete the following statements:

   - One way you can acquire AIDS is _____.

   - One way to prevent getting AIDS is _____.

   - One question I have regarding AIDS is _____.

5. Review the following facts and myths surrounding AIDS.

   - IT IS **NOT** POSSIBLE TO GET AIDS by being around someone with it.

   - IT IS **NOT** POSSIBLE TO GET AIDS by visiting, socializing, or working with someone who has it.

   - IT IS **NOT** POSSIBLE TO GET AIDS by being sneezed upon, coughed upon or breathed upon by anyone who has it.

   - IT IS **NOT** POSSIBLE TO GET AIDS by touching or sharing anything that a person with AIDS has touched: for instance, doorknobs, bed linens, clothing, towels, toilets, telephones, showers, swimming pools, eating utensils, drinking glasses. None of these has been found to carry AIDS.

   - IT IS **NOT** POSSIBLE TO GET AIDS by simply crying with, sweating with, kissing, or hugging people with AIDS.

   - IT IS POSSIBLE TO GET AIDS by sharing needles (for drugs or tattoos) with someone who has the AIDS virus.

   - IT IS POSSIBLE TO GET AIDS by having sex with someone who has the AIDS virus (some people have the virus without symptoms).

   - IT IS POSSIBLE TO GET AIDS by nursing a child from a mother who has the AIDS virus.

- IT IS POSSIBLE TO GET AIDS by being born to a mother who has the AIDS virus (about 60% of those babies will have AIDS).

- IT IS POSSIBLE TO GET AIDS by through artificial insemination from a donor with the AIDS virus.

6. Focus on ways to prevent AIDS. Re-address pregnancy prevention methods and discuss each method and its effectiveness in preventing AIDS.

IF'S, AND'S, OR BUT'S:

1. Talking about AIDS can be very frightening for many people. Present the facts; clarify the myths.

2. Information about AIDS is taken from **AIDS: Questions and Answers** published by Planned Parenthood Federation of America.

3. Sexual activity is an anxious topic for many of us to discuss. Some may feel that discussion of sexual activity is very uncomfortable and to some degree, is prying into their personal life. Conduct the discussion in a non-threatening manner.

4. Be supportive of the individuals who are struggling with discussing sexual activity. Silly behavior exhibited during the discussion should be an indication of how anxious the individual really is.

PARENT ACTIVITY: 29.3 Home Practice Exercise
CONSTRUCT: Empathy
MATERIALS: Parent Handbooks

GOAL:

To reinforce parents' ability to teach concepts of scary touch to their children.

OBJECTIVES:

1. To help children understand scary touch.

2. To empower children with the ability to refuse touch.

3. To empower children with the ability to be in control of their bodies.

4. To maintain a warm and supportive atmosphere.

PROCEDURES:

1. Instruct parents to locate the Home Practice Exercise on page 142 in their Handbooks. Review the exercise with them:

   a. Review with all your children the concepts of scary touch, body part terminology, ownership of body, and permission to touch.

   b. Complete family log.

---

2. Tell parents that in addition to the Home Practice Exercise, they are to spend 30 minutes each day with each of their children in nurturing playtime activities. Playtime is a time with the parent and child alone — no TV, no other distractions. Playing a game or reading books are good activities. From the *Nurturing Book for Babies and Children*, have the parents practice activities listed in the following sections: Activities for Infants, Activities for Toddlers, Activities for Preschoolers, or Infant and Child Massage. Have the parents remember what they did and report the next week.

IF'S, AND'S, OR BUT'S:

Remind the parents that they already practiced teaching the concepts in their role play. Actually teaching the concepts to their children will not be much different.

FAMILY ACTIVITY:	**29.4 Family Nurturing Time**
CONSTRUCT:	**Empathy, Self-Awareness**
MATERIALS:	**Nurturing Book for Babies and Children**

ACTIVITIES FOR INFANTS (Birth to 15 months):

Utilizing the *Nurturing Book for Babies and Children*, select activities from the sections entitled Activities for Infants or Infant and Child Massage. Engage parents in practicing songs, play and stimulation activities, or massage. Vary the activities weekly to sustain interest.

ACTIVITIES FOR TODDLERS (15 months to 3 years):

Utilizing the *Nurturing Book for Babies and Children*, select activities from the sections entitled Activities for Toddlers or Infant and Child Massage. Engage parents in practicing songs, play, language, and movement activities, or massage. Vary the activities weekly to sustain interest.

ACTIVITIES FOR PRESCHOOLERS (3-5 years):

Use the following activities when working with preschool children and their parents. Use the activities as the basis for involving infants and toddlers if you are conducting a home visit with children ages birth to five years.

GOAL:

To reinforce family cohesion.

OBJECTIVES:

1. To personally greet each child and parent.

2. To experience successful interaction in a family setting.

3. To get parents and children to have fun.

PROCEDURES:

1. Have everyone sit on the floor in a circle.

2. Explain that we will take turns singing a song to each person in the group.

3. Go around the circle and sing the following song to each person (to the tune of "This is the Way We Wash Our Clothes").

> We're happy to see you here today,
> Here today, here today.

> We're happy to see you here today,
> Happy to see you,   (name) .

4. After the name, ask the person, "How are you today?"

5. All children and adults should be sung to and asked how they are.

IF'S, AND'S, OR BUT'S:

1. After a person has been sung to, he or she may choose the next person for the group to sing to.

2. Touch each person in some way when they are being greeted (i.e., shake hands, touch their arm, pat their shoulder), but do not force this if a person is uncomfortable. Ask the person how they would like to be touched.

3. In a family setting, parents may be called by their first name or by their role (mom, dad, pop, mother, etc.). Check with the parent to see which they prefer prior to beginning the activity.

FAMILY ACTIVITY:	29.6 Blanket Game
CONSTRUCT:	Age Appropriate Developmental Expectation
MATERIALS:	Large blanket or large bed sheet

GOAL:

To reinforce positive family interactions.

OBJECTIVES:

1. To reinforce positive trusting interactions with adults.

2. To use large muscles.

3. To reinforce creative imagination.

PROCEDURES:

1. Have all children and adults sit close together on the floor.

2. An adult covers the group with a large blanket. Make sure everyone is under the blanket.

3. The adult tells the group (under the blanket) to listen carefully, then says:

   When I take the blanket off, you will be _____(animal name)_____ .
   (i.e., monkeys, birds, lions, cows, etc.)

4. Pull the blanket off the group (be dramatic about it) and encourage them to act like the animal named. Adults in the group should model expected behaviors. Let this go on for about 1/2 minute, then call the children and adults back to sit on the floor again.

5. When the group is sitting on the floor, repeat the activity for a different animal.

IF'S, AND'S, OR BUT'S:

1. Be sure to reassure children who may be frightened of being under the blanket.

2. Call children back to group using the animal name; i.e., "Come on back to your pen, little pigs," or, "All the cows need to return to the barn," etc.

FAMILY ACTIVITY:	29.7 Circle Time: Scary Touch
CONSTRUCT:	Developmental
MATERIALS:	Pictures of nude children, Scary Touch dolls

GOAL:

To increase the child's ability to identify and respond with judgments regarding physical touch.

OBJECTIVES:

1. To increase the child's understanding of appropriate and inappropriate sexual and nonsexual touch.

2. To increase the child's ability to effectively control or manage situations when they are being touched inappropriately.

3. To increase a child's assertiveness regarding not wanting to be touched.

PROCEDURES:

1. Have children and adults sit in a circle on the floor.

2. Let's begin. Today we are going to talk about touching. Touching is very special and most of us like to be touched. Does anyone here not like to be touched? (Process any responses.) Do you remember Ellie and Benny? What did we call that kind of touch? (Hurting touch.) Why was it hurting touch? (Benny was hurt by Ellie.) We are going to talk about a touch that we call "scary touch." Does anyone know what being scared is/feels like?

3. Sometimes other children and adults touch us in places and ways that scare us. Who can remember what boys called the body part between their legs? (Penis.) The body part between the legs of girls? (Vagina.) The place we sit? (Butt.) The place we talk? (Mouth.)

4. These places on our bodies are all very special places. Sometimes adults or other children get confused and want to touch us in these places on our bodies. Just like the rest of our body, we own these parts. Owning them means we don't have to let anyone touch them without our permission. We can use our personal power and say, "No, don't touch me here," or "I don't like being touched here."

5. Being touched in these places without our permission doesn't feel very good. Has anyone ever been kissed by an Aunt or Uncle or other people when you didn't want to be? How did you feel? Has anyone ever been touched in any of these other places when you didn't give your permission? How did that feel?

6. (Hold up pictures of boys and girls with arms crossed.) A good way to remember where you have a right not to be touched without permission and to use your personal power to say "No" is anywhere you can cross your hands. These are special places and no one can touch you there unless you say so.

7. (Holding up the two paper dolls with movable arms.) I have two friends with me today, _____ and _____ (provide names.) Can someone show me where _____ and _____ should not let anyone touch them without their permission? (Let children take turns crossing the arms of the dolls over their mouths, breasts (girls), genitals, and buttocks.)

8. Let's practice pointing to the places on our body by crossing our hands. (Have the children stand up, cross their hands, and place their crossed hands over their mouth, breasts, genitals, and buttocks.)

IF'S, AND'S, OR BUT'S:

1. With permission means no one can touch you without you first allowing them to: the optimal use of personal power.

2. Parents should participate in the discussion reinforcing the concept of the right to say "no" to unwanted touch.

FAMILY ACTIVITY: 29.8 Tear and Paste and Family Hug
CONSTRUCT: Developmental
MATERIALS: Old magazines, phone book pages or tissue paper, glue, cardboard, paper plates, construction paper

GOAL:

To encourage creative expression through the use of developmental capabilities.

OBJECTIVES:

1. To create in art.

2. To enhance fine motor movement.

3. To increase the ability to control finger muscles.

4. To increase the child's awareness of shapes, sizes, and proportions.

5. To reinforce comfort in using nurturing touch.

PROCEDURES:

1. Assemble everyone around a table or on the floor with some protective covering.

2. Provide old magazines, phone book pages, or tissue paper and let the children tear out pieces of paper to their heart's content.

3. Practice tearing together. Talk about the "pinching" fingers. Keep both pinchers together to get the paper to do what you want it to do. Children can learn to control the torn edge by moving their fingers inch by inch as they tear.

4. Practice tearing the paper into shapes. Let's tear a small piece from our big piece. Let's tear our paper right in half. Tear, together, long skinny strips, tiny bits, and so on.

5. Have the children paste their shapes on cardboard, paper plates, or construction paper.

6. Let the children participate in clean up.

FAMILY HUG:

1. End each home visit with a family hug. Everyone get in a circle and put your arms around the people next to you. During the family hug time, anyone can say anything they like. It is a time for free expression.

2. At a natural time, close the activities for the day.

IF'S, AND'S, OR BUT'S:

Have parents assist their child in their art activity.

NURTURING PROGRAM FOR ADULTS AND CHILDREN BIRTH TO FIVE YEARS

SESSION 30

BEHAVIOR CONSTRUCT:	Empathy
SESSION CONCEPT:	Body Map
BRIEF DESCRIPTION:	Parents draw a picture of their bodies and indicate where they have felt good and bad touch. Afterwards, the parents engage in stress reduction by going on a "vacation." Children practice recognizing scary touch, telling someone, and owning their body.
INTENDED USE:	For parents of children birth to 5 years
PREREQUISITE KNOWLEDGE:	Body Bubble, Our Bodies, Scary Touch

AGENDA

Parent Activities	Materials
30.1　Icebreaker and Home Practice Check In	*Parent Handbooks*
30.2　Body Map	Magic markers, large sheets of paper
30.3　Vacation Visualization	None
30.4　Home Practice Exercise	*Parent Handbooks*

Family Activities*	Materials
30.5　Family Nurturing Time	*Nurturing Book for Babies and Children*
30.6　Hello Time: The Farmer in the Dell	None
30.7　I'm a Dynamic Doer	None
30.8　Circle Time: I Own My Body	Puppets, Our Bodies pictures
30.9　Pair It and Family Hug	Dynamic Doer and Pair It Card Games

*For parents with infants or toddlers, use activities presented in *Nurturing Book for Babies and Children*. For parents with preschoolers (ages 3-5), use the activities listed below Family Nurturing Time.

PARENT ACTIVITY: 30.1 Icebreaker and Home Practice Check In
CONSTRUCT: Empathy, Self-Awareness
MATERIALS: Parent Handbooks

GOAL:

To increase parents' awareness of childhood hurts.

OBJECTIVES:

1. To help parents recognize and express feelings.

2. To empower parents to act on their hurts.

PROCEDURES:

1. Begin today's parent activities by having each adult respond to the following:

    *   One childhood hurt that I'm still holding onto is _____ .

    *   I would like to not have this hurt, but _____ .

2. After each parent has had an opportunity to respond to the statements above, review the Home Practice Exercise from the previous meeting. Also discuss perceived changes in family members and their interactions as reported in the family log.

IF'S, AND'S, OR BUT'S:

Childhood hurts are feelings associated with the presence or absence of behavior. Get parents in touch with residual hurts that complicate their current lives.

PARENT ACTIVITY: 30.2 Body Map
CONSTRUCT: Empathy, Self-Awareness
MATERIALS: Magic markers, large sheets of paper

GOAL:

To increase parents' sensitivity to appropriate and inappropriate touch interactions.

OBJECTIVES:

1. To enable parents to be aware of their personal touch histories.

2. To encourage parents to touch their children in positive ways.

3. To increase parents' awareness of uncomfortable feelings they may have about touch.

4. To increase parents' sense of control over their own bodies.

PROCEDURES:

1. Tell the parents they are about to engage in a very difficult exercise. They will determine the impact of good and bad touch in their lives. Ask everyone to sit around a table. Have plenty of magic markers. Give each person a large sheet of paper. Let them know that they are to use the entire sheet of paper in this exercise. Facilitator should also participate in the exercise.

2. Instruct everyone to draw their bodies on the paper — both front view and back view. They are to pay attention to detail, that is, eyes, arms, legs, face, etc., have to be drawn — no stick figures allowed. Although they may choose not to, encourage them to draw themselves nude with genitals. Allow only 5 minutes to complete drawing bodies.

3. When everyone is done, share that touch is an important means of communication. Everyone will now explore touch in their lives.

   a. Instruct everyone to color in stripes all the places of the body that get a lot of touch. It could be self-touch or touch by others — if the body part or area gets touched a lot, color it with stripes. Touch may include anything like sexual touch, pushing up one's glasses on their nose, etc.

   b. Next, have everyone focus on areas of their body that get some touch, but not a lot. Color body parts and areas that get some touch with dots or small circles.

   c. Finally, have everyone focus on areas of their body that seldom get touched at all. Leave areas that seldom get touched white or blank.

4. Ask everyone to share their body maps by holding them up and discussing the areas colored and left blank.

5. After everyone has had a turn, suggest that they are now going to focus on a special type of touch called hurting touch and scary touch. Ask everyone to identify experiences of hurting touch and scary touch on their body as far back as they can remember. Have them place dark, black x's over those areas that have received hurting touch and scary touch. Any touch that didn't feel good can be hurting or scary. Some examples might be a spanking, painful injury, unwanted grabbing, a fight, an operation, etc.

6. When everyone has completed identifying these areas, ask each to share and discuss the x's. How did they feel about themselves and the person doing the hurting? If they were to draw the body maps of their children, would their children's bodies have x's on them that the parents placed?

IF'S, AND'S, OR BUT'S:

1. Touching is both a powerful positive and negative experience. Drawing one's body map is not going to be easy for all parents in the group. Old, painful experiences will surface. Be prepared to offer parents support.

2. Allow parents to share whatever they wish.

GOAL:

To increase parents' ability to take pleasure in their senses.

OBJECTIVES:

1. To help parents recognize and appreciate their own ability to enjoy sensual stimulation.

2. To help them differentiate between sensuality and sexuality.

3. To help parents unwind from body map exercise.

PROCEDURES:

1. Ask parents to lie on the floor or assume a comfortable position in chairs.

2. Tell them this is going to be a short, very short vacation.

3. Begin:

> You can relax now and it might be very pleasant for you to enjoy yourself. Take a few deep breaths to help you center and to help you enjoy the peace of the moment. Relax and let your mind paint the pictures for you that you would most like to see or that would be best for you. Enjoy yourself as we think together. I am going to take you on a remembering fantasy. (Pause after each item.)

Vacation

Remember a beautiful sunset.

Remember the sound of the water in a little creek.

Remember the taste of hot buttered popcorn.

Remember the sight of a cozy campfire.

Remember the feel of clean sheets.

Remember the sound of rain on the roof.

Remember the smell of a meadow in the hot summer sun.

Remember the sound of someone special saying, "I love you."

Remember the stars and the moon in the dark sky on a clear summer's night.

Remember the softness of a baby's skin.

Remember the feeling of the hot sun on your skin.

Remember a cool drink on a hot day when you were thirsty.

Remember the smell of vanilla when you were a kid making cookies.

Remember the taste of your favorite food.

Remember a beautiful song.

Remember the wind on your face on a hot day.

Remember a special kiss.

Remember the feel of a perfectly right bath as you sink into it.

And now remember where you are now and with whom and come back to the group, come back to us now.

(Give them a minute or two to get organized.)

IF'S, AND'S, OR BUT'S:

Tell the parents they have just had a very sensual experience, not **sexual**, but **sensual**. They have experienced stimulation in all of their senses:

SIGHT   SOUND   TOUCH   TASTE   SMELL

A full life is one that experiences an awareness in each of the senses.

PARENT ACTIVITY: 30.4 Home Practice Exercise
CONSTRUCT: Empathy
MATERIALS: Parent Handbooks

GOAL:

To increase parents' experiences with positive touch.

OBJECTIVES:

1. To encourage positive touch with objects.

2. To encourage positive touch with another adult.

3. To encourage positive touch with children.

4. To maintain a warm and supportive atmosphere.

PROCEDURES:

1. Instruct parents to locate the Home Practice Exercise on page 142 in their Handbooks. Review the exercise with them:

   a. Practice positive touch with some **thing** – enjoy touching some**thing**.

   b. Practice positive touch with some **one** – enjoy touching some**one**. (Remember you are a person.)

   c. Touch your child(ren) in a nurturing way.

   d. Complete family log.

2. Tell parents that in addition to the Home Practice Exercise, they are to spend 30 minutes each day with each of their children in nurturing playtime activities. Playtime is a time with the parent and child alone — no TV, no other distractions. Playing a game or reading books are good activities. From the *Nurturing Book for Babies and Children*, have the parents practice activities listed in the following sections: Activities for Infants, Activities for Toddlers, Activities for Preschoolers, or Infant and Child Massage. Have the parents remember what they did and report the next week.

IF'S, AND'S, OR BUT'S:

The touch exercise will not be an easy one for some parents. Encourage them to try.

FAMILY ACTIVITY:	**30.5 Family Nurturing Time**
CONSTRUCT:	**Empathy, Self-Awareness**
MATERIALS:	**Nurturing Book for Babies and Children**

ACTIVITIES FOR INFANTS (Birth to 15 months):

Utilizing the *Nurturing Book for Babies and Children*, select activities from the sections entitled Activities for Infants or Infant and Child Massage. Engage parents in practicing songs, play and stimulation activities, or massage. Vary the activities weekly to sustain interest.

ACTIVITIES FOR TODDLERS (15 months to 3 years):

Utilizing the *Nurturing Book for Babies and Children*, select activities from the sections entitled Activities for Toddlers or Infant and Child Massage. Engage parents in practicing songs, play, language, and movement activities, or massage. Vary the activities weekly to sustain interest.

ACTIVITIES FOR PRESCHOOLERS (3-5 years):

Use the following activities when working with preschool children and their parents. Use the activities as the basis for involving infants and toddlers if you are conducting a home visit with children ages birth to five years.

FAMILY ACTIVITY:	**30.6 Hello Time: The Farmer in the Dell**
CONSTRUCT:	**Empathy**
MATERIALS:	**None**

GOAL:

To build positive parent-child interactions.

OBJECTIVES:

1. To help parents and children relate in a positive, nurturing way.

2. To help parents learn to enjoy their children.

PROCEDURES:

1. This is the traditional version of the Farmer in the Dell circle game.

2. Assemble children and adults holding hands in a circle.

3. Choose one child to stand in the center of the circle and be the "farmer."

4. The group moves in a circle around the "farmer" while singing. As the song calls for the farmer to "take a wife," have the child in the center of the circle choose another child or adult to join him inside the circle.

5. Continue in the same way until the verse "the cheese stands alone." Have the "cheese" stand in the center of the circle while the children sing that verse.

6. If the game is repeated, the person who was the "cheese" becomes the "farmer" for the new game.

The Farmer in the Dell

The farmer in the dell, the farmer in the dell,
Hi ho the dairy-o, the farmer in the dell.

The farmer takes a wife, the farmer takes a wife,
Hi ho the dairy-o, the farmer takes a wife.

The wife takes a child, the wife takes a child,
Hi ho the dairy-o, the wife takes a child.

The child takes a nurse, the child takes a nurse,
Hi ho the dairy-o, the child takes a nurse.

The nurse takes a dog, the nurse takes a dog,
Hi ho the dairy-o, the nurse takes a dog.

The dog takes a cat, the dog takes a cat,
Hi ho the dairy-o, the dog takes a cat.

The cat takes a rat, the cat takes a rat,
Hi ho the dairy-o, the cat takes a rat.

The rat takes the cheese, the rat takes the cheese,
Hi ho the dairy-o, the rat takes the cheese.

The cheese stands alone, the cheese stands alone,
Hi ho the dairy-o, the cheese stands alone.

IF'S, AND'S, OR BUT'S:

In small families you may want to use objects such as dolls or pets to participate in the game.

FAMILY ACTIVITY: 30.7 I'm a Dynamic Doer
CONSTRUCT: Self-Awareness
MATERIALS: None

GOAL:

To increase positive self-worth and self-esteem in children.

OBJECTIVES:

1. To increase self-awareness.

2. To reinforce positive family interactions.

PROCEDURES:

1. Assemble children in a large circle, squatting on the floor.

2. Using the tune of "I'm a Little Tea Pot," conduct the following activity.

I'm a Dynamic Doer

We're dynamic doers, here we stand (Have children stand),

Next to our friends, we all shake hands (Have children shake hands with those standing on left and right),

Telling them they're as nice as they could be (Simulate saying something by cupping hands over mouth to children standing on left and right),

I wish they could come home with me (Grab a partner, skip together).

When we're in school, we all play nice (Lock arms with partner, do square dance move),

Sharing our toys, and saying thanks (Girls curtsy, boys bow to their neighbors),

When we have to go, we all feel sad (Rub eyes with fists),

We'll be back soon, and feel real glad (Smile and laugh).

3. Repeat the song.

IF'S, AND'S, OR BUT'S:

Have fun with the song, keep the action moving. Rehearse the moves with the children so they learn the exercise.

FAMILY ACTIVITY: 30.8 Circle Time: I Own My Body
CONSTRUCT: Developmental
MATERIALS: Puppets, Our Bodies Pictures

GOAL:

To increase the children's ability to identify and respond with judgments regarding physical touch.

OBJECTIVES:

1. To increase the child's understanding of appropriate and inappropriate sexual and non-sexual touch.

2. To increase the child's ability to effectively control or manage situations when they are being touched inappropriately.

3. To increase a child's assertiveness regarding not wanting to be touched.

PROCEDURES:

1. Have children and adults sit in a semicircle on the floor.

2. Leader begin: Who can tell me what scary touch is? What are some things we can do if someone else wants to touch parts of our body and we feel scared? (Say "NO", leave the room, tell mom/dad/teacher, etc.).

3. Play act the following situations with the puppets. Elicit responses after each situation from the children regarding what action they would take.

    a. You and your older brother play a very special game. In fact, it's so special that your older brother tells you not to tell anyone. It's a secret between you and him. The game involves both of you taking off your clothes. When your clothes are off, he asks you to touch him here (use picture of male boy or point to the genitals). He touches you in the same area. He says it makes him and you feel good. But it doesn't make you feel very good at all. You're scared and don't like playing the game. But your brother has told you not to tell anyone. It's a secret. What should you do?

    b. You are in your room alone, getting ready to take a bath. You like taking baths because it means rubbing your body with soap and the warm water feels good. You like to touch all parts of your body because there are certain body parts (generally indicate breast and genital areas) where rubbing feels good. Your mom walks in and sees you touching yourself between your legs. What should you do?

    c. Your uncle (or mother's boyfriend, grandfather, step-father, etc.) likes to wrestle with you. You have fun with him, but sometimes he touches you between the legs and that makes you feel unhappy or scared. You don't want to play with him anymore because he often touches you there. You tell your mom but she likes it when you play with your uncle and thinks you're making a big deal out of nothing. What should you do?

IF'S, AND'S, OR BUT'S:

1. You need to process questions regarding adults touching children during baths, or for rectal temperatures with very young children, etc.

2. The key to the lesson is to inform children how they can use their personal power to protect themselves from scary touch. You may need to clarify scary touch from nonscary touch.

3. Pictures and discussion of nudity, genitals, sex, etc., tend to generate anxiety in children that will be manifested in laughing, silly behavior, jokes, etc. Respect the anxiety and help the children understand the concepts.

4. Work with the parents to get them to a comfort level with the concepts.

FAMILY ACTIVITY: **30.9 Pair It and Family Hug**
CONSTRUCT: **Behavior Management**
MATERIALS: **Dynamic Doer and Pair It Card Games**

GOAL:

To increase interpersonal skills among children.

OBJECTIVES:

1. To have children play cooperatively in a group.

2. To reinforce appropriate social behavior.

3. To increase short-term memory.

4. To reinforce comfort in using nurturing touch.

PROCEDURES:

1. Have parents and children sit on the floor or at a table.

2. Divide cards up so there are approximately three pairs for each player. (Four players would have 12 pairs; six players would have 18 pairs.) There are 24 pairs in a deck and you may want to use more pairs for the older children.

3. Mix the pairs up by shuffling the cards. Lay the cards on the table or floor, picture side down, facing the players.

4. The object of the game is to match pairs. The player turns over one card and leaves it for all to see. S/he then turns over another card. If it matches, the player picks up both cards and takes another turn. If the second card does not match the first, both cards are turned over and the next player takes a turn.

5. The player who ends up with the most pairs wins the game.

FAMILY HUG:

1. End each home visit with a family hug. Everyone get in a circle and put your arms around the people next to you. During the family hug time, anyone can say anything they like. It is a time for free expression.

2. At a natural time, close the activities for the day.

IF'S, AND'S, OR BUT'S:

Children will enjoy matching pictures. At the same time they build their visual memory.

NURTURING PROGRAM FOR PARENTS AND CHILDREN BIRTH TO FIVE YEARS
SESSION 31

BEHAVIOR CONSTRUCT:	Empathy
SESSION CONCEPT:	Criticism and Confrontation
BRIEF DESCRIPTION:	Parents and children both work on understanding the differences between criticizing and confronting someone. Children make a visual differentiations in art by making a warm fuzzy and cold prickly.
INTENDED USE:	For parents of children birth to 5 years
PREREQUISITE KNOWLEDGE:	Behavior Management, Praise

AGENDA

Parent Activities	Materials
31.1 Icebreaker and Home Practice Check In	*Parent Handbooks*
31.2 Criticism and Confrontation	*Parent Handbooks*
31.3 Blue Light Visualization	None
31.4 Home Practice Exercise	*Parent Handbooks*

Family Activities*	Materials
31.5 Family Nurturing Time	*Nurturing Book for Babies and Children*
31.6 Hello Time: Hokey Pokey	None
31.7 Streamer Dance	Cassette player and cassettes or record player and records, streamers
31.8 Circle Time: Criticism	Puppets, Feeling Faces
31.9 Warm Fuzzies/Cold Pricklies and Family Hug	Paper, crayons, magic markers, cotton, glue, sand paper, toothpicks, scissors

*For parents with infants or toddlers, use activities presented in *Nurturing Book for Babies and Children*. For parents with preschoolers (ages 3-5), use the activities listed below Family Nurturing Time.

PARENT ACTIVITY: 31.1 Icebreaker and Home Practice Check in
CONSTRUCT: Empathy, Self-Awareness
MATERIALS: Parent Handbooks

GOAL:

To increase parents' awareness of feelings associated with criticism and praise.

OBJECTIVES:

1. To recognize feelings of criticism and praise.

2. To share feelings of being criticized and praised with group.

3. To share thoughts of criticism and praise.

PROCEDURES:

1. Begin today's parent activities by having each adult respond to the following:

    - When I am criticized, I feel _____ .

    - When I am praised, I feel _____ .

    - When I am criticized, I think _____ .

    - When I am praised, I think _____ .

2. After each parent has had an opportunity to respond to the statements above, review the Home Practice Exercise from the previous meeting. Also discuss perceived changes in family members and their interactions as reported in the family log.

IF'S, AND'S, OR BUT'S:

1. Encourage parents to express their feelings and thoughts related to being criticized and praised. A brief discussion of the difference between feelings and thoughts may be appropriate.

2. With the practice of praising for the past several weeks, it should be easier for the parents to state they enjoy being praised. Keep an ear open for parents who are still having trouble accepting praise.

GOAL:

To increase parents' ability to use confrontation instead of criticism.

OBJECTIVES:

1. To help parents realize destructive effects of criticism.

2. To help parents learn to confront instead of criticize.

3. To provide practice in confrontation for parents.

PROCEDURES:

1. Discuss differences between criticism and confrontation. Criticism leaves a person feeling badly about him/herself. The person feels worthless, terrible, and inadequate as an entire person. Confrontation leaves a person knowing he or she has done something you don't like, but still feels positive about him/herself. The difference between criticism and confrontation is the feelings the person is left with.

2. Explain that the goal of today's session is to introduce them to an easy tool for the hard job of confronting another person about something that they do not like. This important communication tool can help avoid criticism and blaming.

3. Explain these concepts, eliciting examples and discussion:

   a. Blaming. We often blame others when we feel bad. We say "You make me so angry!" or "You're giving me ulcers." or "You make me love you (I didn't want to do it. I didn't want to do it.)" In the Nurturing Program, this is called a blaming you message, or criticism.

   b. You are responsible for your feelings. You choose your own interpretation of an event, and you choose to feel a certain way about it. Two people can experience the same event and each will think about (or interpret) it differently. Each can feel differently about it.

   Example: Two young women are going on blind dates. One feels glad because she believes she can talk to anyone. The other feels scared because she thinks she is a poor conversationalist.

   c. You are responsible for your own behavior. You choose to act a certain way based on what you think and what you feel.

   Example: The first young woman, who believed that she could talk to anyone and was glad for the chance to meet someone new on a blind date, acted in a warm and friendly manner toward her date. The other woman, who thought she had nothing interesting to say and was scared to go on the date, barely spoke to the young man and hardly looked at him when he talked.

d. When you accept that you choose your own feelings, thoughts, and behaviors, then you will be able to take better care of yourself. You will be able to stop blaming others for your bad feelings and start getting what you want and need.

4. Discuss your feelings and fears about being criticized or confronted. Try to think of a time someone confronted you without making you feel terrible.

5. Make a list of what is needed to confront someone and still leave the person feeling okay.

6. Instruct parents to locate the information entitled **Rules for Fair Fighting** on pages 98-99 in their Handbooks. Review the information.

IF'S, AND'S, OR BUT'S:

If people **never** confront others; bad things happen to them, such as getting walked all over, blowing up at their kids when they're angry at someone else, and not getting their own needs met. If people **always** confront others; bad things happen, such as not having any friends or anyone who even dares to be around you. So a balance is necessary.

PARENT ACTIVITY: 31.3 Blue Light Visualization
CONSTRUCT: Self-Awareness
MATERIALS: None

GOAL:

To reinforce internal feelings of success in replacing the internal feelings of failure.

OBJECTIVES:

1. To relax parents.

2. To give parents confidence in their ability to handle situations.

3. To provide parents with a successful relaxation experience.

PROCEDURES:

Instruct the parents to get comfortable. Read the following:

Blue Light

Right now you can just relax and be quiet. Imagine the inside of your head is now becoming a soft blue. Your mind and your self are light blue. Let the blue color flow into every crack and crevice of your mind and see nothing but light sky blue. Let your body inside be blue also, blue in your face, your stomach, your back and a blue light bathing you all over; a blue color inside and out.

Now envision a person you need to confront, someone with whom you need to be more honest about the way you are feeling about something that person is doing. Keep the blue light soft and flowing over both of you. Envision yourself, either with your hand or with your spirit, gently touching the person as you begin to speak. You are telling the person exactly what it is you need to say to the person. You are being clear, in control of yourself and in command of the situation. The other person is listening well to you even though you know the other person would rather not be talking about this. But you are confident and strong and you are saying what it is you need to say.

Now the person is responding to you and as the person begins, you are extra careful to remember the softness and the tranquility of the blue light. You are pulling it over and around you both and breathing in deeply as the person speaks to you.

You are able to hear what the person is saying and you are not getting angry or hurt, you are simply concentrating on trying to understand what the other person is saying. You are seeing the person through the blue light and you are able to be gentle and strong at the same time. You are handling this situation calmly and smoothly.

Now it is your turn to speak and once again you are conscious of the peace of the blue light and the tranquility as you are able to respond to the other person in a constructive way and yet in a way which fully protects your rights.

Now envision the blue light even more brightly as it shimmers through the situation and around both of you. Let the blue light continue to flow and shine as you see that both you and the other person are calm, that you understand each other better. Feel proud that you have done so well in expressing yourself and in hearing the other person. Slowly return to this place and time as you open your eyes when you are ready.

IF'S, AND'S, OR BUT'S:

Encourage parents to process their feelings as a group after the visualization.

PARENT ACTIVITY:	31.4 Home Practice Exercise
CONSTRUCT:	Behavior Management
MATERIALS:	Parent Handbooks

GOAL:

To practice new skills in communication.

OBJECTIVES:

1. To encourage the use of confrontation as a skill.

2. To reinforce appropriate ways to handle anger.

3. To maintain a warm and supportive atmosphere.

PROCEDURES:

1. Instruct parents to locate the Home Practice Exercise on page 142 in their Handbooks. Review the exercise with them:

   a. Practice confrontation twice.

   b. Complete family log.

2. Tell parents that in addition to the Home Practice Exercise, they are to spend 30 minutes each day with each of their children in nurturing playtime activities. Playtime is a time with the parent and child alone – no TV, no other distractions. Playing a game or reading books are good activities. From the *Nurturing Book for Babies and Children*, have the parents practice activities listed in the following sections: Activities for Infants, Activities for Toddlers, Activities for Preschoolers, or Infant and Child Massage. Have the parents remember what they did and report the next week.

IF'S, AND'S, OR BUT'S:

Confrontation is a critical skill in communication. Helping parents to be able to differentiate it from criticism is and important step in becoming a nurturing parent.

FAMILY ACTIVITY: 31.5 Family Nurturing Time
CONSTRUCT: Empathy, Self-Awareness
MATERIALS: Nurturing Book for Babies and Children

ACTIVITIES FOR INFANTS (Birth to 15 months):

Utilizing the *Nurturing Book for Babies and Children*, select activities from the sections entitled Activities for Infants or Infant and Child Massage. Engage parents in practicing songs, play and stimulation activities, or massage. Vary the activities weekly to sustain interest.

ACTIVITIES FOR TODDLERS (15 months to 3 years):

Utilizing the *Nurturing Book for Babies and Children*, select activities from the sections entitled Activities for Toddlers or Infant and Child Massage. Engage parents in practicing songs, play, language, and movement activities, or massage. Vary the activities weekly to sustain interest.

ACTIVITIES FOR PRESCHOOLERS (3-5 years):

Use the following activities when working with preschool children and their parents. Use the activities as the basis for involving infants and toddlers if you are conducting a home visit with children ages birth to five years.

FAMILY ACTIVITY: 31.6 Hello Time: Hokey Pokey
CONSTRUCT: Empathy
MATERIALS: None

GOAL:

To increase positive parent-child interactions through music and dance.

OBJECTIVES:

1. To help parents and children learn to relate in a positive way.

2. To help parents learn to enjoy their children.

3. To provide an opportunity for the children to be with the parents in a safe atmosphere.

PROCEDURES:

Have parents and children stand in a circle. Ask if everyone knows how to do the Hokey Pokey.
If not, model a few verses and movements.

Hokey Pokey

Put your right hand in, take your right hand out,
Put your right hand in, and shake it all about.
Do the hokey pokey; and turn yourself around (hands in air, body swaying as you
turn around in place),
That's what it's all about.

(Repeat words only substituting: left hand, right and left arms, right and left foot,
right and left leg, use all parts, let children suggest.)

IF'S, AND'S, OR BUT'S:

Some parents may feel a little silly at first doing the Hokey Pokey. Have patience, they will get
more comfortable if you are.

FAMILY ACTIVITY: 31.7 Streamer Dance
CONSTRUCT: Age Appropriate Developmental Expectations
MATERIALS: Cassette player and cassettes or record player and records, streamers

GOAL:

To express self through creative expression.

OBJECTIVES:

1. To increase positive adult-child interactions through music and dance.

2. To help children express themselves through positive play.

PROCEDURES:

1. Tie streamers to the wrists of everyone and tell the children that they are going to dance or move slow when the music is slow and dance or move fast when the music is fast. Set boundaries in terms of the area of rooms where children may dance.

2. Play the music and have the adults demonstrate fast and slow dancing with the streamers.

IF'S, AND'S, OR BUT'S:

1. Children who are reluctant to dance or respond to music with their bodies may feel less apprehensive since their attention is placed on the movements of the streamers.

2. Streamers may be attached to ankles, fingers, or around waists for variation.

3. A reluctant child may not want the streamer tied to him, and should be allowed to hold it in his hand. He may change his mind after observing others.

FAMILY ACTIVITY:	**31.8 Circle Time: Criticism**
CONSTRUCT:	**Empathy**
MATERIALS:	**Puppets, Feeling Faces**

GOAL:

To increase children's awareness of the difference between praise and criticism.

OBJECTIVES:

1. To increase children's awareness of criticism.

2. To increase children's sensitivity of the feelings of others.

3. To encourage children to use alternatives to criticism.

PROCEDURES:

1. Assemble everyone in a circle sitting on the floor. Explain that today we are going to learn about a way some kids talk to each other that is not very nice. It's called criticism. Can you say criticism?

2. Criticism means saying something mean to someone else. Can someone tell me something mean? (Get Examples.) Yes, that's something mean — that's criticism.

   Some examples of criticism:

Criticize for being:	I hate you.
	You are no good.
	You are a bad boy/girl.

Criticize for doing:	I hate you because you took my toy.
	I don't like you because...

---

3. Help the children recognize how they feel when someone criticizes them. Criticism feels bad, sad, cold, etc. Hold up a sad face to help the children recognize criticism. You may want to use the following questions to stimulate their comments:

   - When are you criticized by others?

   - How does it feel to be criticized by others?

   - Do you ever criticize others?

   - What do you think other feel when they're criticized?

4. Remind children of the difference between criticism and praise. Ask them which they would rather get. Which would they rather give?

IF'S, AND'S, OR BUT'S:

1. The concepts of criticism and praise may be difficult for some of the younger children. You will want to continue to use the words throughout the program so children can learn to use praise and avoid criticism.

2. Reinforce all attempts when children and parents praise each other.

FAMILY ACTIVITY:	**31.9 Warm Fuzzies/Cold Pricklies and Family Hug**
CONSTRUCT:	**Behavior Management, Self-Awareness**
MATERIALS:	**Paper, crayons, magic markers, cotton, glue, sand paper, toothpicks, scissors**

GOAL:

To increase children's awareness of warm and hurting feelings.

OBJECTIVES:

1. To identify warm feelings.

2. To identify hurting feelings.

3. To characterize warm feelings in an object.

4. To characterize hurting feelings in an object.

5. To help children differentiate between praise and criticism.

6. To reinforce comfort in using nurturing touch.

PROCEDURES:

1. Explain to the children that they are to make objects that represent warm fuzzies and cold pricklies.

2. A warm fuzzy is something that represents praise, acceptance. warmth, feeling good. A cold prickly is something that represents criticism, rejection, coldness, feeling bad.

3. Have materials ready for children to use. The things they make may be drawings, masks, objects, etc.

FAMILY HUG:

1. End each home visit with a family hug. Everyone get in a circle and put your arms around the people next to you. During the family hug time, anyone can say anything they like. It is a time for free expression.

2. At a natural time, close the activities for the day.

IF'S, AND'S, OR BUT'S:

1. Materials listed are only suggested. Be creative. In a family setting, encourage parents to help their children and to make their own fuzzy and prickly.

2. Reinforce praise by asking the children which object they would rather get as a present: a warm fuzzy or a cold prickly.

NURTURING PROGRAM FOR PARENTS AND CHILDREN BIRTH TO FIVE YEARS
SESSION 32

BEHAVIOR CONSTRUCT: Behavior Management

SESSION CONCEPT: I Statements and You Messages

BRIEF DESCRIPTION: Parents learn about taking ownership of a problem and using I statements and you messages. Children review the concepts of praise and criticism.

INTENDED USE: For parents of children birth to 5 years

PREREQUISITE KNOWLEDGE: Behavior Management, Praise, Criticism and Confrontation.

AGENDA

Parent Activities	Materials
32.1 Icebreaker and Home Practice Check In	*Parent Handbooks*
32.2 I Statements and You Messages	*Parent Handbooks*, **I Statements and You Messages** AV presentation, AV equipment
32.3 Home Practice Exercise	*Parent Handbooks*

Family Activities*	Materials
32.4 Family Nurturing Time	*Nurturing Book for Babies and Children*
32.5 Hello Time: Where is _____ ?	None
32.6 Shake Your Booty	Scarf
32.7 Circle Time: Fooler on Praise and Criticism	Puppets
32.8 Finger Painting and Family Hug	Finger paint, paint smocks, finger paint paper

*For parents with infants or toddlers, use activities presented in *Nurturing Book for Babies and Children*. For parents with preschoolers (ages 3-5), use the activities listed below Family Nurturing Time.

PARENT ACTIVITY: 32.1 Icebreaker and Home Practice Check In
CONSTRUCT: Self-Awareness
MATERIALS: Parent Handbooks

GOAL:

To increase parents' awareness of the impact of messages received from parents.

OBJECTIVES:

1. To increase awareness of parental messages.

2. To share feelings with the group.

3. To increase self-concept.

4. To modify negative parental messages.

PROCEDURES:

1. Begin today's parent activities by having each adult respond to the following:

   - One message I received from my mother or father that I definitely do not want to pass on is _____ .

   - As a result of this message, I have (or have not) _____ .

2. After each parent has had an opportunity to respond to the statements above, review the Home Practice Exercise from the previous meeting. Also discuss perceived changes in family members and their interactions as reported in the family log.

IF'S, AND'S, OR BUT'S:

1. Some parents may express difficulty in identifying a parental message they don't want to pass on to their kids. You might try using the technique called "10 Things" presented in the Program Implementation Manual.

2. Some parents may suggest that they already passed the message on. Have them brainstorm what additional message they would also like to pass on.

PARENT ACTIVITY: 32.2 I Statements and You Messages
CONSTRUCT: Behavior Management
MATERIALS: Parent Handbooks, I Statements and You Messages AV presentation, AV equipment

---

GOAL:

To increase parents' knowledge of I statements and You messages as a behavior management technique.

OBJECTIVES:

1. To help parents learn to take responsibility for their own behavior.

2. To help parents focus attention on others at appropriate times.

3. To help parents learn to use I statements and you messages.

4. To help parents learn not to blame others.

PROCEDURES:

1. If you are using the audio-visual programs, present the AV entitled **I Statements, You Messages.**

2. Instruct parents to locate the information entitled **I Statement and You Messages** on pages 107-110 in their Handbooks. Utilize the information presented to discuss the following major concepts with the parents:

   a. I statements are about me — the way I feel, what I need, what I think.

   b. You messages are about someone else — the way someone else feels, needs, or thinks.

   c. Using I Statements entails owning one's feelings and thoughts.

   d. Owning your own feelings and thoughts means you alone are responsible for your behavior.

   e. Inappropriate use of I statements lays guilt on someone else.

   f. Appropriate use of you messages:

   * To ask a question.

   * To get clarification.

   * To give choices.

   g. Inappropriate use of you messages:

   * To blame someone else for your bad feelings.

   h. Proper use of I statements and you messages ensures more positive family communication patterns.

   i. Using I statements can help you negotiate with another person to get your needs met. An I statement is about you — your feelings, thoughts, and needs. Using the I statement formula (will discuss later) helps you think about your feelings and needs, and helps you communicate them clearly to other people.

   j. I statements are used for confronting another person about something he/she does that you are unhappy about. When you confront someone using an I statement, you are taking responsibility both for your part of the problem and for asking for what you want.

   k. A confrontation (I statement) is better than criticism (blaming you message) because it focuses on the problem you have with the person's behavior, or on the person himself.

3. Refer back to the discussion of ownership of problems. Discuss with the parents what the concept of ownership means.

4. Practice with the parents using I statements with the following formula:

The Formula for Communicating with I Statements

When you _____ ,
(describe the exact behavior)

I feel _____
(state a feeling: glad/mad/sad/scared)

because _____ .
(state the need that relates to that feeing and any thought or belief related to it)

What I want is _____ .
(describe the exact behavior that would meet the need)

Examples:

- When you pick up your things each day, I feel glad because I need to have things tidied in order to feel good about our house. I want to thank you for being so considerate of my need for order, even though it is not your need.

- When you did not call me yesterday to let me know that you would be home late, I felt scared because I need to know that you are safe. I believe that it is unsafe to walk in that area after dark. What I want is to understand your plan for keeping yourself safe, and to be contacted whenever you are going to get home more than a half hour late.

  I also felt mad because when you did not call, I believed that you did not really care about my need to know you were OK. What I want is to hear from you, know that you understand my need, and will go out of your way to contact me, even if it is inconvenient for you at the time.

Helpful Hints:

- Take time to think it through before you confront.
- Use a sincere voice that expresses caring.
- Be concrete and use specific examples.
- Use one of the four primary feelings.
- Make eye contact.

5. Have parents pick out one issue that they often get hassled about in their family. Pair them up as partners.

   a. Set up three chairs facing each other — one for the "receiver" and two for the "sender."

   b. The "sender" sits in his first chair and criticizes the "receiver" about the issue, using the words and voice tones that he hears at home. The "receiver" does not respond.

   c. The "sender" then moves to his second chair and confronts the "receiver" about the same issue, using the I Statement Formula. The receiver does not respond.

   d. Do this until everyone participating has a chance to be a "sender" and "receiver."

   e. Afterwards, discuss reactions with the parents.

6. Ask each parent to remember a time when they received a blaming You Message which wasn't their fault. Ask each parent to share that blaming you message. How did they feel?

7. Ask each parent to translate one you message into an I statement. It could be the one they received or one they gave to their kids.

8. Finally, make a list of considerations when to use an I statement; when to use a you message.

IF'S, AND'S, OR BUT'S:

1. Mention that some people define maturity of being grown-up as the ability to delay gratification or the ability to wait to get what you want. When kids need a you message and parents need to give an I statement, maybe giving the you message first and then the I statement is more possible as people get older and wiser.

2. By helping parents differentiate ownership of the problem, you are actually building in the parent the ability to use appropriate communication skills. Reinforce attempts at understanding the concept of ownership.

PARENT ACTIVITY: **32.3 Home Practice Exercise**
CONSTRUCT: **Behavior Management, Self-Awareness**
MATERIALS: **Parent Handbooks**

GOAL:

To reinforce the use of appropriate methods of communication.

OBJECTIVES:

1. To encourage the use of I statements and you messages.

2. To help parents recognize problem ownership.

3. To maintain a warm and supportive atmosphere.

PROCEDURES:

1. Instruct parents to locate the Home Practice Exercise on page 143 in their Handbooks. Review the exercise with them:

   a. Identify ownership in problem situations.

   b. Make three I statements.

   c. Make three you messages.

   d. Complete family log.

2. Tell parents that in addition to the Home Practice Exercise, they are to spend 30 minutes each day with each of their children in nurturing playtime activities. Playtime is a time with the parent and child alone — no TV, no other distractions. Playing a game or reading books are good activities. From the *Nurturing Book for Babies and Children*, have the parents practice activities listed in the following sections: Activities for Infants, Activities for Toddlers, Activities for Preschoolers, or Infant and Child Massage. Have the parents remember what they did and report the next week.

IF'S, AND'S, OR BUT'S:

Encourage parents to work on increasing their skills in using I statements and you messages.

FAMILY ACTIVITY:	**32.4 Family Nurturing Time**
CONSTRUCT:	**Empathy, Self-Awareness**
MATERIALS:	**Nurturing Book for Babies and Children**

ACTIVITIES FOR INFANTS (Birth to 15 months):

Utilizing the *Nurturing Book for Babies and Children*, select activities from the sections entitled Activities for Infants or Infant and Child Massage. Engage parents in practicing songs, play and stimulation activities, or massage. Vary the activities weekly to sustain interest.

ACTIVITIES FOR TODDLERS (15 months to 3 years):

Utilizing the *Nurturing Book for Babies and Children*, select activities from the sections entitled Activities for Toddlers or Infant and Child Massage. Engage parents in practicing songs, play, language, and movement activities, or massage. Vary the activities weekly to sustain interest.

ACTIVITIES FOR PRESCHOOLERS (3-5 years):

Use the following activities when working with preschool children and their parents. Use the activities as the basis for involving infants and toddlers if you are conducting a home visit with children ages birth to five years.

FAMILY ACTIVITY: 32.5 Hello Time: Where is _____?
CONSTRUCT: Empathy
MATERIALS: None

GOAL:

To have children gain an awareness of others in the group.

OBJECTIVES:

1. To greet each child and adult by their first name.

2. To increase recognition of the needs of others.

3. To have fun in family interactions.

PROCEDURES:

1. Children and adults should be seated in a circle on the floor.

2. Ask everyone if they know the tune "Frere Jacques." Hum the tune and see if they recognize the melody. It is a good idea to have the children hum or sing the tune with you without any words a couple of times to ensure they know the song.

3. Using the tune of "Frere Jacques," sing the following words, first alone, and then once with the group. Use your first name (or the name of a parent) and identify an activity (suggest running or hopping).

    Where is _____?

    Where is __(name)__? Where is __(name)__ ?
    Please stand up, please stand up.

    (Dance, hop, run, etc.) around the group __(name)__ .
    (Dance, hop, run, etc.) around the group __(name)__ .

    Then sit down, then sit down.

4. Explain that everyone will have a chance to get up and move when it is their turn.

5. Choose a child to begin. Sing the song, inserting the movement. Allow the child to choose the next person, or the adult may choose who is next.

IF'S, AND'S, OR BUT'S:

1. For variation, ask for movement suggestions from the group. Children especially like to choose movements for adults and view this as a good joke. The response of the adult to this teasing provides a good model for behavior.

2. Noncompliant children may be encouraged if they are allowed to take a turn with a friend. Vary the song to include two people. Example: "Where are Jesse and Chad?"

FAMILY ACTIVITY: 32.6 Shake Your Booty
CONSTRUCT: Behavior Management
MATERIALS: Scarf

GOAL:

To give children experience in leading and following.

OBJECTIVES:

1. To increase child's ability to follow commands.

2. To allow children opportunity to lead family activities.

PROCEDURES:

1. Have children and adults sit in a circle on the floor.

2. Explain the activity. I am going to see how well we follow directions. I am going to drop this scarf from as high as I can reach. While it is in the air, you are to hum, but only while it is in the air. When the scarf reaches the floor, I want you to be as quiet as you can.

3. Drop the scarf two times for the children to catch on.

4. This time, when I drop the scarf, I want you to wiggle all over while the scarf is in the air. When the scarf reaches the floor, I want you to stand at attention.

5. Have children take turns dropping the scarf. Before dropping the scarf, the home visitor is to tell the family what they are to do while the scarf is in the air.

IF'S, AND'S, OR BUT'S:

Permit each child to drop the scarf several times. Notice not only how each leader commands the family, but also the nature of the response.

FAMILY ACTIVITY: 32.7 Circle Time: Fooler on Praise and Criticism
CONSTRUCT: Empathy
MATERIALS: Puppets

GOAL:

To reinforce the concepts of praise and criticism.

OBJECTIVES:

1. To challenge children's ability to recognize praise statements.

2. To challenge children's ability to recognize criticism statements.

3. To practice using praise statements.

PROCEDURES:

1. Assemble children and adults in a circle sitting on the floor.

2. Using the "fooler" approach, have on of the puppets say a variety of things. The goal for the children is to see if they can catch the errors. The following is a sample script:

    Puppet#1: "Hello, boys and girls. I'm gonna see if I can catch you in giving praise. I bet I can fool you guys. I bet you don't know what praise is. I'll say something and you tell me if I'm praising you or not."

    "Hey Bozo, you got big ears!" Children respond: "No."

    "I like your fat legs!" Children respond: "NO."

    "I think you're nice!" Children respond: "Yes."

    "You work well!" Children respond: "Yes."

    "My brother is a dummy!" Children respond: "No."

    "My brother tries real hard!" Children respond: "Yes."

3. Continue with other examples relevant to the group.

4. Ask for volunteers to take the puppet and say something nice to another person in the group.

IF'S, AND'S, OR BUT'S:

The child may want to use the fooler approach in trying to trick other children or adults.

FAMILY ACTIVITY:	**32.8 Finger Painting and Family Hug**
CONSTRUCT:	**Self-Awareness**
MATERIALS:	**Finger paint, paint smocks, finger paint paper**

GOAL:

To participate in creative artistic expression involving tactile stimulation.

OBJECTIVES:

1. To participate in an art activity involving physical and tactile sensory experience.

2. To engage in creative, original self-expression that is appropriate to each child's individual social and developmental level.

3. To give and accept nurturing physical contact appropriately as part of self-help activities.

4. To reinforce comfort in using nurturing touch.

PROCEDURES:

1. Tell the children that today they will be doing finger painting during art. It's best to use something to protect the table or floor from the paint.

2. Demonstrate finger painting with emphasis on various ways of painting: painting with the whole hand, individual finger, fist, elbow, etc. Encourage exploration.

3. Allow the children time to put their hands into the paint unassisted. If a child does not respond, encourage him/her individually in order to get some type of involvement.

4. Talk about the texture and feel of the paint.

5. Finger painting may be done either directly on the table top (or on oilcloth to protect the table) or on finger paint paper. Paper should be wet before painting.

6. Paintings on the tabletop may be saved by placing a piece of paper over the painted surface and rubbing the paper to transfer the design.

FAMILY HUG:

1. End each home visit with a family hug. Everyone get in a circle and put your arms around the people next to you. During the family hug time, anyone can say anything they like. It is a time for free expression.

2. At a natural time, close the activities for the day.

IF'S, AND'S, OR BUT'S:

Utilize clean up time to provide nurturing physical contact.

NURTURING PROGRAM FOR ADULTS AND CHILDREN BIRTH TO FIVE YEARS

SESSION 33

BEHAVIOR CONSTRUCT:	Behavior Management
SESSION CONCEPT:	Problem Solving and Decision Making
BRIEF DESCRIPTION:	Parents learn a process of solving problems and making decisions. Children discuss the concept of keeping secrets and when to learn the difference between a bad secret and a good secret.
INTENDED USE:	For parents of children birth to 5 years
PREREQUISITE KNOWLEDGE:	Behavior Management, I Statements, Praise

AGENDA

Parent Activities   Materials

33.1   Icebreaker and Home Practice Check In   *Parent Handbooks*

33.2   Problem Solving/Decision Making   *Parent Handbooks*

33.3   Home Practice Exercise   *Parent Handbooks*

Family Activities*   Materials

33.4   Family Nurturing Time   *Nurturing Book for Babies and Children*

33.5   Hello Time: This is the Way   None

33.6   Row, Row, Row Your Boat   None

33.7   Circle Time: Keeping Secrets   Puppets

33.8   Food Coloring Painting and Family Hug   Paint brushes, food coloring, paper towels, containers with water, tape

*For parents with infants or toddlers, use activities presented in *Nurturing Book for Babies and Children*. For parents with preschoolers (ages 3-5), use the activities listed below Family Nurturing Time.

PARENT ACTIVITY: 33.1 Icebreaker and Home Practice Check In
CONSTRUCT: Self-Awareness
MATERIALS: Parent Handbooks

GOAL:

To increase parents' awareness of their effectiveness as problem solvers.

OBJECTIVES:

1. To increase parents' awareness of their strengths as problem solvers.

2. To increase parents' awareness of their weaknesses as problem solvers.

PROCEDURES:

1. Begin today's parent activities by having each adult respond to the following:

   ● When it comes to solving problems on a scale of 1 to 10 (1 lousy, 10 great), I rate myself a
     _____ .

   ● My biggest strength in problem solving is _____ .

   ● My biggest weakness in problem solving is _____ .

2. After each parent has had an opportunity to respond to the statements above, review the Home Practice Exercise from the previous meeting. Also discuss perceived changes in family members and their interactions as reported in the family log.

IF'S, AND'S, OR BUT'S:

1. Problem solving and decision making are skills that can be learned. Used as a behavior management strategy, children soon learn how to effectively solve their own problems.

2. Instruct parents that more detail on how to problem solve and make decisions is presented in the following activity.

PARENT ACTIVITY: 33.2 Problem Solving/Decision Making
CONSTRUCT: Self-Awareness, Behavior Management
MATERIALS: Parent Handbooks

GOAL:

To increase parents' abilities in problem solving and decision making.

OBJECTIVES:

1. To help parents examine alternatives to problems.

2. To help parents learn a constructive process in making decisions and solving problems.

PROCEDURES:

1. Instruct parents to locate the information entitled **Problem Solving and Decision Making** on pages 111-113 in their Handbooks.

2. Explain the difference between problem solving and decision making.

   Problem Solving: What you do when you have a problem but don't know what to do.

   Decision Making: What you do when you know what your alternatives are.

3. **Problem Solving.** Solving problems can be a person process or a family process. To reach a point of action in solving problems, both personal and familial, follow these suggested steps:

   a. Identify the problem. Write it down for you or other family members to see.

   b. Determine ownership of the problem. Is your child doing something you don't approve of but does not see the behavior as a problem? Is the problem yours or your child's?

   c. Write down a goal statement. What behavior do you want to see instead? This is the crucial step and perhaps the most difficult of them all. If it is a child's problem, tell him/her the behavior you want the child to perform. Make sure the behavior is reasonable and attainable.

   d. Brainstorm ways to achieve the behavior. Whether your problem or your child's problem, brainstorming ways to achieve the desired behavior, and thus reducing the problem behavior, is an important step in the problem solving process.

   e. Pick out your favorite three and begin working on the desired behavior.

4. From the lists the decision ought to be clear. If not, check the problem statement and goal statement to make certain they are still accurate reflections of what you mean.

5. **Decision Making.**

   a. Make a two column grid for each suggestion, then mark one column POSITIVES and the other NEGATIVES.

   b. Fill in each column with all the positive and all the negative aspects of the suggestion you can think of.

   c. Repeat the step with each of the top three favorites.

IF'S, AND'S, OR BUT'S:

1. Helping parents identify the problem, what they want to see instead, ways to achieve desired behavior, and payoffs for each of the top three ways to achieve the desired behavior should serve as a process for them to use in any problem situation.

2. When the problem is the child's, have the parents help the child brainstorm his/her own desired behaviors and ways to achieve the desired behavior.

GOAL:

To practice problem solving techniques at home.

OBJECTIVES:

1. To encourage family involvement in decision making.

2. To help parents learn new ways to resolve problem situations.

3. To increase ability to handle stressful situations.

4. To maintain a warm and supportive atmosphere.

PROCEDURES:

1. Instruct parents to locate the Home Practice Exercise on page 143 in their Handbooks. Review the exercise with them:

   a. Help your child learn to problem solve.

   b. Solve a problem, make a decision (your own or family's).

   c. Praise each of your children twice: once for being, once for doing.

   d. Complete family log.

2. Tell parents that in addition to the Home Practice Exercise, they are to spend 30 minutes each day with each of their children in nurturing playtime activities. Playtime is a time with the parent and child alone — no TV, no other distractions. Playing a game or reading books are good activities. From the *Nurturing Book for Babies and Children*, have the parents practice activities listed in the following sections: Activities for Infants, Activities for Toddlers, Activities for Preschoolers, or Infant and Child Massage. Have the parents remember what they did and report the next week.

IF'S, AND'S, OR BUT'S:

Reinforce parents' attempts to understand the problem solving process.

FAMILY ACTIVITY: 33.4 Family Nurturing Time
CONSTRUCT: Empathy, Self-Awareness
MATERIALS: Nurturing Book for Babies and Children

ACTIVITIES FOR INFANTS (Birth to 15 months):

Utilizing the *Nurturing Book for Babies and Children*, select activities from the sections entitled Activities for Infants or Infant and Child Massage. Engage parents in practicing songs, play and stimulation activities, or massage. Vary the activities weekly to sustain interest.

ACTIVITIES FOR TODDLERS (15 months to 3 years):

Utilizing the *Nurturing Book for Babies and Children*, select activities from the sections entitled Activities for Toddlers or Infant and Child Massage. Engage parents in practicing songs, play, language, and movement activities, or massage. Vary the activities weekly to sustain interest.

ACTIVITIES FOR PRESCHOOLERS (3-5 years):

Use the following activities when working with preschool children and their parents. Use the activities as the basis for involving infants and toddlers if you are conducting a home visit with children ages birth to five years.

FAMILY ACTIVITY: 33.5 Hello Time: This is the Way
CONSTRUCT: Behavior Management
MATERIALS: None

GOAL:

To build positive social interaction among family members.

OBJECTIVES:

1. To increase children's ability to communicate.

2. To reinforce positive peer interactions.

PROCEDURES:

1. Have children and adults stand in a circle.

2. Explain to them that today we are going to sing hello. Sing the following song to the tune of "This is the Way We Wash Our Clothes" and demonstrate the actions to the children.

This is the Way

This is the way we say hello (wave open hand-fingers pointing up),
Say hello (continue waving), say hello (continue waving),
This is the way we say hello, early in the morning.

This is the way we greet our friends (bow to one another),
Greet our friends, greet our friends,
This is the way we greet our friends, happy to see you here today.

3. Continue with "This is the way we . . . . (smile and laugh, shake other's hands, dance and sing).

IF'S, AND'S, OR BUT'S:

Have a good time with the song. Be creative and add your own lyrics.

FAMILY ACTIVITY:	**33.6 Row, Row, Row Your Boat**
CONSTRUCT:	**Empathy**
MATERIALS:	**None**

GOAL:

To increase positive social interactions through play.

OBJECTIVES:

1. To involve children and adults in active and cooperative musical activities.

2. To foster creative expression through music.

PROCEDURES:

1. Request children and adults to sit in a circle with their legs spread apart so an adult or another child can sit between them.

2. Explain to the group that we are all going to pretend that we are in a boat and we have to row to get to shore.

3. Have the children hold the arms of the person in front of them. When the song begins, everyone will make a rowing movement with their hands.

Row, Row, Row Your Boat

Row, row, row your boat gently down the stream,
Merrily, merrily, merrily, merrily,
Life is but a dream.

4. To add variety, move slow when casually rowing, fast when you are being chased by a shark, etc.

IF'S, AND'S, OR BUT'S:

Ask a child if he or she wants to lead the activity.

FAMILY ACTIVITY: 33.7 Circle Time: Keeping Secrets
CONSTRUCT: Self-Awareness
MATERIALS: Puppets

GOAL:

To help children gain mastery of threatening situations.

OBJECTIVES:

1. To reinforce the concepts of good and bad secrets.

2. To empower children with the ability to handle good and bad secrets.

PROCEDURES:

1. Have children and adults in a circle sitting on the floor.

2. "Who can tell me what is the difference between a good and scary/bad secret?"

3. What do you do when you have a bad/scary secret?" (Tell someone).

4. "What are some bad secrets that you would want to tell someone?"

5. "What are some good secrets that you could keep to yourself and not tell anyone?"

6. Have each child take a turn telling good secrets (those you keep to yourself) and bad secrets (those you tell others.)

7. Have each child make the puppet do what is appropriate.

IF'S, AND'S, OR BUT'S:

It's important that the child identify what should be done with bad secrets. Desirable response is to tell someone.

FAMILY ACTIVITY: 33.8 Food Coloring Painting and Family Hug
CONSTRUCT: Developmental
MATERIALS: Paint brushes, food coloring, paper towels, containers with water, tape

GOAL:

To increase children's self-concept and self-esteem through accomplishment of age appropriate tasks.

OBJECTIVES:

1. To foster creative expression through art.

2. To increase fine motor skills.

3. To reinforce comfort in using nurturing touch.

PROCEDURES:

1. Assemble children around a table.

2. Pour water into small containers and add food coloring.

3. Give each child a plain white paper towel and tape it to the table.

4. Have each child dip their brush into the colored water and paint designs on their paper towels.

FAMILY HUG:

1. End each home visit with a family hug. Everyone get in a circle and put your arms around the people next to you. During the family hug time, anyone can say anything they like. It is a time for free expression.

2. At a natural time, close the activities for the day.

IF'S, AND'S, OR BUT'S:

Hang the finished products to dry and display.

NURTURING PROGRAM FOR PARENTS AND CHILDREN BIRTH TO FIVE YEARS

SESSION 34

BEHAVIOR CONSTRUCT: Empathy

SESSION CONCEPT: Helping Children with Feelings

BRIEF DESCRIPTION: Parents learn a way to help children identify and handle their feelings. Children review the concept of keeping secrets and protecting their bodies.

INTENDED USE: For parents of children birth to 5 years

PREREQUISITE KNOWLEDGE: I Statements and You Messages

AGENDA

Parent Activities	Materials
34.1 Icebreaker and Home Practice Check In	*Parent Handbooks*
34.2 Helping Children with Feelings	*Parent Handbooks*, Feeling Faces, paper, pencils
34.3 Home Practice Exercise	*Parent Handbooks*

Family Activities*	Materials
34.4 Family Nurturing Time	*Nurturing Book for Babies and Children*
34.5 Hello Time: Something Good About Me	None
34.6 Here's One Foot	None
34.7 Circle Time: Protecting My Body	Puppets
34.8 Ask It, Tell It and Family Hug	Ask It, Tell It Game

*For parents with infants or toddlers, use activities presented in *Nurturing Book for Babies and Children*. For parents with preschoolers (ages 3-5), use the activities listed below Family Nurturing Time.

PARENT ACTIVITY: 34.1 Icebreaker and Home Practice Check In
CONSTRUCT: Self-Awareness, Empathy
MATERIALS: Parent Handbooks

GOAL:

To help parents identify feelings that are difficult to handle.

OBJECTIVES:

1. To help parents recognize personal feelings.
2. To help parents become aware of children's feelings.
3. To help parents recognize troublesome feelings.

PROCEDURES:

1. Begin today's parent activities by having each adult respond to the following:

   - One feeling I have difficulty handling is _____ .
   - One feeling I think my child(ren) has (have) difficulty handling is _____ .
   - When he/she has trouble with that feeling, I want to _____ , but what my child could use at that time is _____ .

2. After each parent has had an opportunity to respond to the statements above, review the Home Practice Exercise from the previous meeting. Also discuss perceived changes in family members and their interactions as reported in the family log.

IF'S, AND'S, OR BUT'S:

Try to help parents begin to separate feelings from behavior: feeling angry from throwing toys.

PARENT ACTIVITY: 34.2 Helping Children with Feelings
CONSTRUCT: Empathy
MATERIALS: Parent Handbooks, Feeling Faces, paper, pencils

GOAL:

To teach parents ways to help children handle their feelings.

OBJECTIVES:

1. To help parents identify feelings children have.
2. To teach parents to identify the needs of children.
3. To help parents teach children to handle their own feelings.

PROCEDURES:

1. Explain that today we will discuss the feeling of empathy.

    a. Begin by asking someone to define what empathy means.

    b. Reinforce responses.

2. Share the following definition of empathy: Empathy is the ability to recognize and respond to the feelings of others so that they know that how they feel is important to you. Feeling empathy as a parent means understanding your own feelings, putting them aside for the time, and responding to the needs and feelings of your children. When you pay attention to the feelings of children, you recognize them as human beings. When you ignore children's feelings, you ignore them as people.

3. Displaying the Feeling Faces one at a time, ask the parents to identify the feeling. You may want to paraphrase each face by asking, "What do you suppose he/she is feeling? What do you suppose happened that contributed to his/her feeling?"

4. Afterwards, brainstorm a list of children's feelings. What are some feelings children commonly have? Write down the list.

5. Suggest to the parents that feelings are always okay and feelings can always be accepted, but not behavior. Behavior must be limited.

6. People have children for many reasons. These reasons influence how much empathy the parent will be able to show for the child after he is born. List all the reasons they can think of for having a child. Then divide the list into two groups. In one group put the reasons that you feel will be conducive to showing empathy for the child; put all the leftover reasons in the second group.

7. Suggest ways parents can help children manage their own feelings. Instruct parents to locate the information entitled **Helping Children with Feelings** on pages 114-115 in their Handbooks. Review with the parents the following steps for helping children deal with their feelings:

    a. Label what you see or think you see for the child. "You look angry, or proud, or happy." This will give the child a feeling of being believed and respected.

    b. Don't dominate the conversation. Let the child do the talking. Encourage the child by looking interested in what he/she is saying. Children can think better when someone isn't advising, blaming, or criticizing.

    c. When your child wants something, honor the desire. If you are in the store and your child wants a toy, rather than saying "no", tell the child you wish you could give the child anything he or she wants. "If I had the money, I would buy you 12 toys." Or, "If I could, I'd buy you every kind of cookie there is — a different kind for every hour of the day." This can have almost a magical effect on the situation because you have joined the child, not forbidden the child. The child feels you understand and appreciate his or her desires and that you honor the child.

8. Using the steps just reviewed, have the parents role play the following situations in displaying empathy. Afterwards, discuss the responses.

    a. Your baby is crying in the middle of the night. What can you do? What can you say that can help your baby feel better?

b. Your two-year-old falls down the steps and begins crying. What do you say to him/her that shows you feel empathy? How do you act toward him?

c. Your child wants dessert before dinner. Honor the desire but don't give him/her dessert before dinner.

d. Your child wants a toy but you can't afford the toy. Honor the desire, but don't give in and buy the toy.

e. Your kindergarten child excitedly comes running in the house. He wants to tell you about his first day at school. What do you say to him that shows you feel empathy? How do you act?

f. Your three-year-old daughter comes in the house. Her friends told her she couldn't play with them. What can you say and do that shows her you understand her feelings?

IF'S, AND'S, OR BUT'S:

Help parents understand that sometimes the best solution for helping children handle feelings is to talk to them about what and how they feel.

PARENT ACTIVITY:	34.3 Home Practice Exercise
CONSTRUCT:	Behavior Management, Empathy
MATERIALS:	Parent Handbooks

GOAL:

To practice helping children handle their feelings.

OBJECTIVES:

1. To encourage children to express their feelings.

2. To help parents learn new ways to recognize children's feelings.

3. To increase empathic understanding of children's needs.

4. To maintain a warm and supportive atmosphere.

PROCEDURES:

1. Instruct parents to locate the Home Practice Exercise on page 143 in their Handbooks. Review the exercise with them:

   a. Help your child handle a feeling.

   b. Praise your child for handling/trying to handle the feeling.

   c. Complete family log.

2. Tell parents that in addition to the Home Practice Exercise, they are to spend 30 minutes each day with each of their children in nurturing playtime activities. Playtime is a time with the parent and child alone — no TV, no other distractions. Playing a game or reading books are good activities. From the *Nurturing Book for Babies and Children*, have the parents practice activities listed in the following sections: Activities for Infants, Activities for Toddlers, Activities for Preschoolers, or Infant and Child Massage. Have the parents remember what they did and report the next week.

IF'S, AND'S, OR BUT'S:

Reinforce parents' attempts to understand the needs and feelings of their children.

FAMILY ACTIVITY:	**34.4 Family Nurturing Time**
CONSTRUCT:	**Empathy, Self-Awareness**
MATERIALS:	**Nurturing Book for Babies and Children**

ACTIVITIES FOR INFANTS (Birth to 15 months):

Utilizing the *Nurturing Book for Babies and Children*, select activities from the sections entitled Activities for Infants or Infant and Child Massage. Engage parents in practicing songs, play and stimulation activities, or massage. Vary the activities weekly to sustain interest.

ACTIVITIES FOR TODDLERS (15 months to 3 years):

Utilizing the *Nurturing Book for Babies and Children*, select activities from the sections entitled Activities for Toddlers or Infant and Child Massage. Engage parents in practicing songs, play, language, and movement activities, or massage. Vary the activities weekly to sustain interest.

ACTIVITIES FOR PRESCHOOLERS (3-5 years):

Use the following activities when working with preschool children and their parents. Use the activities as the basis for involving infants and toddlers if you are conducting a home visit with children ages birth to five years.

FAMILY ACTIVITY: 34.5 Hello Time: Something Good About Me
CONSTRUCT: Self-Awareness
MATERIALS: None

GOAL:

To increase positive self-concept and self-esteem.

OBJECTIVES:

1. To reinforce positive verbal self-expression.

2. To increase positive perceptions of self.

PROCEDURES:

1. Children and adults should be seated in a circle on the floor.

2. Have each child and adult respond to the following statements:

   • Right now I am feeling _____ .

   • Something good about me is _____ .

IF'S, AND'S, OR BUT'S:

1. Have the parents help their children come up with something good about themselves. Those who say nothing is good about them need extra praise for being and doing.

2. Encourage parents to be supportive and encouraging.

FAMILY ACTIVITY: 34.6 Here's One Foot
CONSTRUCT: Empathy
MATERIALS: None

GOAL:

To increase positive parent-child interactions through play.

OBJECTIVES:

1. To involve children and parents in active and cooperative musical activities.

2. To foster creative expression through music.

PROCEDURES:

1. Request parents and children stand in a circle to participate in this activity.

2. Ask everyone if they know the song "This Old Man." Sing a few bars so they know the melody.

3. Tell them that we are all going to pretend to be an old man who is going to do a variety of things.

4. Demonstrate what you want to do using the following verse:

> **Here's One Foot**
>
> Here's one foot, here are two.
> Each is wearing one new shoe.
> So I'll stand up, turn around,
> Dance around the floor,
> Dancing is what feet are for.

5. Alter the movement by suggesting or requesting from group the desired change. Some suggested movements: walk, run, tip toe, skip, march, etc.

IF'S, AND'S, OR BUT'S:

See if one of the parents wants to lead the activity.

FAMILY ACTIVITY:	**34.7 Circle Time:Protecting My Body**
CONSTRUCT:	**Behavior Management**
MATERIALS:	**Puppets**

GOAL:

To increase children's awareness of the concept of sharing concerns with others.

OBJECTIVES:

1. To reinforce sharing scary secrets.

2. To empower children with an ability to influence the actions of others.

3. To protect self.

4. To differentiate between good and bad secrets.

PROCEDURES:

1. Have children and adults in a circle sitting on the floor.

2. Today we will review the difference between a good secret and scary/bad secret.

    a. Who can tell me what a secret is?

    b. What is a good secret? Get examples.

    c. What is a bad secret? Get examples.

3. Who can tell me when it's OK to keep a secret and when it's OK to tell a secret?

4. What do you do when you have a scary secret? (Tell someone.)

5. Who do you tell when you have a scary secret?

6. Remember when we talked about scary touch. Can someone tell me what scary touch is? (Wait for response and reinforce.) What did we say to do when someone touches you in a place that makes you feel uncomfortable? (Tell someone.) I want you all to listen to a story about telling someone about scary touch.

> **Puppet #1**: Puppet #2, you look so sad. What's the matter?
>
> **Puppet #2**: Something weird happened to me last night!
>
> **Puppet #1**: Can you tell me what happened?
>
> **Puppet #2**: I'll try, but I'm sure scared. Last night my stepfather (father, mother's boyfriend, uncle, etc.) came into my bedroom again and wanted to touch me.
>
> **Puppet #1**: Well that doesn't sound so terrible. Touch is nice. He probably was just trying to say goodnight.
>
> **Puppet #2**: His touch makes me feel uncomfortable. He wants to touch me in places that I don't like to be touched. He touches me between my legs. I get so scared, all I want him to do is to not touch me there anymore.
>
> **Puppet #1**: Have you told him that touching you there makes you feel scared?
>
> **Puppet #2**: No, I just wish he would stop.
>
> **Leader**: How do you suppose Puppet #2 feels right now? What can Puppet #2 do to get _____ to stop touching her so she won't feel scared anymore? (Reinforce the concept of communication.) Telling him to stop or telling mom or other meaningful adults. The goal is to tell someone. Don't keep it to yourself.
>
> **Puppet #1**: Why don't you tell _____ and your mom that you feel scared when he touches you there and that you don't like it. You want him to stop.
>
> **Puppet #2**: I will. I'll tell _____ and my mom so he will stop touching me.

IF'S, AND'S, OR BUT'S:

1. Children may want to know what happens after she tells. Suggest he stopped touching her and that telling someone really helped.

2. What happens to perpetrator — he gets help.

GOAL:

To increase positive family interactions through awareness.

OBJECTIVES:

1. To increase children's self-awareness.

2. To increase children's awareness of others.

3. To increase children's communication skills.

4. To reinforce comfort in using nurturing touch.

PROCEDURES:

1. Direct children and adults to sit around a small table or in a circle on the floor.

2. Place the Ask It, Tell It game board and cards in the center.

3. Each person will have a turn to spin. If the spinner stops in a yellow area, the person chooses a yellow Ask It Card. If the spinner stops in an orange area, the person chooses an orange Tell It Card. The person should respond to the statement on the chosen card accordingly.

4. When everyone has had a turn, repeat. The game ends when either the cards or time expires.

FAMILY HUG:

1. End each home visit with a family hug. Everyone get in a circle and put your arms around the people next to you. During the family hug time, anyone can say anything they like. It is a time for free expression.

2. At a natural time, close the activities for the day.

IF'S, AND'S, OR BUT'S:

1. Children will like playing this game. If you have a very large group, the game will be more fun if you break into smaller groups with each group having its own game board and cards.

2. Some young children will need help reading the card statements. See if other children can help out.

NURTURING PROGRAM FOR PARENTS AND CHILDREN BIRTH TO FIVE YEARS

SESSION 35

BEHAVIOR CONSTRUCT: Empathy

SESSION CONCEPT: Improving Specific Self-Esteem

BRIEF DESCRIPTION: Parents learn ways to improve their own self-esteem as well as their children's. Children participate in making a family footprint mural.

INTENDED USE: For parents of children birth to 5 years

PREREQUISITE KNOWLEDGE: Praise

AGENDA

Parent Activities	Materials
35.1 Icebreaker and Home Practice Check In	*Parent Handbooks*
35.2 Improving Specific Self-Esteem and Self-Concept	*Parent Handbooks*, pencils
35.3 Home Practice Exercise	*Parent Handbooks*

Family Activities*	Materials
35.4 Family Nurturing Time	*Nurturing Book for Babies and Children*
35.5 Hello Time: Loud and Soft	None
35.6 Circle Time: Dancercise	Cassette player and cassettes or record player and records
35.7 Putting My Best Foot Forward and Family Hug	4 large pie plates, aluminum foil, tempera paint (4 colors), long sheets of butcher block paper, wash pan, towels or rags

*For parents with infants or toddlers, use activities presented in *Nurturing Book for Babies and Children*. For parents with preschoolers (ages 3-5), use the activities listed below Family Nurturing Time.

PARENT ACTIVITY: 35.1 Icebreaker and Home Practice Check In
CONSTRUCT: Self-Awareness
MATERIALS: Parent Handbooks

GOAL:

To increase parents' awareness of times they feel good and bad about themselves as parents.

OBJECTIVES:

1. To help parents differentiate feelings of who they are from what they do.

2. To reinforce parents' ability to build a positive self-esteem.

PROCEDURES:

1. Begin today's parent activities by having each adult respond to the following:

   - Right now I am feeling _____ about myself as a man/woman.

   - Right now I am feeling _____ about myself as a parent.

   - One thing I do to help build my self-esteem as a man/woman is _____ .

   - One thing I do to help build my self-esteem as a parent is _____ .

2. After each parent has had an opportunity to respond to the statements above, review the Home Practice Exercise from the previous meeting. Also discuss perceived changes in family members and their interactions as reported in the family log.

IF'S AND'S OR BUT'S:

Today's icebreaker is a rather long one, but one which helps differentiate the differences between self and roles. Help parents differentiate who they are from what they do.

PARENT ACTIVITY: 35.2 Improving Specific Self-Esteem and Self-Concept
CONSTRUCT: Empathy
MATERIALS: Parent Handbooks, pencils

GOAL:

To help parents increase their children's self-esteem and self-concept.

OBJECTIVES:

1. To help parents realize their ability to impact on a child's feeling of worth.

2. To teach parents ways to help a child improve his/her self-concept.

PROCEDURES:

1. Explain to the parents the terms self-concept and self-esteem.

   a. Self-concept is what people think about themselves: I think I'm a loser; I think I'm strong; I think I can or can't handle this; I think I'm too fat, short, skinny, tall, helpless, etc.

   b. Self-esteem is how people feel about themselves: I feel good about myself; I hate myself; I like myself; I feel strong, weak, depressed, lonely, etc.

   When you think and feel positive about yourself, you are in total control and life is fun. When you think and feel lousy about yourself, others are in control and life is miserable.

2. Instruct parents to locate the information entitled **Improving Specific Self-Esteem** on pages 116-118 in their Handbooks. Ask parents, "Do you, your mate, or your family have a negative label for one or more of your children? If so, write it down."

3. If you do have a negative label, think of a new label you would like instead. If you don't have a negative label, think of a positive label you would like for your child.

4. Share the labels you have written.

5. Discuss with the parents suggestions on how to develop a child's self-esteem in a particular area. Let parents write them down in their Handbook.

   a. Put children in situations where they can succeed at being what you want them to be. For instance, if a child is unsure of him or herself, give the child an opportunity to develop self-confidence by experiencing success such as by weighing the bananas at the grocery store while you look at the lettuce.

   b. Expect the child to succeed in the small specific situation. If you expect children to succeed ALL the time in ALL situations, you will be very disappointed in children. That is not realistic.

   c. If the child does not succeed in a situation be very clear that you expected him or her to and you are disappointed that he or she has chosen not to succeed. You have every right to be disappointed that your child has chosen not to do it; but once the disappointment is expressed, forget it. You are disappointed in the CHOICE the child made, not in the whole child.

   d. Every time you see your child behaving in the desired way, write it down. Try to remember other times in the past when you have seen the desired behavior and then you can have a list or a "story" of successes. You can either read this to the child when the child is feeling down or use it as a bedtime story so the child can go to sleep with this new and successful picture of him or herself in his or her mind.

   e. Call or tell someone else about how well the child is behaving. Make certain the child can hear you. Describe the successes.

   f. Be what you want the child to be and then praise yourself for being that way.

   g. Visualize your child as already being the new label and then relate to the child with the new label as part of the child.

   h. Show respect for the child's feelings and opinions even though you might not agree with them. The child's feelings and opinions are a part of you.

i. Be careful to give children comments on their strengths as well as on their weaknesses. Often we are so intent on helping the children get rid of all their "bad" qualities that we neglect to comment on all the good ones we see. Keep track for a few days of the balance of your comments by dividing a sheet of paper into two columns, one labeled STRENGTHS and the other labeled WEAKNESSES. Then put each comment in the appropriate side and see how you do. Try to balance the columns.

6. Think of three specific ways you can help your child develop a positive label. Write them down.

7. Do you have a negative label that you put on yourself?

8. Think of the label you would like to have. Write it down.

9. Think of three specific ways you can help to change your own self-concept and self-esteem. Write them down.

IF'S AND'S, OR BUT'S:

Reinforce earlier concepts of praise and behavior payoff.

PARENT ACTIVITY: 35.3 Home Practice Exercise
CONSTRUCT: Empathy
MATERIALS: Parent Handbooks

GOAL:

To build children's positive self-concept and self-esteem.

OBJECTIVES:

1. To reinforce desired behaviors.

2. To help children feel good about themselves.

3. To help children think of themselves as winners.

4. To maintain a warm and supportive atmosphere.

PROCEDURES:

1. Instruct parents to locate the Home Practice Exercise on page 143 in their Handbooks. Review the exercise with them:

   a. Do two things to improve your child's self-esteem and self-concept.

   b. Do two things to improve your own self-esteem and self-concept.

   c. Complete family log.

2. Tell parents that in addition to the Home Practice Exercise, they are to spend 30 minutes each day with each of their children in nurturing playtime activities. Playtime is a time with the parent and child alone — no TV, no other distractions. Playing a game or reading books are good activities. From the *Nurturing Book for Babies and Children*, have the parents practice activities listed in the following sections: Activities for Infants, Activities for Toddlers, Activities for Preschoolers, or Infant and Child Massage. Have the parents remember what they did and report the next week.

IF'S, AND'S, OR BUT'S:

1. Remind parents that a positive self-esteem and self-concept are important for children to have. Children who feel good do good things.

2. Self-esteem and self-concept do not change overnight. Remind parents they will have to continue to work on helping children learn to feel good.

FAMILY ACTIVITY:	**35.4 Family Nurturing Time**
CONSTRUCT:	**Empathy, Self-Awareness**
MATERIALS:	**Nurturing Book for Babies and Children**

ACTIVITIES FOR INFANTS (Birth to 15 months):

Utilizing the *Nurturing Book for Babies and Children*, select activities from the sections entitled Activities for Infants or Infant and Child Massage. Engage parents in practicing songs, play and stimulation activities, or massage. Vary the activities weekly to sustain interest.

ACTIVITIES FOR TODDLERS (15 months to 3 years):

Utilizing the *Nurturing Book for Babies and Children*, select activities from the sections entitled Activities for Toddlers or Infant and Child Massage. Engage parents in practicing songs, play, language, and movement activities, or massage. Vary the activities weekly to sustain interest.

ACTIVITIES FOR PRESCHOOLERS (3-5 years):

Use the following activities when working with preschool children and their parents. Use the activities as the basis for involving infants and toddlers if you are conducting a home visit with children ages birth to five years.

FAMILY ACTIVITY: 35.5 Hello Time: Loud and Soft
CONSTRUCT: Self-Awareness
MATERIALS: None

GOAL:

To have family members become aware of their self and others through selected verbal expression of feelings.

OBJECTIVES:

1. To greet each child and adult by first name.

2. To gain sensitivity to the feelings of others.

3. To encourage self-expression and ownership of feelings.

PROCEDURES:

1. Children and adults should be seated in a circle on the floor. A parent or home visitor should act as the leader of the activity.

2. The adult leading the activity explains the rules of the game. Rules: The group will take turns saying hello to everyone individually in either a loud or soft voice. The adult may say, "When it is your turn, you can tell us if you want us to say hello in a loud voice or a soft voice. When we ask, 'how are you?' you can answer in a loud or soft voice. After your turn you can choose the next person for us to say hello to."

3. The adult asks whether they'd like a loud or soft voice. After the child indicates his choice, the group responds in a loud or soft voice by saying, "Hello __(name)__ ."

4. The adult asks, "How are you?" and the child is encouraged to respond. The adult may remark that the child appears happy, sad, etc., in response to the child's feeling.

5. The child chooses the next person to be greeted, and Steps 3 and 4 are repeated.

IF'S AND'S, OR BUT'S:

1. Remind children that loud voices are for outside use but that it is okay to yell during this special activity.

2. When a child doesn't respond to "How are you?" or "Do you want loud or soft?" the group may be enlisted to interpret how the child is feeling and how they should talk to them.

> **Example:** Are you feeling sad, happy, etc.?
> How does Chad look? How do you think he feels?
> How you think he'd like us to say hello?

FAMILY ACTIVITY: 35.6 Circle Time: Dancercise
CONSTRUCT: Developmental
MATERIALS: Cassette player and cassettes or record player and records

GOAL:

To increase family interactions through music.

OBJECTIVES:

1. To involve children and parents in group cooperative musical activities.

2. To use large muscle movements.

3. To foster creative expression through dance.

4. To enhance self-awareness through dance.

5. To have fun.

PROCEDURES:

1. This activity will serve as a mini-dancercise movement. Have children and adults assemble in a circle.

2. Play music on a cassette player or a record player.

3. Demonstrate easy dance activities that generally use gross motor movements. The movements should change every 30 seconds to one minute to keep the interest going. Some gross motor movements may include the following:

   30 seconds, jumping jacks
   30 seconds, standing leg lifts (bending leg at hip and knee to form right angle)
   30 seconds, body twisting (turning at waist with hands on hips)
   The intent is to create gross motor movement to music.

IF'S AND'S OR BUT'S:

1. Some parents may feel silly dancing around. Have patience and encourage the parents to participate. Soon they will see it's fun.

2. Select music that will encourage movement. You may want to ask one of the children to pick out their favorite song to dance to.

FAMILY ACTIVITY: 35.7 Putting My Best Foot Forward and Family Hug
CONSTRUCT: Self-Awareness
MATERIALS: 4 large pie plates, aluminum foil, tempera paint (4 colors), long sheets of butcher block paper, wash pan, towels or rags

GOAL:

Spontaneous creative expression through exploration of color and design.

OBJECTIVES:

1. Children will be provided an emotional release to be messy in an appropriate manner.

2. Increase social interactions.

3. Increase tactile stimulation.

4. Promote positive parent-child interactions.

5. To reinforce comfort in using nurturing touch.

PROCEDURES:

1. Line the bottom of pie pans with aluminum foil.

2. Put the tempera paints in the various pie pans. Place large sheets of butcher paper close by.

3. Have each child and adult take turns stepping in pie pans to coat bottom of feet in two colors (1 right foot, 1 left foot).

4. Take turns walking across the paper making footprints in various directions.

5. At the end of the paper, set up a wash pan, plenty of towels or rags, and a chair for children to wash their feet off. An adult situated to help children clean their feet would be a good idea.

FAMILY HUG:

1. End each home visit with a family hug. Everyone get in a circle and put your arms around the people next to you. During the family hug time, anyone can say anything they like. It is a time for free expression.

2. At a natural time, close the activities for the day.

IF'S, AND'S, OR BUT'S:

1. Have each child make his/her own mural and have them make a family mural. First make his/her own then walk a few times on family mural.

2. Some children will be very squeamish about stepping in paint with bare feet. Don't force anyone who doesn't want to participate. Allow them to watch.

NURTURING PROGRAM FOR PARENTS AND CHILDREN BIRTH TO FIVE YEARS

SESSION 36

BEHAVIOR CONSTRUCT: **Child Development**

SESSION CONCEPT: **Stimulating and Communicating**

BRIEF DESCRIPTION: **Parents learn new ways to stimulate children's growth and increase their language development. Children draw their silhouettes and fill them with pictures, drawings, and objects that represent them.**

INTENDED USE: **For parents of children birth to 5 years**

PREREQUISITE KNOWLEDGE: **Praise, Helping Children with Feelings, Touch and Talk**

AGENDA

Parent Activities	Materials
36.1 Icebreaker and Home Practice Check In	*Parent Handbooks*, pencils, small pieces of paper
36.2 Stimulate and Communicate	*Parent Handbooks*, **Touch and Talk** AV presentation, AV equipment
36.3 Home Practice Exercise	*Parent Handbooks*

Family Activities*	Materials
36.4 Family Nurturing Time	*Nurturing Book for Babies and Children*
36.5 Hello Time: Good Morning to You	None
36.6 Circle Time: Feeling Song	None
36.7 Silhouettes and Family Hug	Large sheets of paper, strong flashlight or lamp, magic markers, crayons, tape, pencil, magazine

*For parents with infants or toddlers, use activities presented in *Nurturing Book for Babies and Children*. For parents with preschoolers (ages 3-5), use the activities listed below Family Nurturing Time.

PARENT ACTIVITY: 36.1 Icebreaker and Home Practice Check In
CONSTRUCT: Empathy, Self-Awareness
MATERIALS: Parent Handbooks, pencils, small pieces of paper

GOAL:

To increase parents' awareness of their strengths as perceived by others.

OBJECTIVES:

1. To increase parents' awareness of self.

2. To share feelings with others.

3. To increase sharing.

4. To reinforce positive feelings of self.

5. To practice praise for being and doing.

PROCEDURES:

1. Begin today's parent activities by handing out pieces of paper and pencils to each parent.

2. Ask each parent to write a nice message, which could be a wish, a compliment, or affectionate message, to each person in the group.

3. Parents may sign their names to their messages or not as they choose. Have them write the person's name on the outside.

4. Have parents read their messages. Process the activity. How do the parents feel about their message(s).

5. After each parent has had an opportunity to respond to the statements above, review the Home Practice Exercise from the previous meeting. Also discuss perceived changes in family members and their interactions as reported in the family log.

IF'S, AND'S, OR BUT'S:

1. This short exercise is one of the most powerful in the program. Parents will enjoy receiving positive statements.

2. If there is only you and the parent, you can tell each other your message.

PARENT ACTIVITY: 36.2 Stimulate and Communicate
CONSTRUCT: Child Development
MATERIALS: Parent Handbooks, Touch and Talk AV presentation, AV equipment

---

GOAL:

To increase parents' ability to enhance child growth and development.

OBJECTIVES:

1. To increase parents' ability to foster positive growth in their children through stimulation.

2. To increase parents' ability to foster language development through communication.

3. To increase parents' ability to touch and talk to their children.

PROCEDURES:

1. If you are using the audio-visual programs, present the AV entitled **Touch and Talk.**

2. Instruct parents to locate the information entitled **Stimulate and Communicate** on pages 119-121 in their Handbooks. Utilize the information presented to discuss the following major concepts with the parents:

   a. Talking to and touching your baby are excellent ways to develop positive feelings toward self and others.

   b. Children are born with the capacity to understand words and learn to talk.

   c. Baby's first sounds are e's, eh's, and a's. These sounds are called discomfort sounds.

   d. Babies soon make sounds like ah, oh, oo. These sounds are called comfort sounds.

   e. Paying attention to the different comfort/discomfort sounds helps establish a system of communication.

   f. Praise children for all the sounds they make.

   g. Ways to help develop language:

   • Putting words to behavior.

   • Describing feelings.

   h. Stimulate your child:

   • Allow children to touch safe objects of different texture, size, color.

   • Hang mobiles; tape colored shapes and pictures of animals to walls by crib and changing table.

   • Dance and sing with your children.

   • Give baby massages.

3. Ask the parents to complete the following:

   • Familiar words or sounds I hear my child make are _____.

   • He/she usually makes these noises (say these words) when _____.

   • One thing I do that stimulates my child is _____.

IF'S, AND'S, OR BUT'S:

It takes time to want to communicate and stimulate children. It also takes empathy. If parents still seem reluctant about touching and talking to their children, keep working on building empathy.

PARENT ACTIVITY: 36.3 Home Practice Exercise
CONSTRUCT: Child Development, Empathy
MATERIALS: Parent Handbooks

GOAL:

To provide parent with practice time to stimulate growth and communicate with their children.

OBJECTIVES:

1. To initiate stimulating experiences between infant and parent.
2. To encourage parents to communicate with their children.
3. To increase positive parent-child interactions.
4. To increase comfort in nurturing touch.

PROCEDURES:

1. Instruct parents to locate the Home Practice Exercise on page 143 in their Handbooks. Review the exercise with them:

   a. Do one activity with your child that is stimulating.

   b. Practice talking to your child by describing his/her feelings during feeding time, bath time, and changing time.

   c. Pay attention to your child's ways of communicating to you.

   d. Complete family log.

2. Tell parents that in addition to the Home Practice Exercise, they are to spend 30 minutes each day with each of their children in nurturing playtime activities. Playtime is a time with the parent and child alone — no TV, no other distractions. Playing a game or reading books are good activities. From the *Nurturing Book for Babies and Children*, have the parents practice activities listed in the following sections: Activities for Infants, Activities for Toddlers, Activities for Preschoolers, or Infant and Child Massage. Have the parents remember what they did and report the next week.

IF'S, AND'S, OR BUT'S:

At this stage in the program, parents should be capable of completing the Home Practice Exercise.

FAMILY ACTIVITY: 36.4 Family Nurturing Time
CONSTRUCT: Empathy, Self-Awareness
MATERIALS: Nurturing Book for Babies and Children

ACTIVITIES FOR INFANTS (Birth to 15 months):

Utilizing the *Nurturing Book for Babies and Children*, select activities from the sections entitled Activities for Infants or Infant and Child Massage. Engage parents in practicing songs, play and stimulation activities, or massage. Vary the activities weekly to sustain interest.

ACTIVITIES FOR TODDLERS (15 months to 3 years):

Utilizing the *Nurturing Book for Babies and Children*, select activities from the sections entitled Activities for Toddlers or Infant and Child Massage. Engage parents in practicing songs, play, language, and movement activities, or massage. Vary the activities weekly to sustain interest.

ACTIVITIES FOR PRESCHOOLERS (3-5 years):

Use the following activities when working with preschool children and their parents. Use the activities as the basis for involving infants and toddlers if you are conducting a home visit with children ages birth to five years.

FAMILY ACTIVITY: 36.5 Hello Time: Good Morning to You
CONSTRUCT: Empathy
MATERIALS: None

GOAL:

To increase children's awareness of the presence and feelings of others.

OBJECTIVES:

1. To increase children's self-awareness.

2. To allow children to share how they feel.

3. To increase listening skills.

PROCEDURES:

1. Begin this activity with children and adults seated on the floor in a circle.

2. Take turns singing the following song to each child, to the tune of "Happy Birthday."

    Good Morning to you, Good Morning to you,
    Good Morning to___(child's name)___, How are you today?

3. Each child should be encouraged to tell how he/she is feeling or he/she may choose to sing his/her response, to the tune of "Happy Birthday."

> I'm happy today, I'm happy today,
> I'm happy today, I'm happy today.

> Other feeling words may he used: grumpy, sleepy, sad, silly, lonely, etc.

4. An adult may choose to model the sung response for the children, but allow them to choose how they express their feelings to the group.

5. Be sure to focus the attention on the person being greeted; i.e., "Where's Adam? Let's all sing to him."

IF'S, AND'S, OR BUT'S:

If a child does not respond by saying how he feels, try to elicit from others how they think he may be feeling; i.e., "Look at Adam. How do you think he may be feeling? I see a smile. Do you think he's happy or sad?"

FAMILY ACTIVITY: 36.6 Circle Time: Feeling Song
CONSTRUCT: Empathy
MATERIALS: None

GOAL:

To reinforce appropriate adult/child interactions.

OBJECTIVES:

1. To help parents and children learn to enjoy each other.

2. To provide an opportunity for the children to be with the parents in a safe atmosphere.

3. To physically and emotionally nourish children and parents.

4. To increase awareness of feelings.

PROCEDURES:

1. Have adults and children stand in a circle.

2. Explain the activity of singing a song that has lots of feelings. The song goes like this:

Feeling Song

> When you're happy and you know it, clap your hands,
> When you're happy and you know it, clap your hands,
> When you're happy and you know it, then your face
> will surely show it,
> When you're happy and you know it, clap your hands.

3. Repeat singing the song with the children clapping their hands.

4. Repeat the song with the following stanzas:

> When you're mad...stamp your feet.
> When you're sad...wipe your eyes.
> When you're scared...scream out loud (Ahh!).
> When you're cold...shake and shiver (shake body).
> When you're hot...sweat and faint (bend to knees).

IF'S, AND'S, OR BUT'S:

1. Encourage everyone to participate even though some may feel somewhat hesitant.

2. Ask children for suggestions for additional activities.

FAMILY ACTIVITY:	**36.7 Silhouettes and Family Hug**
CONSTRUCT:	**Self-Awareness**
MATERIALS:	**Large sheets of paper, strong flashlight or lamp, magic markers, crayons, tape, pencil, magazines**

GOAL:

To increase children's awareness of self and others.

OBJECTIVES:

1. Children will increase awareness of their appearance.

2. Children will increase use of fine motor skills.

3. Children will increase awareness of "best" characteristics.

4. Children will became aware of the characteristics of others.

5. To reinforce comfort in using nurturing touch.

PROCEDURES:

1. Tell the group that today they will be making silhouettes.

2. Tape some butcher block paper to the walls. Place a chair 3-4 feet from the wall, parallel with the wall.

3. Have child sit on chair. Using a strong flashlight or lamp, have someone hold a light to the side of the child's face forming a shadow (silhouette) on the paper.

4. Trace the silhouette of the child with a pencil. Have adults get their silhouette made as well.

5. Instruct everyone to cut out their silhouette.

6. Instruct each to place in his/her silhouette words or pictures that describe experiences or feelings they have. These can only be positive feelings and experiences. The intent is to have everyone see the "good" in him/herself.

7. Paste/tape silhouettes to a sheet of construction paper and tape to wall.

8. Let everyone discuss their silhouettes.

FAMILY HUG:

1. End each home visit with a family hug. Everyone get in a circle and put your arms around the people next to you. During the family hug time, anyone can say anything they like. It is a time for free expression.

2. At a natural time, close the activities for the day.

IF'S, AND'S, OR BUT'S:

Draw a silhouette of everyone in the family present—even the children birth to 3 years. Ask brothers/sisters to fill in silhouette, or have very young children scribble/color lines in their silhouettes.

NURTURING PROGRAM FOR PARENTS AND CHILDREN BIRTH TO FIVE YEARS

SESSION 37

BEHAVIOR CONSTRUCT: Child Development

SESSION CONCEPT: Toilet Training

BRIEF DESCRIPTION: Parents learn a nurturing way to train children in using the potty. Children review anger, ways to handle it and make monster masks to display anger.

INTENDED USE: For parents of children birth to 5 years

PREREQUISITE KNOWLEDGE: Ages and Stages, Praise, I Statements

AGENDA

Parent Activities	Materials
37.1 Icebreaker and Home Practice Check In	*Parent Handbooks*
37.2 Toilet Training	*Parent Handbooks*, **Toilet Teaching** AV presentation, AV equipment
37.3 Home Practice Exercise	*Parent Handbooks*

Family Activities*	Materials
37.4 Family Nurturing Time	*Nurturing Book for Babies and Children*
37.5 Hello Time: London Bridge	None
37.6 Hopping Song	None
37.7 Circle Time: The Angry Hulk	Puppets
37.8 Monster Masks and Family Hug	Paper bag, scissors, materials for decorating: magic markers, crayons, cotton, glue

*For parents with infants or toddlers, use activities presented in *Nurturing Book for Babies and Children*. For parents with preschoolers (ages 3-5), use the activities listed below Family Nurturing Time.

PARENT ACTIVITY: 37.1 Icebreaker and Home Practice Check In
CONSTRUCT: Self Awareness
MATERIALS: Parent Handbooks

GOAL:

To increase parents' awareness of various aspects of adulthood and childhood.

OBJECTIVES:

1. To identify advantages of being a grown-up.

2. To identify disadvantages of being a grown-up.

3. To reinforce a sharing relationship between parents and home visitor.

PROCEDURES:

1. Begin today's parent activities by having each adult respond to the following:

   • The thing I like least about being grown-up is _____ .

   • The thing I like best about being grown-up is _____.

2. After each parent has had an opportunity to respond to the statements above, review the Home Practice Exercise from the previous meeting. Also discuss perceived changes in family members and their interactions as reported in the family log.

IF'S, AND'S, OR BUT'S:

In this exercise, statements related to the phenomenon of role reversal may arise. Good insight into an adult's childhood can be gathered by listening attentively to parents' comments.

PARENT ACTIVITY: 37.2 Toilet Training
CONSTRUCT: Child Development, Empathy
MATERIALS: Parent Handbooks, Toilet Teaching AV presentation, AV equipment

GOAL:

To increase parents' skill in properly teaching children to use the toilet.

OBJECTIVES:

1. To increase parents' knowledge of when to initiate toilet training.

2. To develop a nurturing routine in teaching children to use the toilet.

PROCEDURES:

1. If you are using the audio-visual progams, present the AV entitled **Toilet Teaching**.

2. Instruct parents to locate the information entitled **Toilet Training** on pages 122-127 in their Handbooks. Utilize the information presented to discuss the following major concepts with the parents:

   a. Is your child ready to be taught?

      ● Age — at least 2 years or older.

      ● Muscle control — physical coordination.

      ● Physical development — bladder maturity.

      ● Communication — words or facial movements and the ability to follow verbal directions.

      ● Desire — the desire to learn to use the potty.

   b. Before you begin your teaching:

      ● Choose words to use for urinating and bowel movements.

      ● Model the bathroom behavior you desire.

      ● Buy a potty chair that sits on the floor.

      ● Buy training pants.

   c. Pick a day both you and your child are feeling good.

   d. In teaching potty training:

      ● Be aware of natural potty times — after eating, after a nap, etc.

      ● Just before starting, help your child pull his training pants down and guide him to the potty.

      ● Talk to your child and use the words you selected for urinating and bowel movements.

      ● Stay with your child in the bathroom the first few times.

      ● Praise all efforts in using the potty.

      ● Praise all accomplishments.

      ● Teach your child how to wipe himself.

      ● Empty the potty.

   e. Don't make a big deal about accidents.

   f. Never use punishment in potty training.

   g. Keep the potty in the bathroom.

   h. Establishing a nurturing routine will help build in your child a positive sense of self.

3. Ask each parent to respond to the following:

   ● What does the parent remember about his/her own toilet training?

   ● What are some messages parents remember about toilet training that they received from others?

- What has been the experience of the parents so far related to teaching their children to use the toilet?
- What are the parents' expectations regarding potty training?

IF'S, AND'S, OR BUT'S:

Toilet training can often be a time of conflict between parents and their children. It is one of the few areas children can have complete control of their lives. You may need to spend a couple of sessions with parents discussing and developing skills in toilet training.

PARENT ACTIVITY:	**37.3 Home Practice Exercise**
CONSTRUCT:	**Child Development, Empathy**
MATERIALS:	**Parent Handbooks**

GOAL:

To increase parents' ability to train their child in using the potty.

OBJECTIVES:

1. To establish a nurturing routine for toilet training.

2. To give parents new toilet training skills.

3. To allow parents to practice their new skills.

4. To maintain a warm, close supportive environment.

PROCEDURES:

1. Instruct parents to locate the Home Practice Exercise on page 143 in their Handbooks. Review the exercise with them:

   a. Practice potty training your child with the techniques and steps identified in the resource material.

   b. Complete family log.

2. Tell parents that in addition to the Home Practice Exercise, they are to spend 30 minutes each day with each of their children in nurturing playtime activities. Playtime is a time with the parent and child alone – no TV, no other distractions. Playing a game or reading books are good activities. From the *Nurturing Book for Babies and Children*, have the parents practice activities listed in the following sections: Activities for Infants, Activities for Toddlers, Activities for Preschoolers, or Infant and Child Massage. Have the parents remember what they did and report the next week.

IF'S, AND'S, OR BUT'S:

Before assigning toilet training as home practice, make sure the child has the prerequisite abilities.

FAMILY ACTIVITY:	37.4 Family Nurturing Time
CONSTRUCT:	Empathy, Self-Awareness
MATERIALS:	Nurturing Book for Babies and Children

ACTIVITIES FOR INFANTS (Birth to 15 months):

Utilizing the *Nurturing Book for Babies and Children*, select activities from the sections entitled Activities for Infants or Infant and Child Massage. Engage parents in practicing songs, play and stimulation activities, or massage. Vary the activities weekly to sustain interest.

ACTIVITIES FOR TODDLERS (15 months to 3 years):

Utilizing the *Nurturing Book for Babies and Children*, select activities from the sections entitled Activities for Toddlers or Infant and Child Massage. Engage parents in practicing songs, play, language, and movement activities, or massage. Vary the activities weekly to sustain interest.

ACTIVITIES FOR PRESCHOOLERS (3-5 years):

Use the following activities when working with preschool children and their parents. Use the activities as the basis for involving infants and toddlers if you are conducting a home visit with children ages birth to five years.

FAMILY ACTIVITY:	37.5 Hello Time: London Bridge
CONSTRUCT:	Empathy
MATERIALS:	None

GOAL:

To reinforce appropriate adult-child interactions.

OBJECTIVES:

1. To help parents and children enjoy each other.

2. To increase positive touch.

PROCEDURES:

1. Choose two persons to be the "bridge" by facing each other and holding hands with their arms lifted high enough for others to pass under.

2. Have the rest of the people form a line and pass under the bridge as everyone sings:

London Bridge

London Bridge is falling down, falling down, falling down,
London Bridge is falling down, My fair __(name)__ .

3. As the group sings "my fair ___(name)___," the two people who are the bridge should lower their arms and "catch" someone. Have the group sing that person's name in the line "my fair _____."

4. The person who gets "caught" in the bridge takes the place of one of the people making up the bridge and that person joins the group moving under the bridge.

IF'S, AND'S, OR BUT'S:

Allow all children a chance to be a part of the bridge.

FAMILY ACTIVITY:	**37.6 Hopping Song**
CONSTRUCT:	**Empathy**
MATERIALS:	**None**

GOAL:

To increase positive family interactions through music.

OBJECTIVES:

1. To involve children in active and cooperative musical activities.

2. To foster creative expression through music.

PROCEDURES:

1. Assemble children and adults in a circle to participate in the song activity.

2. Sing words to the tune of "99 Bottles of Beer."

Hopping Song

There is one person hopping, hopping all around,
Hopping, hopping, hopping,
Hopping, hopping all around.

Movement: Kids hop and increase to 2 kids, 3 kids, etc. OR have everyone participate at the same time. Ask the children what activity should be performed.

Example: There is one family hopping, hopping all around.

IF'S, AND'S, OR BUT'S:

Use gross motor movements such as hopping, skipping, jumping, running backwards, etc. The idea is movement.

GOAL:

To encourage children to effectively express and control their anger.

OBJECTIVES:

1. To increase a child's ability to express anger in socially acceptable ways.

2. Recall some of the important ideas discussed during Circle Time about things that make them angry, and how they (the children) express their anger.

PROCEDURES:

1. Have children and adults sit in a circle on the floor.

2. Ask the group to remember last time we talked about anger and how we can control our anger. "Who can tell me what we said we could do to control our anger?"

3. Choose one of the puppets and let him/her represent the feeling of "Anger." Explain briefly to the children: "We all have feelings inside us that need to come out. This feeling (pointing to the puppet) is ANGER (make a loud, growling sound like a tiger with the last syllable — Grrrrr.) (In a quieter voice) "We all feel anger occasionally, but most of the time anger (pointing to the puppet) is sleeping. Can anyone tell us why we need to control our anger? (Wait for response that suggest we can hurt ourselves and others; others don't like talking or playing with us; etc.)

4. Use all three puppets for the upcoming situations. Two puppets will be engaged in a situation, one puppet will represent the feeling anger — "The Hulk." When one of the two puppets in the upcoming situations becomes angry, as will happen, puppet who feels angry will turn into the "anger" puppet. The change of appearance (e.g, the mild doctor turning into the Hulk) will help illustrate the concept of controlling an "enraged" feeling.

5. Situation #1: Not having ice cream before dinner. Puppet #1 is the child, Puppet #2 is the mother.

    Puppet #1: Mommy, I want some ice cream.

    Puppet #2: No, you can't have any ice cream just before dinner.

    Puppet #1: (Getting angry) But mommy, chocolate is my favorite flavor and we are not going to eat for another hour.

    Puppet #2: You heard what I said, no ice cream before dinner.

    Puppet #1: (Changing into "Hulk") I want ice cream NOW! I hate you! (Throwing things, yelling, kicking, hitting mom). I want ice cream!

Leader: Boy-o-boy! Puppet #1 (child) is really angry. He/she was so angry that he/she turned into the Hulk. How did Puppet #1 handle the anger? What did he/she do? What could Puppet #1 have done that would have helped him/her express his/her anger about not having ice cream more appropriately than hitting, kicking, throwing things? (Get ideas that suggest: going outside, going into their room, expressing their feelings to mom about not being allowed ice cream, etc.)

GROUP LEADER, PLEASE NOTE: It is not the intent of the exercise to tell children they can't or shouldn't get angry. The intent is to help them find ways to appropriately express their anger.

6. Situation #2: Going to bed. Puppet #1 is the child, Puppet #2 is the mother.

Puppet #2: (Calling to her son/daughter) It's time to go to bed. Make sure you wash your face and brush your teeth before you get into bed.

Puppet #1: But mommy, I don't want to go to sleep now. I'm watching TV.

Puppet #2: You know that 9 p.m. is your time to go to bed. Now hurry up, get washed and into bed.

Puppet #1: (Getting angry) No, I don't want to! I'm not going to bed and you can't make me!

Puppet #2: You have a choice. You can get into bed in the next 5 minutes, or else you can't watch TV tomorrow. It's your choice.

Puppet #1: (Changing into "Hulk") You can't do this to me. It's my favorite program (yelling, kicking, throwing a temper tantrum.) I hate this house. I'm old enough to sit up and watch TV.

Leader: What could Puppet #1 have done that would have helped him/her express his/her anger about having to go to bed more appropriately than throwing temper tantrums? Seek alternatives from the children to temper tantrums.

7. Situation #3: Group's Choice. Have children act out a skit of their choice with the puppets. Encourage participation.

IF'S, AND'S, OR BUT'S:

1. It will help get the concept of anger across if you can become a little animated when being the angry puppet.

2. It also will help the activity if the puppet who represents anger is different in some way than the other puppets: different color or bigger eyes, more/less hair, etc.

FAMILY ACTIVITY: **37.8 Monster Masks and Family Hug**
CONSTRUCT: **Self-Awareness**
MATERIALS: **Paper bag, scissors, materials for decorating: magic markers, crayons, cotton, glue**

GOAL:

To encourage children to release fears through play.

OBJECTIVES:

1. Children will increase their awareness of fear.

2. Children will increase their group interactions.

3. To reinforce comfort in using nurturing touch.

PROCEDURES:

1. Explain today we will be making monster masks. "Who can tell me what a monster is? Has anyone ever seen a monster? Are monsters good or bad?"

2. Provide each child with a paper bag to make a mask. Let them decorate it any way they want. They will make a monster mask.

3. Cut openings for eyes.

4. Ask children how monsters act.

5. Let them act like monsters for awhile.

6. When completed, tell them the monsters have to be put away; it's time for little boys and little girls to play.

FAMILY HUG:

1. End each home visit with a family hug. Everyone get in a circle and put your arms around the people next to you. During the family hug time, anyone can say anything they like. It is a time for free expression.

2. At a natural time, close the activities for the day.

IF'S, AND'S, OR BUT'S:

Encourage the children to verbalize their fears.

NURTURING PROGRAM FOR PARENTS AND CHILDREN BIRTH TO FIVE YEARS

SESSION 38

BEHAVIOR CONSTRUCT Behavior Management

SESSION CONCEPT: Verbal Management

BRIEF DESCRIPTION: Parents learn to use verbal management as a means of helping children gain self-control. Children have fun with shaving cream and identifying others.

INTENDED USE: For parents of children birth to 5 years

PREREQUISITE KNOWLEDGE: Praise, Problem Solving, Choices and Consequences, Behavior Management, Time-Out

AGENDA

Parent Activities	Materials
38.1 Icebreaker and Home Practice Check In	*Parent Handbooks*
38.2 Verbal Management	*Parent Handbooks*
38.3 Home Practice Exercise	*Parent Handbooks*

Family Activities*	Materials
38.4 Family Nurturing Time	*Nurturing Book for Babies and Children*
38.5 Hello Time: I Spy	None
38.6 Circle Time: Are You Sleeping?	Blanket, pillow, bell, rug or mat
38.7 Shaving Cream and Family Hug	Shaving cream, food coloring

*For parents with infants or toddlers, use activities presented in *Nurturing Book for Babies and Children*. For parents with preschoolers (ages 3-5), use the activities listed below Family Nurturing Time.

PARENT ACTIVITY: 38.1 Icebreaker and Home Practice Check In
CONSTRUCT: Self-Awareness
MATERIALS: Parent Handbooks

GOAL:

To encourage parents to share their feelings of parenthood.

OBJECTIVES:

1. To increase awareness of the positive payoffs of parenthood.

2. To increase awareness of the negative payoffs of parenthood.

PROCEDURES:

1. Begin today's parent activities by having each adult respond to the following:

   • Right now I am feeling _____ .

   • As a parent, my greatest joy is when _____ , and my greatest frustration is when _____ .

2. After each parent has had an opportunity to respond to the statements above, review the Home Practice Exercise from the previous meeting. Also discuss perceived changes in family members and their interactions as reported in the family log.

IF'S, AND'S, OR BUT'S:

Pay close attention to the joys and frustrations of being a parent. Insight into the identity of needed remedial work can be recognized.

PARENT ACTIVITY: 38.2 Verbal Management
CONSTRUCT: Behavior Management
MATERIALS: Parent Handbooks

GOAL:

To teach parents an alternative method of behavior management to physical punishment.

OBJECTIVES:

1. To provide parents with a verbal process to replace physical punishment.

2. To increase the appropriate use of verbal management.

3. To increase parents' sense of competence with their children.

PROCEDURES :

1. Remark that we have already learned a number of behavior management techniques: praise, time-out, choices and consequences, I statements and You messages, and now verbal management.

2. Instruct parents to locate the information entitled **Verbal Management** on pages 128-130 in their Handbooks.

3. Discuss each of the steps of verbal management with the parents.

4. Ask the parents if there is a situation they would like to offer as a trial.

5. Role play by using the steps of verbal management to the specific problem. Encourage the parents to ask for assistance when they need it.

IF'S, AND'S, OR BUT'S:

1. If time allows, select another situation and repeat steps 4 through 7.

2. Verbal management is an excellent technique in helping children manage their behavior.

PARENT ACTIVITY:	38.3 Home Practice Exercise
CONSTRUCT:	**Behavior Management, Self-Awareness**
MATERIALS:	**Parent Handbooks**

GOAL:

To reinforce parents' use of appropriate behavior management techniques.

OBJECTIVES:

1. To reinforce the use of verbal management skills.

2. To reinforce attempts to use choices and consequences.

3. To reinforce the use of self praise.

4. To reinforce the use of problem solving techniques.

5. To maintain a warm supportive atmosphere.

PROCEDURES:

1. Instruct parents to locate the Home Practice Exercise on page 143 in their Handbooks. Review the exercise with them:

   a. Use verbal management at least once.

   b. Model self praise: Praise self out loud in front of child.

   c. Try the problem solving techniques.

   d. Complete family log.

---

2. Tell parents that in addition to the Home Practice Exercise, they are to spend 30 minutes each day with each of their children in nurturing playtime activities. Playtime is a time with the parent and child alone — no TV, no other distractions. Playing a game or reading books are good activities. From the *Nurturing Book for Babies and Children*, have the parents practice activities listed in the following sections: Activities for Infants, Activities for Toddlers, Activities for Preschoolers, or Infant and Child Massage. Have the parents remember what they did and report the next week.

IF'S, AND'S, OR BUT'S:

Remind parents that praise is the most powerful verbal management technique. Reinforce children for desirable behaviors.

FAMILY ACTIVITY: 38.4 Family Nurturing Time
CONSTRUCT: Empathy, Self-Awareness
MATERIALS: Nurturing Book for Babies and Children

ACTIVITIES FOR INFANTS (Birth to 15 months):

Utilizing the *Nurturing Book for Babies and Children*, select activities from the sections entitled Activities for Infants or Infant and Child Massage. Engage parents in practicing songs, play and stimulation activities, or massage. Vary the activities weekly to sustain interest.

ACTIVITIES FOR TODDLERS (15 months to 3 years):

Utilizing the *Nurturing Book for Babies and Children*, select activities from the sections entitled Activities for Toddlers or Infant and Child Massage. Engage parents in practicing songs, play, language, and movement activities, or massage. Vary the activities weekly to sustain interest.

ACTIVITIES FOR PRESCHOOLERS (3-5 years):

Use the following activities when working with preschool children and their parents. Use the activities as the basis for involving infants and toddlers if you are conducting a home visit with children ages birth to five years.

FAMILY ACTIVITY: 38.5 Hello Time: I Spy
CONSTRUCT: Empathy
MATERIALS: None

GOAL:

To describe simple, tangible characteristics of both self and others.

OBJECTIVES:

1. To increase children's awareness of self.

2. To increase children's awareness of others.

PROCEDURES:

1. Have children and adults sit in a circle on the floor.

2. Explain that today we will be playing a guessing game called "I Spy." We all take turns describing something someone has in the room, and everyone else tries to guess who it is. For example, I say, "I spy someone wearing glasses," and everyone else has to guess who I spy.

IF'S AND'S OR BUT'S:

If a child is having difficulty describing another child, give a prompt.

FAMILY ACTIVITY: 38.6 Circle Time: Are You Sleeping?
CONSTRUCT: Empathy
MATERIALS: Blanket, pillow, bell, rug or mat

GOAL:

To express and accept nurturing gestures appropriately among children and their parents.

OBJECTIVES:

1. To increase positive parent-child nurturing interactions.

2. To engage in cooperative activity between children and parents.

PROCEDURES:

1. Have children and parents sit in a circle on the floor.

2. Begin to discuss the concept of nurturing. Start by using examples:

   a. When they are frightened, the feeling of comfort when someone holds them.

   b. The feelings of comfort after someone helped them do a difficult task. In this instance, nurturing is being equated to the feeling of being comforted.

3. Describe the game for parents and children. One child lies down on the rug and pillow and is covered with the blanket by the parent. Appropriate nurturing-type interactions may be demonstrated, such as tucking the blanket around the child, touching him/her and saying "good night" softly. The small bell should be placed near the pillow. The child on the rug pretends to sleep while the group sings softly:

Are You Sleeping?

Are you sleeping, Are you sleeping,
Brother (Sister) _____ , Brother (Sister) _____ .

4. The group sings loudly and claps:

Morning bells are ringing, Morning bells are ringing,
Ding, dong, ding; ding, dong, ding.

(The sleeping person jumps up and rings the bell.)

5. Activity continues until all children have been tucked in by their parents.

IF'S, AND'S, OR BUT'S:

This is a good activity to use to provide appropriate physical contact in a nurturing way to children and their parents who may not ordinarily be receptive to it.

FAMILY ACTIVITY:	38.7 Shaving Cream and Family Hug
CONSTRUCT:	Self-Awareness
MATERIALS:	Shaving cream, food coloring

GOAL:

To participate in creative artistic expression involving tactile stimulation.

OBJECTIVES:

1. To participate in an art activity involving physical and tactile sensory experience.

2. To engage parents and children in creative, original self-expression.

3. To increase parents' ability to foster creative expression in their children.

4. To reinforce comfort in using nurturing touch.

PROCEDURES:

1. Get everyone to stand around the kitchen table. Introduce the activity by holding up and shaking a can of shaving cream.

2. Inform parents that children and adults simply do not get enough time to have fun with touch. This activity is designed to experience positive touch and to promote positive touch with your children.

3. (*PLEASE NOTE:* We recommend covering your table with a nonabsorbent material such as plastic garbage bags cut open or butcher block paper. Tape edges down to prevent movement during smearing.) Demonstrate painting with shaving cream by squirting it onto the table and smearing it around.

4. Squirt some shaving cream on the table for each person. Encourage parents and children to finger paint with the shaving cream on the table.

5. Add interest to the activity by adding a bit of food coloring to various piles of shaving cream. Encourage everyone to share their piles of shaving cream blending the colors.

FAMILY HUG:

1. End each home visit with a family hug. Everyone get in a circle and put your arms around the people next to you. During the family hug time, anyone can say anything they like. It is a time for free expression.

2. At a natural time, close the activities for the day.

IF'S, AND'S, OR BUT'S:

1. Parents will feel a bit awkward "playing" like children. Encourage parents to participate by suggesting to them that knowing how to play like a child will encourage them to play with their children.

2. Children might get really excited. Help them manage their behavior but remain nurturing.

NURTURING PROGRAM FOR PARENTS AND CHILDREN BIRTH TO FIVE YEARS

SESSION 39

BEHAVIOR CONSTRUCT:	Self-Awareness
SESSION CONCEPT:	Self-Expression
BRIEF DESCRIPTION:	Parents and children engage in free self-expression through painting.
INTENDED USE:	For parents of children birth to 5 years
PREREQUISITE KNOWLEDGE:	None

AGENDA

Parent Activities

		Materials
39.1	Icebreaker and Home Practice Check In	*Parent Handbooks*
39.2	Self-Expression	Paint brushes, paper, cups to rinse brushes, newspaper for floor, tempera paints
39.3	Home Practice Exercise	*Parent Handbooks*

Family Activities*

		Materials
39.4	Family Nurturing Time	*Nurturing Book for Babies and Children*
39.5	Hello Time: Happy to See You	None
39.6	Boat Song	None
39.7	Circle Time: What should I do?	Puppets
39.8	Marble Painting and Family Hug	Marbles, shoe boxes, white paper, tempera paint

*For parents with infants or toddlers, use activities presented in *Nurturing Book for Babies and Children*. For parents with preschoolers (ages 3-5), use the activities listed below Family Nurturing Time.

PARENT ACTIVITY: 39.1 Icebreaker and Home Practice Check In
CONSTRUCT: Self-Awareness
MATERIALS: Parent Handbooks

GOAL:

To increase parents' awareness of life tasks yet to be accomplished.

OBJECTIVES:

1. To increase parents' use of their positive personal power to affect changes in their lives.

2. To increase parents' awareness of the value of life.

PROCEDURES:

1. Begin today's parent activities by having each adult respond to the following:

    • If you knew you would die tomorrow, what regrets would you have?

    • Is there anything you can do now to avoid feeling this way?

2. After each parent has had an opportunity to respond to the statements above, review the Home Practice Exercise from the previous meeting. Also discuss perceived changes in family members and their interactions as reported in the family log.

IF'S, AND'S, OR BUT'S:

A rather morbid thought, but none-the-less provoking. Engage parents to use their personal power to change their lifestyle now while they are still alive.

PARENT ACTIVITY: 39.2 Self-Expression
CONSTRUCT: Empathy, Self-Awareness
MATERIALS: Paint brushes, paper, cups to rinse brushes, newspaper for floor, tempera paints

GOAL:

To increase self-expression in parents through painting.

OBJECTIVES:

1. To enable parents to express self.

2. To help parents experience their own creativity.

3. To provide parents reinforcement in expressing self.

PROCEDURES:

1. Cover floor or table with newspaper.

2. Hand out paints and paper to each parent.

3. Explain that parents are going to paint their past, present, and future. Begin by having parents paint pictures of their current selves. The picture can be splotches of color or a specific design. Given parents 5 minutes to paint their present selves.

4. Using the same guidelines, have parents paint pictures of their childhood. They can take any aspect of their childhood but the goal is to have them paint their overall feelings.

5. Last, have them paint their future—what is in store for them.

6. After all those pictures are painted, ask the parents to share their pictures. Have them draw similarities, observations, etc.

IF'S, AND'S, OR BUT'S:

1. Home visitors are also asked to paint their pictures.

2. Listen for optimistic or pessimistic responses.

PARENT ACTIVITY:	39.3 Home Practice Exercise
CONSTRUCT:	Child Development
MATERIALS:	Parent Handbooks

GOAL:

To increase positive parent-child interactions.

OBJECTIVES:

1. To maintain a supportive atmosphere.

2. To reinforce creativity and self-expression.

3. To foster communication.

PROCEDURES:

1. Instruct parents to locate the Home Practice Exercise on page 143 in their Handbooks. Review the exercise with them:

   a. Have one playtime activity per child that encourages self-expression and creativity.

   b. Complete family log.

2. Tell parents that in addition to the Home Practice Exercise, they are to spend 30 minutes each day with each of their children in nurturing playtime activities. Playtime is a time with the parent and child alone—no TV, no other distractions. Playing a game or reading books are good activities. From the *Nurturing Book for Babies and Children*, have the parents practice activities listed in the following sections: Activities for Infants, Activities for Toddlers, Activities for Preschoolers, or Infant and Child Massage. Have the parents remember what they did and report the next week.

IF'S, AND'S, OR BUT'S:

Any play time activity could encourage creativity and self-expression. The goal is to get parents to play with their children.

FAMILY ACTIVITY: **39.4 Family Nurturing Time**
CONSTRUCT: **Empathy, Self-Awareness**
MATERIALS: **Nurturing Book for Babies and Children**

ACTIVITIES FOR INFANTS (Birth to 15 months):

Utilizing the *Nurturing Book for Babies and Children*, select activities from the sections entitled Activities for Infants or Infant and Child Massage. Engage parents in practicing songs, play and stimulation activities, or massage. Vary the activities weekly to sustain interest.

ACTIVITIES FOR TODDLERS (15 months to 3 years):

Utilizing the *Nurturing Book for Babies and Children*, select activities from the sections entitled Activities for Toddlers or Infant and Child Massage. Engage parents in practicing songs, play, language, and movement activities, or massage. Vary the activities weekly to sustain interest.

ACTIVITIES FOR PRESCHOOLERS (3-5 years):

Use the following activities when working with preschool children and their parents. Use the activities as the basis for involving infants and toddlers if you are conducting a home visit with children ages birth to five years.

FAMILY ACTIVITY: 39.5 Hello Time: Happy to See You
CONSTRUCT: Empathy
MATERIALS: None

GOAL:

To reinforce family cohesion.

OBJECTIVES:

1. To personally greet each child and parent.

2. To experience successful interactions in a family setting.

3. To get parents and children to have fun.

PROCEDURES:

1. Have everyone sit on the floor in a circle.

2. Explain that we will take turns singing a song to each person in the group.

3. Go around the circle and sing the following song to each person (to the tune of "This is the Way We Wash Our Clothes").

    We're happy to see you here today, here today, here today,
    We're happy to see you here today, happy to see you, ___(name)___ .

4. After the name, ask the person, "How are you today?"

5. All children and adults should be sung to and asked how they are.

IF'S, AND'S, OR BUT'S:

After a person has been sung to, he or she may choose the next person for the group to sing to.

FAMILY ACTIVITY: 39.6 Boat Song
CONSTRUCT: Empathy
MATERIALS: None

GOAL:

To increase positive parent-child interactions through music and touch.

OBJECTIVES:

1. To increase parents' ability to enjoy fun times with their children.

2. To have children practice gross motor coordination.

PROCEDURES:

1. This activity takes place on the floor. Adults and children pretend to be "boats" by sitting with their legs extended in front of them and spread apart. One or two children sit in each "boat" by sitting between an adult's legs, with their backs to the adult. The children hold onto the adult's hands and pretend that they are oars.

2. Sing the song "Michael, Row Your Boat Ashore," substituting each child's name for "Michael." As you sing, move your arms in a forward/backward movement simulating rowing a boat while holding hands with the children in each boat. Repeat the song until each person's name has been used once.

IF'S, AND'S, OR BUT'S:

1. Repeat the activity with children in pairs. They can take turns being the "boat" or the "rower."

2. Emphasize taking turns by having the person whose name has been sung choose the next person to be sung about.

3. This is a good activity to provide appropriate physical contact between adults and children in a nonthreatening way. The activity also emphasizes cooperation in taking turns and waiting.

FAMILY ACTIVITY: **39.7 Circle Time: What Should I Do?**
CONSTRUCT: **Behavior Management**
MATERIALS: **Puppets**

GOAL:

To reinforce children's ability to take responsibility for their behavior.

OBJECTIVES:

1. To empower children to use their personal power to make wise decisions.

2. To reinforce the concept of cause and effect.

3. To reinforce appropriate behavior.

4. To reinforce concepts of personal power and positive self-talk.

PROCEDURES:

1. Assemble children and adults in a circle sitting on the floor.

2. Utilizing two puppets, play act the following:

>   **Puppet #1:** Hello. _____. What's new?

>   **Puppet #2:** Oh, my brother makes me so mad. He is just mean. I was playing with one of his toys and he hit me.

>   **Puppet #1:** Why did he hit you?

Puppet #2: Because he doesn't like me playing with his toys without asking first.

Puppet #1: Did you ask him if you could play with his toys?

Puppet #2: No — he never asks me if he can play with my toys. He just takes them, so I took his.

Puppet #1: What did you do after he hit you?

Puppet #2: I hit him back and he started crying and my mom told me to take a time-out. He didn't get in trouble, I did.

Leader: What happened to Puppet #2 for playing with her brother's toys without asking? (He hit her.) Was that a good way to use his personal power? (No.) What would be a better way to use his personal power? (Tell his mom; tell his sister not to play with his toys.) What happened to Puppet #1 after he hit his sister? (She hit him back.) Was that a good way to use her personal power? (No.) What could she have done? (Asked permission; told her brother not to hit.) Sometimes the consequences to things we choose to do hurt us, make us angry, make us cry, and get us into trouble. Good things happen to us when we use our personal power in a nice way. Let's see if Puppet #2 and Puppet #1 could use their personal power and get good consequences and not bad ones.

3. Play act a situation where the sister asks her brother if she can play with his toys. He says yes, both play together nicely, parents notice how nicely the two play together and reward them with a hug.

IF'S, AND'S, OR BUT'S:

The main theme of the activity is to review the concepts of personal power and choices and consequences. If the family is currently dealing with an issue, you may want to substitute that topic and play act the skit with the puppets.

FAMILY ACTIVITY: **39.8 Marble Painting and Family Hug**
CONSTRUCT: **Appropriate Developmental Expectations**
MATERIALS: **Marbles, shoe boxes, white paper, tempera paint**

GOAL:

To reinforce creative expression through art.

OBJECTIVES:

1. To foster creativity in children.

2. To enhance social interactions.

3. To reinforce comfort in using nurturing touch.

PROCEDURES:

1. Do this activity at tables. It may be easier to have children and adults work in pairs.

2. Children drop marbles into paint and then into a shoe box or a shallow dish with paper cut to fit the bottom. By moving the box or plate, the children can roll the marbles from side to side and from top to bottom to make a design. Using different colors gives an exciting contrast.

FAMILY HUG:

1. End each home visit with a family hug. Everyone get in a circle and put your arms around the people next to you. During the family hug time, anyone can say anything they like. It is a time for free expression.

2. At a natural time, close the activities for the day.

IF'S, AND'S, OR BUT'S:

1. Good for physically handicapped child because even the slightest movement produces a design.

2. Use different sizes of boxes and different sizes of marbles to get various effects.

3. The finished product could be used as greeting cards or wrapping paper.

NURTURING PROGRAM FOR PARENTS AND CHILDREN BIRTH TO FIVE YEARS

SESSION 40

BEHAVIOR CONSTRUCT:	Empathy
SESSION CONCEPT:	People and Possessions
BRIEF DESCRIPTION:	Parents discuss how children can be used as possessions. Parents experience their feelings of being a possession through the towel pull exercise. Children will put on makeup to portray their feelings.
INTENDED USE:	For parents of children birth to 5 years
PREREQUISITE KNOWLEDGE:	None

AGENDA

Parent Activities	Materials
40.1 Icebreaker and Home Practice Check In	*Parent Handbooks*
40.2 Towel Pull	Bath towels (one for every two persons)
40.3 People and Possessions	None
40.4 Home Practice Exercise	*Parent Handbooks*

Family Activities*	Materials
40.5 Family Nurturing Time	*Nurturing Book for Babies and Children*
40.6 Hello Time: The Farmer in the Dell	None
40.7 Circle Time: In and Out the Window	None
40.8 Facing Up and Family Hug	White facial mask, makeup, washable magic markers, paints, mirrors, washcloths, and warm water

*For parents with infants or toddlers, use activities presented in *Nurturing Book for Babies and Children*. For parents with preschoolers (ages 3-5), use the activities listed below Family Nurturing Time.

PARENT ACTIVITY: 40.1 Icebreaker and Home Practice Check In
CONSTRUCT: Empathy
MATERIALS: Parent Handbooks

GOAL:

To reinforce positive perceptions of self.

OBJECTIVES:

1. To increase awareness of feelings of self.

2. To increase positive expression of self.

3. To identify personal strengths.

PROCEDURES:

1. Begin today's parent activities by having each adult respond to the following:

    *   Right now I am feeling _____ .

    *   The nicest or best thing about me is _____ .

2. After each parent has had an opportunity to respond to the statements above, review the Home Practice Exercise from the previous meeting. Also discuss perceived changes in family members and their interactions as reported in the family log.

IF'S, AND'S, OR BUT'S:

Parents should be able to express positive elements of self. Listen for those parents who are still having difficulty.

PARENT ACTIVITY: 40.2 Towel Pull
CONSTRUCT: Empathy, Self-Awareness
MATERIALS: Bath towels (one for every two persons)

GOAL:

To enable parents to become aware of their feelings about possessions.

OBJECTIVES:

1. To help parents determine whether they are more powerful in the getting or the keeping.

2. To encourage parents to understand control and possessions in their lives.

3. To help parents make choices about control and possessions.

PROCEDURES:

1. Inform the parents that today the focus will be on loss of power and ownership. Generally people operate on the basic principle of "what you can't have is what you want most. And, the moment you get it, you don't want it anymore."

2. Ask parents to give examples of how they have sought to have and/or own something and the moment they got it, it didn't seem that big of a deal. Give some of your own examples.

3. Ask parents to form pairs and hand out one towel to each pair.

4. Ask each pair of parents to sit on the floor facing each other with their legs extended in front of them so the soles of their shoes (or their feet) are touching each other.

5. Share the following:

   (To person A) — You own the towel. It is yours. He/she wants to take it from you, but you own it. When he/she tries to take it, say, "It's mine, you can't have it, it's mine" and pull the towel toward you.

   (To person B) — You want the towel. Take it from him/her. Say, "Give it to me. I want it." and pull the towel toward you.

6. Begin the exercise and continue it for three minutes.

7. Switch roles — A becomes B, B becomes A.

8. Begin again in new roles and pull for three minutes.

9. Afterwards process the exercise. Were you stronger when you "owned" it or when you "wanted" it? Do you see any parallels to this in your life? Make references to how children operate on this principle.

IF'S AND'S, OR BUT'S:

1. Issues of control and possessions may be very relevant in families where children are manipulated, encouraged to "side" with one parent, or used to undermine the control of the other parents.

2. If you're working with a single parent, you become the other pull partner.

PARENT ACTIVITY:	40.3 People and Possessions
CONSTRUCT:	Empathy, Self-Awareness
MATERIALS:	None

GOAL:

To increase parents' awareness of their treatment of their children, mates, and friends.

OBJECTIVES:

1. To enable parents to recognize times they were treated as possessions.

2. To help parents recognize times when they treated other people as possessions.

PROCEDURES:

1. Leader begin: Parents find a comfortable position in your chair or on the floor for an internal interview.

   a. Relax and close your eyes.

   b. I'll ask you some questions and you answer them quietly inside yourself, with pictures or without, however it happens to you.

   c. Have you ever been treated by anyone as if you were a possession and not a person? (Pause)

   d. By how many people? (Pause)

   e. What did "they" do to make you feel that way? (Pause)

   f. How did that make you feel? (Pause)

   g. Knowing you would never want to treat anyone as a possession but that sometimes we do things we don't intend to, have you ever treated anyone as a possession? (Pause)

   h. How many people? (Pause)

   i. What did you do to treat them that way? (Pause)

   j. How did you feel doing it? (Pause)

   k. How did that person react? (Pause)

2. Now visualize the person who was most apt to treat you as a possession standing in front of you.

3. Visualize yourself saying to that person, "I am a person and not a thing. I do not need to be possessed. I am a changing, loving human being and I hereby declare my independence from your possession." (Pause)

4. Have parent visualize the person they are most apt to treat as a possession.

5. Internally visualize yourself saying to that person, "You are a person and not a thing. I hereby release you from my possession. I now see you as a person in your own right and I do not want to possess you." (Pause)

6. Now tell the parents to enjoy the feeling of having given up possessing someone and of declaring their freedom from being possessed for a moment; to be proud of themselves for being liberated and for liberating.

7. Congratulations and open your eyes.

8. Process with the group.

IF'S, AND'S, OR BUT'S:

1. There may be a parent who is unable to complete the exercise. Advise the parent that there is no hurry, the parent can practice by seeing the person, and then by saying the words until the parent is ready to put them together. Stress that there is no need to force anything.

2. Some parents may have more difficulty liberating than being liberated. Dependency needs often inhibit liberation.

PARENT ACTIVITY:	40.4 Home Practice Exercise
CONSTRUCT:	Empathy, Self-Awareness
MATERIALS:	Parent Handbooks

GOAL:

To encourage the parent to critically examine the concept of possessions in their lives.

OBJECTIVES:

1. To identify instances of treating someone as a possession.

2. To identify instances of being treated as a possession by someone.

PROCEDURES:

1. Instruct parents to locate the Home Practice Exercise on page 144 in their Handbooks. Review the exercise with them:

   a. Notice someone treating another person as a possession.

   b. Notice yourself treating or about to treat someone as a possession.

   c. Notice someone treating or about to treat you as a possession.

   d. Complete family log.

2. Tell parents that in addition to the Home Practice Exercise, they are to spend 30 minutes each day with each of their children in nurturing playtime activities. Playtime is a time with the parent and child alone—no TV, no other distractions. Playing a game or reading books are good activities. From the *Nurturing Book for Babies and Children*, have the parents practice activities listed in the following sections: Activities for Infants, Activities for Toddlers, Activities for Preschoolers, or Infant and Child Massage. Have the parents remember what they did and report the next week.

IF'S, AND'S, OR BUT'S:

You may want to also encourage parents to be aware of instances where they don't treat others as possessions.

FAMILY ACTIVITY:	**40.5 Family Nurturing Time**
CONSTRUCT:	**Empathy, Self-Awareness**
MATERIALS:	**Nurturing Book for Babies and Children**

ACTIVITIES FOR INFANTS (Birth to 15 months):

Utilizing the *Nurturing Book for Babies and Children*, select activities from the sections entitled Activities for Infants or Infant and Child Massage. Engage parents in practicing songs, play and stimulation activities, or massage. Vary the activities weekly to sustain interest.

ACTIVITIES FOR TODDLERS (15 months to 3 years):

Utilizing the *Nurturing Book for Babies and Children*, select activities from the sections entitled Activities for Toddlers or Infant and Child Massage. Engage parents in practicing songs, play, language, and movement activities, or massage. Vary the activities weekly to sustain interest.

ACTIVITIES FOR PRESCHOOLERS (3-5 years):

Use the following activities when working with preschool children and their parents. Use the activities as the basis for involving infants and toddlers if you are conducting a home visit with children ages birth to five years.

FAMILY ACTIVITY:	**40.6 Hello Time: The Farmer in the Dell**
CONSTRUCT:	**Empathy**
MATERIALS:	**None**

GOAL:

To build positive parent-child interactions.

OBJECTIVES:

1. To help parents and children relate in a positive, nurturing way.

2. To help parents learn to enjoy their children.

PROCEDURES:

1. This is the traditional version of the Farmer in the Dell circle game.

2. Assemble children and adults holding hands in a circle.

3. Choose one child to stand in the center of the circle and be the "farmer."

4. The group moves in a circle around the farmer while singing. As the song calls for the "farmer to take a wife," have the child in the center of the circle choose another child or adult to join him inside the circle.

5. Continue in the same way until the verse "the cheese stands alone." Have the "cheese" stand in the center of the circle while the children sing that verse.

6. If the game is repeated, the person who was the "cheese" becomes the " farmer" for the new game.

The Farmer in the Dell

The farmer in the dell, the farmer in the dell,
Hi ho the dairy-o the farmer in the dell.

The farmer takes a wife, the farmer takes a wife,
Hi ho the dairy-o the farmer takes a wife.

The wife takes a child, the wife takes a child,
Hi ho the dairy-o the wife takes a child.

The child takes a nurse, the child takes a nurse,
Hi ho the dairy-o the child takes a nurse.

The nurse takes a dog, the nurse takes a dog,
Hi ho the dairy-o the nurse takes a dog.

The dog takes a cat, the dog takes a cat,
Hi ho the dairy-o the dog takes a cat.

The cat takes a rat, the cat takes a rat,
Hi ho the dairy-o the cat takes a rat.

The rat takes the cheese, the rat takes the cheese,
Hi ho the dairy-o the rat takes the cheese.

The cheese stands alone, the cheese stands alone,
Hi ho the dairy-o the cheese stands alone.

IF'S AND'S OR BUT'S:

In small families you may want to use objects such as dolls or pets to participate in the game.

FAMILY ACTIVITY: 40.7 Circle Time: In and Out the Window

CONSTRUCT: Empathy

MATERIALS: None

GOAL:

To build positive parent-child interactions.

OBJECTIVES:

1. To help parents and children relate in a positive, nurturing way.

2. To help parents learn to enjoy their children.

PROCEDURES:

1. Have all children and parents stand in a large circle without holding hands.

2. Choose one person to start the game by walking around the circle weaving behind and in front of each person as the group sings:

> Go in and out the window,
> Go in and out the window,
> Go in and out the window,
> As we have done before.

3. The person stops and stands in front of someone in the circle as the group sings:

> Now stand and face your partner,
> Now stand and face your partner,
> Now stand and face your partner,
> As we have done before.

4. The person takes the hands of his partner and they weave in and out of the circle as the group sings:

> Now take her off to London,
> Now take her off to London,
> Now take her off to London,
> As we have done before.

5. This game continues until everyone has a turn.

IF'S, AND'S, OR BUT'S:

Have parents act as partners with each of their children.

FAMILY ACTIVITY:	40.8 Facing Up and Family Hug
CONSTRUCT:	Self-Awareness and Empathy
MATERIALS:	White facial mask, make-up, washable magic markers, paints, mirrors, washcloths, and warm water

GOAL:

To increase children's awareness in recognizing and expressing feelings.

OBJECTIVES:

1. Children will be able to portray a feeling through facial make-up.

2. Children will increase their awareness of other's feelings.

3. Children will increase their tactile awareness.

4. To reinforce comfort in using nurturing touch.

PROCEDURES:

1. You need to purchase the substance that forms a facial mask (the kind that dries white and washes off with warm water.) The product is available at drug stores.

2. Put some facial lotion or cream on the children's faces before the facial mask. Using the substance to form a facial mask, place some on the faces of children. Tell the children that the substance will dry and get hard in a few minutes.

3. Once the facial mask is formed, use washable paints, magic markers, or make-up to draw/paint an expression on each child's face. Have adults draw the faces on the children; let the children draw the faces on the adults.

4. The themes can be several. Each can draw or paint a feeling face, a famous person, what they see the person as, their impressions of the person, or just lines.

5. After the masks are completed, allow everyone to see themselves in a mirror.

FAMILY HUG:

1. End each home visit with a family hug. Everyone get in a circle and put your arms around the people next to you. During the family hug time, anyone can say anything they like. It is a time for free expression.

2. At a natural time, close the activities for the day.

IF'S, AND'S, OR BUT'S:

Although adults may not want to have a face drawn on them, letting kids draw a face on you is an excellent sharing activity. Come on—don't be bashful; have a face drawn like everyone.

NURTURING PROGRAM FOR PARENTS AND CHILDREN BIRTH TO FIVE YEARS
SESSION 41

BEHAVIOR CONSTRUCT: Behavior Management

SESSION CONCEPT: Situations and Solutions, and Review of Behavior Management

BRIEF DESCRIPTION: Parents discuss specific problems they are having with their children's behavior and ways to solve the problems. Parents are also involved in reviewing the behavior management strategies learned to determine if further instruction is needed. Children create pictures with crayon shavings.

INTENDED USE: For parents of children birth to 5 years

PREREQUISITE KNOWLEDGE: All behavior management strategies presented in the program.

AGENDA

Parent Activities	Materials
41.1 Icebreaker and Home Practice Check In	*Parent Handbooks*
41.2 Situations and Solutions	None
41.3 Review of Behavior Management	*Parent Handbooks*
41.4 Home Practice Exercise	*Parent Handbooks*

Family Activities*	Materials
41.5 Family Nurturing Time	*Nurturing Book for Babies and Children*
41.6 Hello Time: Where is _____ ?	None
41.7 Circle Time: Blanket Game	Large blanket or large bed sheet
41.8 Crayon Shavings and Family Hug	Crayons, crayon sharpener or vegetable grater, clothes iron, wax paper, newspaper

*For parents with infants or toddlers, use activities presented in *Nurturing Book for Babies and Children*. For parents with preschoolers (ages 3-5), use the activities listed below Family Nurturing Time.

PARENT ACTIVITY: 41.1 Icebreaker and Home Practice Check In
CONSTRUCT: Self-Awareness
MATERIALS: Parent Handbooks

GOAL:

To increase parents' awareness of changes made in themselves and in their role as mothers or fathers.

OBJECTIVES:

1. To increase empathic awareness of self.

2. To increase parental awareness of self change.

3. To promote feelings of accomplishment.

PROCEDURES:

1. Begin today's parent activities by having each adult respond to the following:

   ● One change I've noticed in me as a person is _____ .

   ● One change I've noticed in me as a parent is _____ .

2. After each parent has had an opportunity to respond to the statements above, review the Home Practice Exercise from the previous meeting. Also discuss perceived changes in family members and their interactions as reported in the family log.

IF'S, AND'S, OR BUT'S:

A good indicator of growth in self-esteem and self-concept is to observe the ease or difficulty a parent has in identifying perceptions of change.

PARENT ACTIVITY: 41.2 Situations and Solutions
CONSTRUCT: Behavior Management
MATERIALS: None

GOAL:

To help parents develop a behavior management strategy for specific troublesome behaviors.

OBJECTIVES:

1. To enable parents to think of alternative ways to handle problem situations.

2. To reinforce parent sharing.

3. To increase parents' ability to problem solve and carry out a plan of action.

PROCEDURES:

1. Begin the activity with the following open-ended statement:

   - Something my child is doing which still drives me crazy and I can't handle is _____ .

2. Write down the problem on a sheet of paper. One problem per sheet of paper. If a parent is having the big problem with themselves, s/he can use that, but try to keep the problem child oriented.

3. After the parents have stated their problems, use the problem solving method discussed on pages 111-113 in the Handbook. Discuss what they would like to see instead and go around and have each person offer one suggestion to the problem. The person with the problem should also offer suggestions.

4. Write down all the suggestions and give the paper to the parent.

IF'S, AND'S, OR BUT'S:

When specific problems are stated, most parents will be looking for an immediate action they can take to resolve the problem. You may need to state that most problems don't have immediate solutions but consistent application of appropriate behavior management techniques will eventually reduce the problem behavior(s).

PARENT ACTIVITY: 41.3 Review of Behavior Management
 CONSTRUCT: Behavior Management
MATERIALS: Parent Handbooks

GOAL:

To provide an opportunity to review concepts of behavior management.

OBJECTIVES:

1. To allow parents to review techniques for behavior management.

2. To remediate any perceived deficiencies in understanding the concepts.

PROCEDURES:

1. Instruct parents to locate the information entitled **Behavior Management Review Sheet** on pages 131-132 in their Handbooks. Allow parents an opportunity to discuss all the behavior management strategies they learned. Indicate that the purpose of reviewing the strategies is to determine which techniques/areas need more discussion.

2. Ask each parent to verbally state the areas which s/he needs a lot more work.

3. Identify strengths and weaknesses and focus future parent meetings to remediating deficiencies.

The needs analyses will help you plan future parent meetings. Provide parents with the review of techniques they indicate "need more work."

PARENT ACTIVITY: 41.4 Home Practice Exercise
CONSTRUCT: Behavior Management
MATERIALS: Parent Handbooks

GOAL :

To encourage parents to practice specific behavior management strategies.

OBJECTIVES:

1. To reinforce parents' attempts in nonabusive behavior management.

2. To continue to build personal power in parents as care givers.

3. To maintain a supportive environment.

PROCEDURES:

1. Instruct parents to locate the Home Practice Exercise on page 144 in their Handbooks. Review the exercise with them:

   a. Practice the techniques in behavior management identified as needing more work.

   b. Complete family log.

2. Tell parents that in addition to the Home Practice Exercise, they are to spend 30 minutes each day with each of their children in nurturing playtime activities. Playtime is a time with the parent and child alone—no TV, no other distractions. Playing a game or reading books are good activities. From the *Nurturing Book for Babies and Children*, have the parents practice activities listed in the following sections: Activities for Infants, Activities for Toddlers, Activities for Preschoolers, or Infant and Child Massage. Have the parents remember what they did and report the next week.

IF'S, AND'S, OR BUT'S:

Your encouragement and support are necessary for parents to continue to attempt new skills. Help them succeed.

FAMILY ACTIVITY: 41.5 Family Nurturing Time
CONSTRUCT: Empathy, Self-Awareness
MATERIALS: Nurturing Book for Babies and Children

ACTIVITIES FOR INFANTS (Birth to 15 months):

Utilizing the *Nurturing Book for Babies and Children*, select activities from the sections entitled Activities for Infants or Infant and Child Massage. Engage parents in practicing songs, play and stimulation activities, or massage. Vary the activities weekly to sustain interest.

ACTIVITIES FOR TODDLERS (15 months to 3 years):

Utilizing the *Nurturing Book for Babies and Children*, select activities from the sections entitled Activities for Toddlers or Infant and Child Massage. Engage parents in practicing songs, play, language, and movement activities, or massage.

ACTIVITIES FOR PRESCHOOLERS (3-5 years):

Use the following activities when working with preschool children and their parents. Use the activities as the basis for involving infants and toddlers if you are conducting a home visit with children ages birth to five years.

FAMILY ACTIVITY: 41.6 Hello Time: Where is _____ ?
CONSTRUCT: Empathy
MATERIALS: None

GOAL:

To have children gain an awareness of others in the group.

OBJECTIVES:

1. To greet each child and adult by their first name.

2. To increase recognition of the needs of others.

3. To have fun in family interactions.

PROCEDURES:

1. Children and adults should be seated in a circle on the floor.

2. Ask everyone if they remember the tune "Frere Jacques." Hum the tune and see if they recognize the melody. It is a good idea to have the children hum or sing the tune with you without any words a couple of times to ensure they know the song.

3. Using the tune of "Frere Jacques," sing the following words, first alone, and then once with the group. Use your first name (or the name of a parent) and identify an activity (suggest running or hopping).

> Where is __(name)__ ? Where is __(name)__ ?
> Please stand up, please stand up.
>
> Dance (hop, run, etc.) around the group __(name)__ .
> Dance (hop, run, etc.)around the group __(name)__ .
>
> Then sit down, then sit down.

4. Explain that everyone will have a chance to get up and move when it is their turn.

5. Choose a child to begin. Sing the song, inserting the movement. Allow the child to choose the next person, or the adult may choose who is next.

IF'S, AND'S, OR BUT'S:

1. For variation, ask for movement suggestions from the group. Children especially like to choose movements for adults and view this as a good joke. The response of the adult to this teasing provides a good model for behavior.

2. Noncompliant children may be encouraged if they are allowed to take a turn with a friend. Vary the song to include two people.

   Example: "Where are Jesse and Chad?"

FAMILY ACTIVITY:	**41.7 Circle Time: Blanket Game**
CONSTRUCT:	**Age Appropriate Development Expectations**
MATERIALS:	**Large blanket or large bed sheet**

GOAL:

To reinforce positive family interactions.

OBJECTIVES:

1. To reinforce positive trusting interactions with adults.

2. To use large muscles.

3. To reinforce creative imagination.

PROCEDURES:

1. Have all children and adults sit close together on the floor.

2. An adult covers the entire group with a large blanket. Make sure everyone is under the blanket.

3. The adult tells the group (under the blanket) to listen carefully, then says:

> When I take the blanket off, you will be ____(animal name)____.
> (i.e., monkeys, birds, lions, cows, etc.).

4. Pull the blanket off the group (be dramatic about it) and encourage them to act like the animal named. Adults in the group should model expected behaviors. Let this go on for about 1/2 minute then call the children and adults back to sit on the floor again.

5. When the group is sitting on the floor, repeat the activity for a different animal.

IF'S, AND'S, OR BUT'S:

1. Be sure to reassure children who may be frightened of being under the blanket.

2. Call children back to group using the animal name; i.e. "Come on back to your pen, little pigs," or, "All the cows need to return to the barn," etc.

FAMILY ACTIVITY:	**41.8 Crayon Shavings and Family Hug**
CONSTRUCT:	**Developmental**
MATERIALS:	**Crayons, crayon sharpener or vegetable grater, clothes iron, wax paper, newspaper**

GOAL:

To increase the children's self-concept through completion of art activity.

OBJECTIVES :

1. To increase the child's ability to visualize art.

2. To increase social interactions.

3. To reinforce comfort in using nurturing touch.

PROCEDURES:

1. Plug in the clothes iron prior to the start of the activity. Heat the iron to medium temperature.

2. Have the children make crayon shavings. This can be accomplished by using a crayon sharpener, vegetable grater, or a heavy object to smash the crayons into shavings.

3. Hand out two sheets of wax paper or newsprint. Tell the children to make a design on one sheet of the wax paper by placing the crayon shavings on top. The design can be their choice.

4. Place the second sheet of wax paper over the first. Place the two sheets of wax paper with the crayon shavings between two sheets of newspaper.

5. Using the hot iron, iron the newspaper.

6. The result will be a waxed design between two sheets of wax paper.

FAMILY HUG:

1. End each home visit with a family hug. Everyone get in a circle and put your arms around the people next to you. During the family hug time, anyone can say anything they like. It is a time for free expression.

2. At a natural time, close the activities for the day.

IF'S, AND'S, OR BUT'S:

1. Supervise the use of the hot iron.

2. Have plenty of crayons.

3. Encourage children to use their creativity. Initials, portraits, etc. are all good ideas.

NURTURING PROGRAM FOR PARENTS AND CHILDREN BIRTH TO FIVE YEARS

SESSION 42

BEHAVIOR CONSTRUCT: Empathy

SESSION CONCEPT: Positive Self-Talk

BRIEF DESCRIPTION: Parents and children learn how to use positive self-talk as a way of building their self-esteem and self-concept

INTENDED USE: For parents of children birth to 5 years

PREREQUISITE KNOWLEDGE: Personal Power, Praise

AGENDA

Parent Activities	Materials
42.1 Icebreaker and Home Practice Check In	*Parent Handbooks*
42.2 Positive Self-Talk	None
42.3 Home Practice Exercise	*Parent Handbooks*

Family Activities*	Materials
42.4 Family Nurturing Time	*Nurturing Book for Babies and Children*
42.5 Hello Time: This is the Way	None
42.6 I'm a Dynamic Doer	None
42.7 Circle Time: Positive Self-Talk	Puppets
42.8 Dippy Do and Family Hug	Food colors or tempera paints, paper towels, 4 small containers, newspapers

*For parents with infants or toddlers, use activities presented in *Nurturing Book for Babies and Children*. For parents with preschoolers (ages 3-5), use the activities listed below Family Nurturing Time.

PARENT ACTIVITY: 42.1 Icebreaker and Home Practice Check In
CONSTRUCT: Self-Awareness
MATERIALS: Parent Handbooks

GOAL:

To encourage parents to recognize the positive changes that have occurred in their lives.

OBJECTIVES:

1. To recognize roadblocks in life.

2. To have parents share their successes in life.

3. To continue to reinforce positive use of personal power.

PROCEDURES:

1. Begin today's parent activities by having each adult respond to the following:

   • What two roadblocks in your life did you (or do you) have to overcome?

   • What success did you have (or are you having) in overcoming these roadblocks?

2. After each parent has had an opportunity to respond to the statements above, review the Home Practice Exercise from the previous meeting. Also discuss perceived changes in family members and their interactions as reported in the family log.

IF'S, AND'S, OR BUT'S:

Focus the question either on the past or present. The goal is to get people to use (or recognize the use of) their personal power in a positive way.

PARENT ACTIVITY: 42.2 Positive Self-Talk
CONSTRUCT: Empathy
MATERIALS: None

GOAL:

To encourage parents to build their self-concept through cognitive self-behavior modification.

OBJECTIVES:

1. To increase parents' awareness of the power of self-talk.

2. To increase parents' ability to self-talk themselves into positive feelings.

3. To increase parents' awareness of differentiating what they do from who they are.

PROCEDURES:

1. Share with the parents the power of self-talk. Self-talk is essentially messages we send to ourselves that tell us something about ourselves: we are too fat, thin, tall, mean, happy, uncaring, nurturing, etc. The messages we send to ourselves are ways we use our personal power to build ourselves up, or tear ourselves down. Our focus today is to use the power of self-talk to continue to build our self-esteem, self-concept, and self-perceptions.

2. Ask parents to share times they heard their self-messages tell them they were good/bad people; they did good/bad things. Process the information.

3. Ask parents to relax, close their eyes, and recall the face of someone who either is or has possessed them, put them down, treated them mean, gave them a negative label, etc. This person may be a spouse, friend, teacher, parent, neighbor, boss, fellow worker, or child.

4. Still in a relaxed position, have parents verbally repeat the following statements while visualizing the face of the person: "No matter what you say about me, or do to me, I am still a good person."

5. Have parents repeat the statement louder and louder with more conviction each time they say it.

6. Now, with their eyes still closed, ask parents to recall a time they failed at something, lost something, caused hurt to someone else unintentionally, or disappointed themselves by their own behavior. Visualize something about the experience, get in touch with the feelings, and say out loud: "No matter what I do, I am still a good person."

7. Again, have parents repeat the statement louder and louder each time they say it.

8. Have parents open their eyes, return their attention to you, and begin to process the activity. Inform the parents that when they feel down on themselves, they should use positive self-talk to help build their self-concept.

IF'S, AND'S, OR BUT'S:

Parents may feel uncomfortable at first in chanting the statements out loud. Model the intensity you want, and encourage the parents to use self-talk to help themselves.

PARENT ACTIVITY:	42.3 Home Practice Exercise
CONSTRUCT:	Empathy, Self-Awareness
MATERIALS:	Parent Handbooks

GOAL:

To build parents' self-esteem and self-concept through self-talk.

OBJECTIVES:

1. To reinforce positive feelings of self.

2. To practice positive self-talk.

---

3. To avoid criticizing self.

4. To maintain a supportive environment.

PROCEDURES:

1. Instruct parents to locate the Home Practice Exercise on page 144 in their Handbooks. Review the exercise with them:

    a. Notice a time when you start becoming overly critical of yourself.

    b. Practice using positive self-talk at times when you begin being self-critical.

    c. Complete family log.

2. Tell parents that in addition to the Home Practice Exercise, they are to spend 30 minutes each day with each of their children in nurturing playtime activities. Playtime is a time with the parent and child alone—no TV, no other distractions. Playing a game or reading books are good activities. From the *Nurturing Book for Babies and Children*, have the parents practice activities listed in the following sections: Activities for Infants, Activities for Toddlers, Activities for Preschoolers, or Infant and Child Massage. Have the parents remember what they did and report the next week.

IF'S, AND'S, OR BUT'S:

Positive self-talk is not the easiest thing to do when parents feel lousy about themselves. Encourage parents to practice using positive self-talk.

FAMILY ACTIVITY: 42.4 Family Nurturing Time
CONSTRUCT: Empathy, Self-Awareness
MATERIALS: Nurturing Book for Babies and Children

ACTIVITIES FOR INFANTS (Birth to 15 months):

Utilizing the *Nurturing Book for Babies and Children*, select activities from the sections entitled Activities for Infants or Infant and Child Massage. Engage parents in practicing songs, play and stimulation activities, or massage. Vary the activities weekly to sustain interest.

ACTIVITIES FOR TODDLERS (15 months to 3 years):

Utilizing the *Nurturing Book for Babies and Children*, select activities from the sections entitled Activities for Toddlers or Infant and Child Massage. Engage parents in practicing songs, play, language, and movement activities, or massage. Vary the activities weekly to sustain interest.

ACTIVITIES FOR PRESCHOOLERS (3-5 years):

Use the following activities when working with preschool children and their parents. Use the activities as the basis for involving infants and toddlers if you are conducting a home visit with children ages birth to five years.

FAMILY ACTIVITY: 42.5 Hello Time: This is the Way
CONSTRUCT: Behavior Management
MATERIALS: None

GOAL:

To build positive social interactions among family members.

OBJECTIVES:

1. To increase children's ability to communicate.

2. To reinforce positive peer interactions.

PROCEDURES:

1. Have children and adults stand in a circle.

2. Explain to them that today we are going to sing hello. Sing the following song to the tune of "This is the Way We Wash Our Clothes" and demonstrate the actions to the children.

This is the Way

This is the way we say hello (wave open hand-fingers pointing up),
Say hello (continue waving) say hello (continue waving),
This is the way we say hello, early in the morning.

This is the way we greet our friends (bow to one another),
Greet our friends, greet our friends,
This is the way we greet our friends, happy to see you here today.

3. Continue with "This is the way we.... (smile and laugh, shake other's hands, dance and sing).

IF'S, AND'S, OR BUT'S:

Have a good time with the song. Be creative and add your own lyrics.

FAMILY ACTIVITY: 42.6 I'm a Dynamic Doer
CONSTRUCT: Self-Awareness
MATERIALS: None

GOAL:

To increase positive self-worth and self-esteem in children.

OBJECTIVES:

1. To increase self-awareness.

2. To reinforce positive family interactions.

PROCEDURES:

1. Assemble children in a large circle, squatting on the floor.

2. Using the tune of "I'm a Little Tea Pot," conduct the following activity.

> We're dynamic doers, here we stand (Have children stand),
> Next to our friends, we all shake hands (Have children shake hands with those standing on left and right),
> Telling them they're as nice as they could be (Simulate saying something by cupping hands over mouth to children standing on left and right),
> I wish they could come home with me. (Grab a partner, skip together)

> When we're in school, we all play nice (Lock arms with partner, do square dance move),
> Sharing our toys, and saying thanks (Girls curtsy, boys bow to their neighbors),
> When we have to go, we all feel sad (Rub eyes with fists),
> We'll be back soon, and feel real glad. (Smile and laugh)

3. Repeat the song.

IF'S, AND'S, OR BUT'S:

Have fun with the song, keep the action moving. Rehearse the moves with the children so they learn the exercise.

FAMILY ACTIVITY: 42.7 Circle Time: Positive Self-Talk
CONSTRUCT: Behavior Management
MATERIALS: Puppets

GOAL:

To encourage children to increase their self-concept through cognitive self-behavior modification.

OBJECTIVES:

1. Children will increase their awareness of the power of self-talk.

2. Children will increase their ability to self-talk themselves into positive feelings.

3. Children will increase their awareness of differentiating what they do from who they are.

PROCEDURES:

1. Have children and adults sit in a circle.

2. Today we are going to talk about the feelings other kids and adults have about themselves. There are probably a lot of times we do good things which help us feel good about ourselves. Does anybody here like themselves? (Reinforce positive response). What are some things that you do that are good? How does that make you feel? (Reinforce "good behavior helps me feel good").

3. Does anybody here sometimes do bad things? How do you feel after you do a bad thing? We're going to learn how to feel better about ourselves even after we did something bad. Because even though we did something bad, we're still good people.

4. Using the puppets, play act the following:

    Two puppets are drawing pictures. One puppet draws good and has a nice picture. The other puppet doesn't draw very good and has a scribbly picture.

    Puppet #1: I sure made a good picture. I used the prettiest colors and have a nice picture.

    Puppet #2: (Puppet #2 didn't do such a hot job and criticizes himself,) I'm no good, I'm one of the dumbest kids I know. Bad — that's what I am — just plain ol' bad, I can't do anything right — I can't even make a nice picture.

    Leader: How do you think Puppet #2 feels about himself? How does Puppet #1 feel about himself? Just because Puppet #2 can't draw too well, does that make him a bad person? Does that ever happen to anyone here? After you did something bad did you say bad things about yourself? (Wait for responses.) Even though we might do bad things, each of us is still a good person. Let's practice saying, "even though I did something bad, I'm still a good person."

5. Have each person (including parents) say the phrase, then as a group. Reinforce the concept by providing examples relevant to the family. Play act with the puppets.

IF'S, AND'S, OR BUT'S:

1. If the kids can handle it, let them use the puppets to play act their own skit, saying the phrase afterwards.

2. Continue to have both parents and children repeat the phrase aloud when they need personal support.

FAMILY ACTIVITY:	42.8 Dippy Do and Family Hug
CONSTRUCT:	Appropriate Developmental Expectations
MATERIALS:	Food colors or tempera paints, paper towels, 4 small containers newspapers

GOAL:

To increase children's self-concept and self-esteem through accomplishment of age appropriate tasks.

OBJECTIVES:

1. To foster creative expression through art.

2. To increase fine motor skills.

3. To reinforce comfort in using nurturing touch.

PROCEDURES:

1. Assemble children and adults around a table.

2. Fill 4 small containers with various liquid colors (food colors or watered down tempera paints).

3. Each child should receive a fan-folded paper towel (either fan-fold them before activity or have children fan-fold). The folds should be approximately 1 inch wide, running lengthwise along the paper towel.

4. Start at one end of the fan and fold across 1/2 inches up. Repeat folding over and over to the end, ending with a square.

5. Dip each corner in a different color allowing it to soak on the corner. Leave some white in the middle.

6. Unfold carefully and lay out to dry on newspapers.

FAMILY HUG:

1. End each home visit with a family hug. Everyone get in a circle and put your arms around the people next to you. During the family hug time, anyone can say anything they like. It is a time for free expression.

2. At a natural time, close the activities for the day.

IF'S, AND'S, OR BUT'S:

1. Children will love to do several designs. Hang up for all to see.

2. Make sure parents also complete their own design.

NURTURING PROGRAM FOR PARENTS AND CHILDREN BIRTH TO FIVE YEARS
SESSION 43

BEHAVIOR CONSTRUCT: Self-Awareness

SESSION CONCEPT: Families and Chemical Use

BRIEF DESCRIPTION: Parents discuss how chemical use can negatively impact upon their relationships with their children. Children review ways to build their positive feelings about themselves.

INTENDED USE: For parents of children birth to 5 years

PREREQUISITE KNOWLEDGE: None

AGENDA

Parent Activities	Materials
43.1 Icebreaker and Home Practice Check In	*Parent Handbooks*
43.2 Families and Chemical Use	*Parent Handbooks*, **Chemicals and Kids Don't Mix** AV presentation, AV equipment
43.3 Home Practice Exercise	*Parent Handbooks*

Family Activities*	Materials
43.4 Family Nurturing Time	*Nurturing Book for Babies and Children*
43.5 Hello Time: Loud and Soft	None
43.6 Streamer Dance	Cassette player and cassettes, record player and records or streamers
43.7 Circle Time: Review on I'm a Good Person	Puppets
43.8 Dynamic Doer Card Game and Family Hug	Dynamic Doer and Pair It Card Games

*For parents with infants or toddlers, use activities presented in *Nurturing Book for Babies and Children*. For parents with preschoolers (ages 3-5), use the activities listed below Family Nurturing Time.

GOAL :

To increase parents' awareness regarding messages they received about chemicals.

OBJECTIVES :

1. To help parents recognize how their parents modeled the use of chemicals.

2. To help parents recognize discrepancies between the messages they received and the models they observed.

3. To become aware of feelings that could influence chemical use.

PROCEDURES:

1. Begin today's parent activities by having each adult respond to the following:

   • The message my parents gave me regarding the use of alcohol was _____ .

   • The model my parents provided me with was _____ .

   • When my mom/dad would use alcohol, he/she probably was feeling _____ .

2. After each parent has had an opportunity to respond to the statements above, review the Home Practice Exercise from the previous meeting. Also discuss perceived changes in family members and their interactions as reported in the family log.

IF'S, AND'S, OR BUT'S:

Chemical use may be a difficult concept for parents to discuss. The discussion should reflect an awareness only — not a moral interpretation.

GOAL:

To increase parental awareness of the impact chemical usage has in their lives.

OBJECTIVES:

1. To help parents recognize danger signals of chemical dependency, including alcohol dependency.

2. To help parents understand the relationship between chemical usage and parent-child interactions.

3. To help parents identify chemical abuse in their immediate families and friends.

PROCEDURES:

1. If you are using audio-visual programs, present the AV entitled **Chemicals and Kids Don't Mix**.

2. Instruct parents to locate the information entitled **Families and Chemical Use Questionnaire** on pages 133-134 in their Handbooks.

3. Have each parent complete the questionnaire. Suggest that the purpose of the questionnaire is to increase awareness of chemical usage with self and with family members. Review the parents' responses on the questionnaires.

4. Discuss with parents that using chemicals (alcohol, pot, speed, etc.) often changes their reactions to what their children do and who they are. The chemicals alter our moods and these changes are reflected in the quality of the relationships we have with our children.

5. Have parents share feelings they had when mom and dad drank and argued, when brother used chemicals and ran away, when parents discussed the sick relative, when people were grumpy "the morning after," etc.

6. Have parents suggest things they needed while family members were engaged in chemical use; i.e., safety, strokes, freedom from fighting, money, etc. Ask how they got these things.

7. Ask the parents if they can think of any times when any of their children might have felt these ways as a result of their chemical use, including the way they felt on the morning after.

IF'S, AND'S, OR BUT'S:

We are socialized to view chemical use, and even some kinds of chemical abuse, as desirable behavior. We often view alcohol as a "social lubricant" and chemical use as a social ritual. The American Medical Association clearly states alcoholism is a disease. What is not well advertised is that one out of ten Americans becomes alcoholic. Only 5% per year recover from alcoholism. Whether the chemical in question is alcohol, uppers, downers, tranquilizers, pot, or cocaine, chemical dependency (the process of addiction) is possible and very damaging.

PARENT ACTIVITY: 43.3 Home Practice Exercise
CONSTRUCT: Self-Awareness
MATERIALS: Parent Handbooks

GOAL:

To increase parents' awareness regarding the relationship between chemicals and feelings.

OBJECTIVES:

1. To increase parents' awareness of the types of chemicals used by family members.

2. To increase parents' awareness of feelings that influence chemical use.

3. To maintain a warm and supportive home environment.

PROCEDURES:

1. Instruct parents to locate the Home Practice Exercise on page 144 in their Handbooks. Review the exercise with them:

   a. Identify how you are feeling just prior to and after taking a chemical of choice (aspirin, alcohol, pot, speed, sedatives, etc.).

   b. Identify all the types of chemicals that are used regularly by family members during the week.

   c. Complete family log.

2. Tell parents that in addition to the Home Practice Exercise, they are to spend 30 minutes each day with each of their children in nurturing playtime activities. Playtime is a time with the parent and child alone—no TV, no other distractions. Playing a game or reading books are good activities. From the *Nurturing Book for Babies and Children*, have the parents practice activities listed in the following sections: Activities for Infants, Activities for Toddlers, Activities for Preschoolers, or Infant and Child Massage. Have the parents remember what they did and report the next week.

IF'S, AND'S, OR BUT'S:

Defensiveness may result in some parents regarding their chemical use. Remember, the goal of the exercise is awareness, not chemical use assessment.

FAMILY ACTIVITY: 43.4 Family Nurturing Time
CONSTRUCT: Empathy, Self-Awareness
MATERIALS: Nurturing Book for Babies and Children

ACTIVITIES FOR INFANTS (Birth to 15 months):

Utilizing the *Nurturing Book for Babies and Children*, select activities from the sections entitled Activities for Infants or Infant and Child Massage. Engage parents in practicing songs, play and stimulation activities, or massage. Vary the activities weekly to sustain interest.

ACTIVITIES FOR TODDLERS (15 months to 3 years):

Utilizing the *Nurturing Book for Babies and Children*, select activities from the sections entitled Activities for Toddlers or Infant and Child Massage. Engage parents in practicing songs, play, language, and movement activities, or massage. Vary the activities weekly to sustain interest.

ACTIVITIES FOR PRESCHOOLERS (3-5 years):

Use the following activities when working with preschool children and their parents. Use the activities as the basis for involving infants and toddlers if you are conducting a home visit with children ages birth to five years.

FAMILY ACTIVITY: 43.5 Hello Time: Loud and Soft
CONSTRUCT: Self-Awareness
MATERIALS: None

GOAL:

To have family members become aware of their self and others through selected verbal expression of feelings.

OBJECTIVES:

1. To greet each child and adult by first name.

2. To gain sensitivity to the feelings of others.

3. To encourage self-expression and ownership of feelings.

PROCEDURES:

1. Children and adults should be seated in a circle on the floor. A parent or home visitor should act as the leader of the activity.

2. The adult leading the activity explains the rules of the game. Rules: The group will take turns saying hello to everyone individually in either a loud or soft voice. The adult may say, "When it is your turn, you can tell us if you want us to say hello in a loud voice or a soft voice. When we ask, 'how are you?' you can answer in a loud or soft voice. After your turn, you can choose the next person for us to say hello to."

3. The adult chooses a child and asks whether they'd like a loud or soft voice. After the child indicates his choice, the group responds in a loud or soft voice by saying, "Hello (name) ."

4. The adult asks, "How are you?" and the child is encouraged to respond. The adult may remark that the child appears happy, sad, etc., in response to the child's feeling.

5. The child chooses the next person to be greeted and Steps 3 and 4 are repeated.

1. Remind children that loud voices are for outside use but that it is okay to yell during this special activity.

2. When a child doesn't respond to "How are you?" or "Do you want loud or soft?" the group may be enlisted to interpret how the child is feeling and how they should talk to them.

   Example: Are you feeling sad, happy, etc,?
   How does Chad look?
   How do you think he feels?
   How do you think he'd like us to say hello?

FAMILY ACTIVITY:	**43.6 Streamer Dance**
CONSTRUCT:	**Age Appropriate Developmental Expectations**
MATERIALS:	**Cassette player and cassettes or record player and records, streamers**

GOAL:

To express self through creative expression.

OBJECTIVES:

1. To increase positive adult-child interactions through music and dance.

2. To help children express themselves through positive play.

PROCEDURES:

1. Tie streamers to the wrists of everyone and tell the children that they are going to dance or move slow when the music is slow and dance or move fast when the music is fast. Set boundaries in terms of the area of rooms where children may dance.

2. Play the music and have the adults demonstrate fast and slow dancing with the streamers.

IF'S, AND'S, OR BUT'S:

1. Children who are reluctant to dance or respond to music with their bodies may feel less apprehensive since their attention is placed on the movements of the streamers.

2. Streamers may be attached to ankles, fingers, or around waists for variation.

3. A reluctant child may not want the streamer tied to him, and should be allowed to hold it in his hand. He may change his mind after observing others.

FAMILY ACTIVITY: 43.7 Circle Time: Review on I'm a Good Person
CONSTRUCT: Age-Appropriate Developmental Expectations
MATERIALS: Puppets

GOAL:

To reinforce positive self-growth through cognitive behavior modification.

OBJECTIVES:

1. To increase the children's ability to think of themselves as capable.

2. To build feelings of self-confidence.

3. To increase personal power.

PROCEDURES:

1. Have children and adults sit in a circle on the floor.

2. Ask the group if anyone can recall the words we should say when we're not feeling good about ourselves.

3. Calling puppets by their names, act out the following situations. At the end of each skit, ask the children what the puppet should say. Have the children repeat: "No matter what I do, I'm still a good person."

   a. Puppet gets in trouble by breaking a family rule (no acting silly at dinner table, no throwing things) and has to spend 2 minutes in time-out. While in time-out, he talks to him/herself with ridicule:

      • "I'm no good. I threw the blocks. I am a bad boy/girl."

   b. Puppet makes an error/mistake in a school activity and feels badly. He says to him/herself:

      • "What a dummy I am, I can't do anything right. I'm just stupid."

   c. Puppet drops a dish accidentally and breaks it. He/she feels badly and says to him/herself:

      • "What a clumsy kid I am. I am just rotten. "

IF'S, AND'S, OR BUT'S:

It is important that children learn they can make a mistake, be punished, have an accident but still remain a good person. Use the puppets to help reinforce this concept.

GOAL:

To reinforce the value of positive family interaction.

OBJECTIVES:

1. To allow family members to play cooperatively.

2. To reinforce appropriate social interactions.

3. To reinforce appropriate behaviors in a competitive situation.

4. To reinforce comfort in using nurturing touch.

PROCEDURES:

1. This game follows the same rules as "Old Maid" except players try to end up with the Dynamic Doer card. The objective is to get rid of all your cards while trying to keep the Dynamic Doer card.

2. Allow approximately 8 cards for each player.

3. Add the Dynamic Doer card to the deck, shuffle, and deal the cards to all players.

4. Players may hold their pairs in front of them after all cards have been dealt. The Dynamic Doer card holder must not tell that s/he has that card, in hopes that someone else will not draw it.

5. The first player then draws a card from the player on his/her right. If it is a match to one of his/her cards, the pair can be laid down in front of the player. If not, the player adds the card to his/her hand.

6. Continue drawing from the player on the right until all cards have been matched and only the Dynamic Doer card remains.

FAMILY HUG:

1. End each home visit with a family hug. Everyone get in a circle and put your arms around the people next to you. During the family hug time, anyone can say anything they like. It is a time for free expression.

2. At a natural time, close the activities for the day.

IF'S, AND'S, OR BUT'S:

Competitive games may generate feelings about losing. Some children may need support.

NURTURING PROGRAM FOR PARENTS AND CHILDREN BIRTH TO FIVE YEARS

SESSION 44

BEHAVIOR CONSTRUCT: Self-Awareness

SESSION CONCEPT: Emergency Parenting and Survival Kits

BRIEF DESCRIPTION: Parents brainstorm things to do when parenting becomes difficult and when they begin to do feel down. Children practice positive interactions through the Nurturing Game.

INTENDED USE: For parents of children birth to 5 years

PREREQUISITE KNOWLEDGE: None

AGENDA

Parent Activities	Materials
44.1 Icebreaker and Home Practice Check In	*Parent Handbooks*
44.2 Emergency Parenting Kit	*Parent Handbooks*
44.3 Emergency Survival Kit	*Parent Handbooks*

Family Activities*	Materials
44.4 Family Nurturing Time	*Nurturing Book for Babies and Children*
44.5 Hello Time: Happy and Sad	None
44.6 Circle Time: Row, Row, Row Your Boat	None
44.7 Nurturing Game and Family Hug	Nurturing Game

*For parents with infants or toddlers, use activities presented in *Nurturing Book for Babies and Children*. For parents with preschoolers (ages 3-5), use the activities listed below Family Nurturing Time.

PARENT ACTIVITY: **44.1 Icebreaker and Home Practice Check In**
CONSTRUCT: **Self-Awareness**
MATERIALS: **Parent Handbooks**

GOAL:

To begin the process of separation.

OBJECTIVES:

1. To discuss feelings associated with leaving.

2. To encourage parents to deal with loss.

PROCEDURES:

1. Begin today's parent activities by having each adult respond to the following:

   - Right now I am feeling _____ .

   - Separating from someone always _____ .

   - The part of the program I will miss the most is _____ .

2. After each parent has had an opportunity to respond to the statements above, review the Home Practice Exercise from the previous meeting. Also discuss perceived changes in family members and their interactions as reported in the family log.

IF'S, AND'S, OR BUT'S:

The next session is the last scheduled session in the program. The process of separating needs to be dealt with and discussed.

PARENT ACTIVITY: **44.2 Emergency Parenting Kit**
CONSTRUCT: **Self-Awareness**
MATERIALS: **Parent Handbooks**

GOAL:

To help parents develop strategies to support self in difficult times with their children.

OBJECTIVES:

1. To increase parents' competence in handling tough times with their kids.

2. To increase parents' abilities to handle tough times with their kids.

PROCEDURES:

1. Instruct parents to locate the information entitled **Emergency Parenting Kit** on page 136 in their Handbooks.

2. Have each parent write down five things to do with kids when times are tough.

3. Go around and share items from list. Continue until everyone has had a chance to suggest their five things.

4. Encourage parents to add to their list of things to do from the suggestions of others and try to list 10 things to do with kids when times get tough being a parent.

5. Then when it does get tough with the children, start at the top and go down the list until times are less tense.

IF'S, AND'S OR BUT'S:

Stress the importance of developing a plan of action when children become intolerable.

PARENT ACTIVITY: 44.3 Emergency Survival Kit
CONSTRUCT: Self-Awareness
MATERIALS: Parent Handbooks

GOAL:

To enable parents to develop strategies to support self in times of personal difficulty.

OBJECTIVES:

1. To help parents prepare a specific list of things to do when they are feeling down.

2. To increase parents' competence in supporting self.

3. To help parents understand the value in developing a support plan.

PROCEDURES:

1. Instruct parents to locate the information entitled **Emergency Survival Kit** on page 137 in their Handbooks.

2. On the sheet of paper, have each parent write five things they can do when they are feeling down to make themselves feel better.

3. Have each parent read what they would do when parents begin to feel down. Encourage parents to add to their list of 5 things to do and list 10 things to do when they begin to feel down.

4. Instruct parents that the next time they feel badly they should start at the top of the list and go right down it until they feel better. If they don't feel better by the time they have gone through every suggestion, then start at the top again and keep going.

IF'S, AND'S, OR BUT'S:

Stress the importance of developing a plan to have when the parents are beginning to feel down.

FAMILY ACTIVITY: 44.4 Family Nurturing Time
CONSTRUCT: Empathy, Self-Awareness
MATERIALS: Nurturing Book for Babies and Children

ACTIVITIES FOR INFANTS (Birth to 15 months):

Utilizing the *Nurturing Book for Babies and Children*, select activities from the sections entitled Activities for Infants or Infant and Child Massage. Engage parents in practicing songs, play and stimulation activities, or massage. Vary the activities weekly to sustain interest.

ACTIVITIES FOR TODDLERS (15 months to 3 years):

Utilizing the *Nurturing Book for Babies and Children*, select activities from the sections entitled Activities for Toddlers or Infant and Child Massage. Engage parents in practicing songs, play, language, and movement activities, or massage. Vary the activities weekly to sustain interest.

ACTIVITIES FOR PRESCHOOLERS (3-5 years):

Use the following activities when working with preschool children and their parents. Use the activities as the basis for involving infants and toddlers if you are conducting a home visit with children ages birth to five years.

FAMILY ACTIVITY: 44.5 Hello Time: Happy and Sad
CONSTRUCT: Self-Awareness
MATERIALS: None

GOAL:

To increase family members' sensitivity to the feelings of others.

OBJECTIVES:

1. To increase children's awareness of things that make them happy.

2. To increase children's awareness of things that make them sad.

PROCEDURES:

1. Have children and adults sit in a circle on the floor.

2. Have each child and adult respond to the following statements:

   - Something that makes me happy is _____ .

   - Something that makes me sad is _____ .

IF'S, AND'S, OR BUT'S:

The question of happy and sad was asked earlier in the program. Determine if the things that made children and parents happy and sad earlier in the program remain the same.

FAMILY ACTIVITY: **44.6 Circle Time: Row, Row, Row Your Boat**
CONSTRUCT: **Empathy**
MATERIALS: **None**

GOAL:

To increase positive social interactions through play.

OBJECTIVES:

1. To involve children and adults in active and cooperative musical activities.

2. To foster creative expression through music.

PROCEDURES:

1. Request children and adults to sit in a circle with their legs spread apart so an adult or another child can sit between them.

2. Explain to the group that we are all going to pretend that we are in a boat and we have to row to get to shore.

3. Have the children hold the arms of the person in front of them. When the song begins, everyone will make a rowing or movement with their hands.

          Row, Row, Row Your Boat

    Row, row, row your boat gently down the stream,
    Merrily, merrily, merrily, merrily,
    Life is but a dream.

4. To add variety, move slow when casually rowing, fast when you are being chased by a shark, etc.

IF'S, AND'S, OR BUT'S:

Ask a child if he or she wants to lead the activity.

GOAL :

To reinforce appropriate social interactions through cooperative play.

OBJECTIVES :

1. To reinforce concepts of behavior management.

2. To increase self-awareness.

3. To foster positive touch interactions.

4. To reinforce comfort in using nurturing touch.

PROCEDURES:

1. Assemble children and adults in a circle sitting on the floor.

2. The goal of the game is to all begin at start and end up at "home." To get home, each player has to roll one die and move his/her game piece the appropriate number of squares.

3. Players land on colored squares that correspond to the following:

> **Orange** squares represent **self-awareness.**
>
> **Green** squares represent **behavior management.**
>
> **Pink** squares represent **touch.**
>
> **Yellow** squares represent **praise.**
>
> **Blue** squares represent **feelings.**
>
> When a player lands on a square s/he has to pick up a card and complete the activity. There are no cards for pink and yellow squares. Each time a player (adult or child) lands on a pink square, s/he has to hug or touch someone in a nice way. Each time a player lands on a yellow square, s/he has to praise someone else.

4. The behavior management cards indicate a particular behavior occurred appropriately or inappropriately. A player may be rewarded by moving ahead one to three squares or penalized one to three squares for inappropriate behavior. Chance dictates behavior management.

5. Blue feeling cards and orange self-awareness cards are action cards that the players have to respond to. When the behavior is completed, the next person rolls the die.

FAMILY HUG:

1. End each home visit with a family hug. Everyone get in a circle and put your arms around the people next to you. During the family hug time, anyone can say anything they like. It is a time for free expression.

2. At a natural time, close the activities for the day.

IF'S, AND'S, OR BUT'S:

1. The goal is to encourage interactions between children and adults. The game is based on the programs' constructs and reinforces concepts presented throughout the program.

2. Younger children will need help playing the game and should be encouraged to play.

NURTURING PROGRAM FOR PARENTS AND CHILDREN BIRTH TO FIVE YEARS

SESSION 45

BEHAVIOR CONSTRUCT: **Self-Awareness**

SESSION CONCEPT: **Closing Program Activities**

BRIEF DESCRIPTION: **Families participate in reaching closure on program involvement. Parents complete assessment measures.**

INTENDED USE: **For parents of children birth to 5 years**

PREREQUISITE KNOWLEDGE: **Program participation**

AGENDA

Parent Activities

		Materials
45.1	Icebreaker	None
45.2	Assessing Parenting Strengths	Pencils, Adult-Adolescent Parenting Inventory, Nurturing Quiz, Family Social History Questionnaire
45.3	Hopes and Fears	List of Hopes and Fears from first week

Family Activities*

		Materials
45.4	Family Nurturing Time	*Nurturing Book for Babies and Children*
45.5	Hello Time: London Bridge	None
45.6	Circle Time: Here's One Foot	Song words
45.7	Certificate Awards and Family Hug	Completion Certificates, snacks

*For parents with infants or toddlers, use activities presented in *Nurturing Book for Babies and Children*. For parents with preschoolers (ages 3-5), use the activities listed below Family Nurturing Time.

PARENT ACTIVITY: 45.1 Icebreaker
CONSTRUCT: Empathy, Self-Awareness
MATERIALS: None

GOAL:

To increase parents' awareness of changes in self.

OBJECTIVES

1. To increase awareness of parent gains.

2. To increase awareness of parent losses.

3. To begin termination process of meetings.

PROCEDURES:

1. Begin today's parent activities by having each adult respond to the following:

    • Something I have lost in taking this course is _____ .

    • Something I have gained in taking this course is _____ .

2. After each parent has had an opportunity to respond to the statements above, discuss perceived changes in family members and their interactions as reported in the family log. Ask parents to summarize the changes that have taken place, and those they still need to work on.

IF'S, AND'S, OR BUT'S:

Parents may begin to express some concerns about follow-up meetings. Be prepared to respond appropriately.

PARENT ACTIVITY: 45.2 Assessing Parenting Strengths
CONSTRUCT: Self-Awareness
MATERIALS: Pencils, Adult-Adolescent Parenting Inventory, Nurturing Quiz,
                   Family Social History Questionnaire

GOAL:

To gather post program information.

OBJECTIVE:

To provide parents an opportunity to assess their knowledge about the program content.

PROCEDURES:

1. Distribute the Adult-Adolescent Parenting Inventory (AAPI), Nurturing Quiz, and the Family Social History Questionnaire (FSHQ) to each parent.

---

2. Remind parents that testing is useful for measuring the impact of the program instruction.

3. Administer the AAPI first, then the Nurturing Quiz, then the FSHQ.

4. Allow parents to discuss process very briefly, if needed.

IF'S, AND'S, OR BUT'S:

If parents are concerned about their test scores, such information should be made available to them in a summary, not in raw scores.

PARENT ACTIVITY:	**45.3 Hopes and Fears**
CONSTRUCT:	**Empathy, Self-Awareness**
MATERIALS:	**List of Hopes and Fears from first week**

GOAL:

To attain closure on initial hopes and fears.

OBJECTIVES:

1. To provide opportunity for parents to evaluate program in view of initial concerns and hopes.

2. To enable parents to review their expectations and outcomes of program.

PROCEDURES:

1. Read list of hopes and fears made by the parent in the first week.

2. Process the parent's responses to the initial hopes and fears.

IF'S, AND'S, OR BUT'S:

As parents will discover, many of the fears expressed in Session 1 are no longer a source of anxiety.

FAMILY ACTIVITY:	**45.4 Family Nurturing Time**
CONSTRUCT:	**Empathy, Self-Awareness**
MATERIALS:	**Nurturing Book for Babies and Children**

ACTIVITIES FOR INFANTS (Birth to 15 months):

Utilizing the *Nurturing Book for Babies and Children*, select activities from the sections entitled Activities for Infants or Infant and Child Massage. Engage parents in practicing songs, play and stimulation activities, or massage. Vary the activities weekly to sustain interest.

ACTIVITIES FOR TODDLERS (15 months to 3 years):

Utilizing the *Nurturing Book for Babies and Children*, select activities from the sections entitled Activities for Toddlers or Infant and Child Massage. Engage parents in practicing songs, play, language, and movement activities, or massage. Vary the activities weekly to sustain interest.

ACTIVITIES FOR PRESCHOOLERS (3-5 years):

Use the following activities when working with preschool children and their parents. Use the activities as the basis for involving infants and toddlers if you are conducting a home visit with children ages birth to five years.

FAMILY ACTIVITY: 45.5 Hello Time: London Bridge
CONSTRUCT: Empathy
MATERIALS: None

GOAL:

To reinforce appropriate adult-child interactions.

OBJECTIVES:

1. To help parents and children enjoy each other.

2. To increase positive touch.

PROCEDURES:

1. Choose two people to be the "bridge" by facing each other and holding hands with their arms lifted high enough for others to pass under.

2. Have the rest of the people form a line and pass under the bridge as everyone sings:

London Bridge

London Bridge is falling down, falling down, falling down,
London Bridge is falling down, my fair___(name)___ .

3. As the group sings "my fair __(name)__ ," the two people who are the bridge should lower their arms and "catch" someone. Have the group sing that person's name in the line "my fair _____."

4. The person who gets "caught" in the bridge takes the place of one of the people making up the bridge and that person joins the group moving under the bridge.

IF'S, AND'S, OR BUT'S:

Allow all children a chance to be a part of the bridge.

GOAL:

To increase positive parent-child interactions through play.

OBJECTIVES:

1. To involve children and parents in active and cooperative musical activities.

2. To foster creative expression through music.

PROCEDURES:

1. Request parents and children to stand in a circle to participate in this activity.

2. Ask everyone if they know the song "This Old Man." Sing a few bars so they know the melody.

3. Tell them that we are all going to pretend to be an old man who is going to do a variety of things.

4. Demonstrate what you want to do using the following verse:

Here's One Foot

Here's one foot, here are two.
Each is wearing one new shoe.
So I'll stand up, turn around,
Dance around the floor,
Dancing is what feet are for.

5. Alter the movement by suggesting or requesting from group the desired change. Some suggested movements: walk, run, tip toe, skip, march, etc.

IF'S, AND'S, OR BUT'S:

See if one of the parents wants to lead the activity.

FAMILY ACTIVITY: 45.7 Certificate Awards and Family Hug
CONSTRUCT: Self-Awareness and Child Development
MATERIALS: Completion Certificates, snacks

GOAL:

To celebrate completion of program activities.

OBJECTIVES:

1. To honor parents and children for successfully completing the program.

2. To provide closure in a warm, supportive environment.

3. To provide an opportunity for parents and children to share their feelings.

PROCEDURES:

1. Have family members sit around the table or floor with a snack. Explain to them that today you are going to have a party to celebrate completion of the program.

2. Hand out parents' and children's certificates indicating they have successfully completed the program.

3. When each person gets his/her award, encourage applause from others.

4. Have parents, children, and facilitators stand in a circle. Model by putting your arms around those on either side of you.

5. Allow time for comments, observations, unfinished feelings, or silence.

6. Encourage parents and children to talk about their progress in the program.

7. When appropriate, adjourn.

IF'S, AND'S, OR BUT'S:

1. Fill out a completion certificate for each family member before the session. Make sure you check the names on the certificates for correct spelling.

2. Certificates are also included in the program for facilitators and volunteers. You may choose to hand out these certificates along with the family certificates.

3. Parents and/or children may want to make special arrangements to call or see you in the following weeks. Such thoughts are usually made as a result of some separation anxiety. Be sensitive to the family having a difficult time separating.

Congratulations to you — a job well done!